FINANCING DEVELOPMENT

DEVELOPMENT

THE POWER OF REGIONALISM

EDITED BY NANCY BIRDSALL AND
LILIANA ROJAS-SUAREZ

FINANCING
DEVELOPMENT

THE POWER OF REGIONALISM

CENTER FOR GLOBAL DEVELOPMENT
Washington, DC
September 2004

Nancy Birdsall is the founding president of the Center for Global Development. Before launching the center in 2001, she served for three years as senior associate and director of the Economic Reform Project at the Carnegie Endowment for International Peace. From 1993 to 1998, she was executive vice president of the Inter-American Development Bank. She spent 14 years at the World Bank, including as director of the Policy Research Department. Among her books is *Delivering on Debt Relief: From IMF Gold to a New Aid Architecture* (Washington: Center for Global Development and Institute for International Economics, 2002, with John Williamson).

Liliana Rojas-Suarez is a senior fellow at the Center for Global Development. She is also the chair of the Latin American Shadow Financial Regulatory Committee. She served as managing director and chief economist for Latin America at Deutsche Bank (1998–2000) and as principal adviser in the Office of the Chief Economist at the Inter-American Development Bank. She held various posts at the International Monetary Fund (1984–94), including as deputy chief of the Capital Markets and Financial Studies Division of the Research Department. She was also a professor at Anahuac University. Among her recent works is *Can International Capital Standards Strengthen Banks in Emerging Markets?* (*The Capco Institute Journal of Finance* 2002).

CENTER FOR GLOBAL DEVELOPMENT
1776 Massachusetts Avenue, NW, Suite 301
Washington, DC 20036
(202) 454-1305 FAX: (202) 454-1534
www.cgdev.org

Nancy Birdsall, *President*

Typesetting by Sandra F. Watts
Printing by United Book Press, Inc.

Printed in the United States of America
06 05 04   5 4 3 2 1

Library of Congress Cataloging-in-Publication Data

Financing development : the power of regionalism / Nancy Birdsall, Liliana Rojas-Suarez, editors.
 p. cm.
 Includes bibliographical references and index.
 ISBN 0-88132-353-5
 1. Finance—Development countries.
2. Economic development—Finance.
3. Development banks.   4. Regionalism.
5. International economic integration.
I. Birdsall, Nancy.   II. Rojas-Suarez, Liliana.   III. Title.

HG195.F539   2004
332'.042'091724—dc22   2004057001

The views expressed in this publication are those of the authors. This publication is part of the overall program of the Center, as endorsed by its Board of Directors, but does not necessarily reflect the views of individual members of the Board or the Advisory Committee.

Contents

Foreword   vii
Hilde Frafjord Johnson

Preface   ix

1 **Regionalism for Financing Development:**
   The Unexploited Potential   1
   Nancy Birdsall and Liliana Rojas-Suarez

2 **Regional Banks and Regionalism: A New Frontier**
   for Development Financing   41
   Robert Devlin and Lucio Castro

   Comment   83
   Enrique Iglesias

   Comment   87
   C. Fred Bergsten

   Comment   91
   Willem Buiter

   Comment   96
   Gary Clyde Hufbauer

3 **Regional Public Goods: The Comparative Edge**
   of Regional Development Banks   101
   Marco Ferroni

Comment   123
Todd Sandler

Comment   128
Omar Kabbaj

Comment   131
Gun-Britt Andersson

4   **International Standards for Strengthening
Financial Systems: Can Regional Development
Banks Address Developing Countries' Concerns?**   137
Liliana Rojas-Suarez

Comment   164
Charles W. Calomiris

Comment   169
Eduardo Aninat

Comment   174
Helmut Reisen

5   **Role of Regional Development Banks in
Rebuilding the International Financial Architecture**   179
Manuel Hinds

Comment   206
Roberto Zahler

Comment   213
Guillermo Calvo

Comment   216
Allan Meltzer

Comment   221
Jurgen Stark

About the Contributors   225

Index   233

Foreword

HILDE FRAFJORD JOHNSON

I am extremely pleased that the proceedings of the roundtable *What Role for Regional Development Banks in Financing for Development?*, which took place in Washington on February 18, 2002, organized by the Center for Global Development and the Institute for International Economics, are now being published.

The roundtable convened with two particularly important goals in mind—both related to the preparations for the Monterrey Conference, which was to take place later the same year. The first goal was to address the role of regional cooperation in financing for development, an issue that until then had been largely overlooked. The second was to identify other issues that should be considered at the political level in Monterrey.

At the start of the roundtable, we found ourselves in a rather unusual situation. We had already agreed on a final document to be issued at Monterrey, the Monterrey Consensus, even before the conference had convened. The document struck a good balance, illustrating a need for contributions from both industrialized and developing countries in combating poverty. It reflected an important conceptual convergence between the United Nations and the Bretton Woods institutions and made clear that considerable additional efforts will have to be made by *all* countries if the Millennium Development Goals are to be achieved.

Although the Monterrey Consensus covers important ground, it is conspicuously silent on specific commitments on the part of industrialized countries. The roundtable discussion provided an opportunity to explore how we could move beyond the agreed document, keeping in mind what was missing from it: in short, to achieve the Millennium Development Goals.

We convened, therefore, in Washington to reflect on the role of the regional development banks and our own role in this effort. For Monterrey

Hilde Frafjord Johnson is Norway's minister of international development.

to move beyond the status quo, we had to arrive well prepared to this historic event, which marked the first time that world leaders gathered to discuss financing for development.

An issue of particular significance, at the roundtable and in this book, is the regional dimension of the emerging new international financial architecture. Recent events have shown that a better-functioning financial system is in the best interests of rich and poor countries alike. International standards are one element of strengthening the financial system. At the same time, there is growing awareness of the fact that one size does not fit all and that reforms are costly and take time.

There is a need for initiatives that take into account different national and regional circumstances and that are thoughtfully sequenced. For instance, we have been made aware of the risks of financial liberalization when the necessary institutions are not in place. The regional development banks can undoubtedly play a constructive role in tailoring standards and institutional reforms to regional and national circumstances.

Another important issue, about which I feel strongly, is the management of global public goods. These goods, which could and should benefit all peoples, need to be protected. Neither the private sector nor the governments can, individually, do that. At the regional level, there are also important public goods that national governments cannot easily or sufficiently safeguard or provide for. Not enough emphasis has been given to regional programs to safeguard or provide crucial public goods like environment, health, transport, or energy.

These initiatives are not only important for the development of the participating countries but are also essential instruments for preventing and resolving regional conflicts and are a prerequisite for development: Peace and development are inextricably linked.

Thus, the challenge addressed by the valuable papers and discussions published in this book goes beyond Monterrey: It encompasses the vicious cycle of poverty and conflict in Africa and elsewhere. It encompasses the need to formulate clear ideas and programs for what regional institutions and regional cooperation can do to confront poverty and conflict. And thus it illuminates the need to ensure adequate financial instruments to address these challenges.

At the roundtable, we succeeded in raising the issue of the role of regional institutions in the fight to achieve the Millennium Development Goals. There is still some way to go, but the issue is on the agenda, and this book will help us keep it there.

The challenge now is for all nations, in the developing and industrialized worlds, to deliver on the commitments we made at Monterrey. It is my hope that the work presented in this book will be one small contribution toward forging the proper tools for our great, common endeavor. We have been challenged by poverty, and we should stand to meet it.

Preface

In the early weeks of 2002, the development community was gearing up for the first United Nations Conference on Financing for Development, to be held in March in Monterrey, Mexico. That conference was to set ambitious benchmarks for both rich-country donors and developing countries for financing the investments critical to achieving the Millennium Development Goals. Discussions about those benchmarks focused on the obligations of the rich countries, especially to increase foreign aid, and the obligations of the developing countries, especially to improve their policies and implement sound programs.

Much of the technical work to back up the policy discussions at the United Nations was undertaken, not surprisingly, at the World Bank—the global financial institution. For the first time in decades, foreign affairs ministers and other officials active in UN affairs and financing and central bank officials active at the World Bank and the International Monetary Fund (IMF) were collaborating on the politics and policies for international development.

But the focus on country responsibilities and global communities was overlooking the centrality of *regional* issues to the development challenge and the ongoing and potential contribution of *regional development* institutions. Norway's international development minister, Hilde Frafjord Johnson, therefore asked her colleagues to take steps to rectify that situation. With the advice and collaboration of Norwegian officials and Enrique Iglesias, the president of the Inter-American Development Bank (IDB), and in close cooperation with the Institute for International Economics, the Center for Global Development thus planned and undertook the conference on regional development issues and the role of regional development banks in financing development. The technical work for the conference forms the core of this book.

We convened a small number of the world's most distinguished current and former ministers of finance and development and central bank governors to join with leading policy and academic experts in two days of informal and frank interaction. The enormous interest in the subject was reflected in the broad partnership that was formed in the organization and sponsoring of the meetings, including not only the government of Norway and the IDB but also the Mexican government and the Group of 24.

This book consists of four main papers prepared as background for discussion and the edited transcripts of the invited discussants' comments. Liliana Rojas-Suarez, who played a key role for the Center in planning the agenda and who wrote one of the background papers, joined me in preparing the introductory chapter after the conference. That chapter identifies the common thread that runs through the different aspects of regionalism as a tool for financing development analyzed in the following chapters.

As in any collective endeavor, the list of institutions and people to whom Liliana and I owe our gratitude is large. This book would not exist without the support and collaboration of many colleagues. We are indebted to Fred Bergsten, director of the Institute for International Economics, for his close collaboration on one of the Center's earliest major undertakings. The government of Norway and the Inter-American Development Bank (IDB) provided both financial and technical support. We are grateful to Jan Erik Leikvang and Trond Lindberg of the Ministry of Foreign Affairs, Norway, and to Minister Council Kristian Oedegaard, who, in the initial stages of planning this project, convinced us of the importance of carrying it to completion. We also thank Leiv Lunde of ECON, Norway, who, as a consultant to the government of Norway, was a continuous source of ideas in identifying the major themes that are discussed in this book. Leiv's colleague, Per Schreiner, lent us a valuable hand in summarizing the major conclusions from the conference. All of them were active in attracting the key participants and motivating the discussion and debate reflected in this book. We are particularly grateful to Minister Hilde Frafjord Johnson who, in addition to her initial inspiration, was a key participant in the final session of the conference and wrote the foreword for this book.

The key role of the IDB needs to be deeply acknowledged. President Enrique Iglesias embraced this project from its conception and provided numerous ideas that helped shape this book. He was also the reason behind the active participation of high-level officials from regional development banks in the conference. Some of them, including Omar Kabbaj, president of the African Development Bank, and President Iglesias himself contributed to this book. As always, Euric Bobb, the chief of staff to the president at the IDB, was a driving force in the initial stages of organization and planning of the project. Thanks are also due to the executive directors of the IDB, Paal Aavastmark of Norway, and Augustin Garcia-Lopez of Mexico for their energy and efforts to ensure the success of the meetings.

A number of conference participants provided critical and useful comments that helped Liliana and me to write the introductory chapter. Among those were Burke Dillon, former vice president of the IDB; Oscar DeRojas, executive director, UN Financing for Development Secretariat, United Nations; Barry Herman, chief of the finance and development branch, United Nations; Roberto Junguito, former minister of finance of Colombia; William Larralde, director, Group of 24; Karti Sandilya from the Asian Development Bank; Gerald Ssenduala, minister of finance of Uganda; and Richard Webb, former president of the Central Bank of Peru.

Albert Fishlow and Rudolf Hommes reviewed the entire manuscript and made important comments that significantly improved the quality of the book, especially the introductory chapter.

The conference could not have been successful without the excellent help provided by Sarah Lucas and Angela Gillespie of the Center and Isabella Obnial Platon, who were deeply involved in every aspect of the organization of the conference and made themselves available well beyond the call of duty. We are also grateful to our production and publishing team at the Center, especially Andrew Stober and Noora-Lisa Aberman, as well as Marla Banov, Madona Devasahayam, and Valerie Norville at the Institute for International Economics. With his usual proficiency, Michael Treadway brilliantly edited the first version of the book.

Finally, our deepest gratitude goes to the contributors of this edited volume, in which the reader will find a candid and forthright debate on the relevance of regionalism to the politically charged issue of how to better finance development. Exchange of views rather than consensus characterizes the tone of this volume. We are enormously grateful to our colleagues for their willingness to express their opinions and proposals in a straightforward manner and for dealing with difficult issues in a way that reflects both excellence and ability to communicate innovative and complex ideas.

* * *

The Center for Global Development is an independent, nonprofit policy research organization dedicated to reducing global poverty and inequality and to making globalization work for the poor. Through a combination of research and strategic outreach, the Center actively engages policymakers and the public to influence the policies of the United States, other rich countries, and such institutions as the World Bank, the IMF, and the World Trade Organization (WTO), to improve the economic and social development prospects in poor countries.

The Center's Board of Directors bears overall responsibility for the Center and includes distinguished leaders of nongovernmental organizations, former officials, business executives, and some of the world's leading scholars of development. The Center receives advice on its research and policy programs from the Board and from an Advisory Committee that comprises respected development specialists and advocates.

The Center's president works with the Board, the Advisory Committee, and the Center's senior staff in setting the research and program priorities and approves all formal publications. The Center is supported by an initial significant financial contribution from Edward W. Scott Jr. and by funding from individuals, philanthropic foundations, and other organizations.

NANCY BIRDSALL
President
August 2004

Regionalism for Financing Development: The Unexploited Potential

NANCY BIRDSALL and LILIANA ROJAS-SUAREZ

We argue in this essay that developing countries, in their pursuit of sustainable growth, could much more fully exploit the benefits of a more open and radical regionalism. Open regionalism refers to the idea (see chapter 2 in this volume, and Birdsall and Lawrence 1999) that agreements among countries within regions can be a step toward greater integration into a global trading and financial system, as opposed to a step back from an open multilateral system. By a more radical regionalism we mean much greater integration of economies within regions, through more shared infrastructure, reduced trade barriers, enhanced policy cooperation among countries in a region, and mechanisms to achieve neighborhood objectives such as elimination of infectious diseases and the resolution of border conflicts.[1] Our emphasis is on regionalism as a strategy —as well as an opportunity—to speed the development of domestic institutions, and thus generate faster and steadier growth, and to improve developing countries' ability to cope with the challenges and the risks of deeper integration into the global economy.

We do not pretend to justify completely the logic of a more radical regionalism. We confine our argument largely to the benefits of regionalism for the financing of countries' development needs and to the role

---

Nancy Birdsall is the president of the Center for Global Development. Liliana Rojas-Suarez is a senior fellow at the Center for Global Development. The authors would like to thank Trond Augdal for excellent research support and valuable comments. The errors that remain are, of course, ours.

1. See IDB (2002) for a comprehensive discussion about the geopolitical benefits of regional integration.

of the regional development banks (RDBs) in that process. These are the topics explored in the other essays and commentaries in this volume, on which we rely for some—although not all—of our arguments.

Among economists, the benefits of eliminating borders and thus increasing market transactions and gains from economies of specialization (or scope) are self-evident. As an apparent result of these benefits, dedication to the ideal of a global or multilateral system of trade has been steadfast. In addition, regional trade agreements before the 1990s often involved increasing barriers to nonregional parties, so that regionalism seemed to violate the ideal of overall openness, diverting rather than creating trade.[2] That has changed in the last decade (Robert Devlin and Lucio Castro, in chapter 2 of this volume, conclude that the regionalism of the 1990s has generally supported global integration). The benefits of the new open regionalism are not so readily dismissed, although there is certainly still concern that proliferation of trade agreements, especially on a bilateral basis, would contribute to the "spaghetti bowl" of conflicting rules and interests.[3] Nor is trade the only issue for which economists are revisiting the potential benefits of open regionalism. Other issues include the financing of infrastructure at the regional level, the regional management of monetary affairs to limit vulnerability to financial crises, and the adaptation of regulatory standards to meet regional needs. On these and other considerations, however, there is still only a small body of work on the benefits of the new regionalism, and on its limits. That is the gap we hope this and the other essays in this volume will begin to fill.

---

2. Some of the early initiatives in Latin America after World War II involved a concept of trade integration, in which preferential tariff elimination among trading partners was combined with high barriers to extraregional imports and a strong government intervention in economic activity. These regional arrangements fell into crisis in the 1980s because of the perceptions among some country members that the high levels of protection were a source of trade diversion. Indeed, as documented by José Antonio Ocampo (2001), Chile was the first country in the region to withdraw from a regional trade agreement: the Andean Pact.

3. Bhagwati has been one of the most vocal critics of the recent proliferation of trade agreements. His views are summarized in the following statement: "By the end of 2002, 250 FTAs [free trade agreements] had been notified to the WTO [World Trade Organization]. If those currently under negotiation are concluded, that number will approach 300. The result is a 'spaghetti bowl of rules,' arbitrary definitions of which products comes from where and a multiplicity of tariffs depending on source" (Jagdish Bhagwati and Arvind Panagariya, "Bilateral Treaties are a Sham," *Financial Times*, July 13, 2003, 27).

We do not disagree with that statement. A number of recent FTAs belong to the bilateral rather than the regional category, and there are significant differences between the two types. It is certainly true that a multiplicity of bilateral trade agreements, each one with its own peculiarities (including regarding external tariffs), could lead to a fragmentation of the world market, becoming an obstacle to, rather than a facilitator of, both regionalism and multilateralism. At the same time, however, Jagdish Bhagwati (1992) has recognized that if properly designed to avoid trade diversion, regionalism can lead to the achievement of multilateral trade for all.

We begin with a discussion of the sources of financing for development, focusing on their stability and sustainability. Our discussion highlights the limitations of the current system, in which external flows of development finance are limited or volatile (and often dangerously procyclical) or both. We also analyze internal sources of finance, noting that they are as much an outcome of as an input to the development process. We highlight the differences across regions both in access to external finance and in domestic saving ratios and taxation capabilities. Next we turn to the benefits of regional arrangements for attracting and retaining sources of financing, for reducing the risks and vulnerability associated with participation in the global financial system, and for increasing access to external funds via increased trade and export diversification. We argue that differences among regions indicate some justification for more region-specific strategies toward global integration than what immediate and unilateral liberalization implies. Finally we discuss the existing and unexploited potential for the RDBs to assist their member countries in developing and extending regional arrangements and in increasing their investments in regional public goods.

Three Pillars of Development Finance: An Assessment of Their Reliability and Sustainability

For the more than five decades of the postwar era, the international community has sought ways to increase levels of income and rates of economic growth in the poorer countries. The effort began with the creation of the World Bank as a sister organization to the International Monetary Fund (IMF). The Fund was instituted to assist countries with temporary balance of payments problems; the Bank was instituted to help finance reconstruction (in Europe) and to support critical investments to increase growth and thus raise income levels and promote human advancement (in the developing countries).

In many respects the development project has been successful, particularly in terms of improvement in such indicators as health and education. However, except for the East Asian region, income gains in the developing world have been relatively limited, particularly in the last two decades. Although many countries of East Asia are converging in income terms with the advanced economies, most countries outside that region have been growing more slowly, if at all, over the last two decades, so the income gap between the richest and poorest countries of the world has continued to increase—to a difference of more than 50 to 1 between western Europe and parts of sub-Saharan Africa.

Development thus remains one of the greatest challenges of the 21st century. Financing the process—including the investments in people and institutions that are necessary (although by no means sufficient) for development—is a critical part of that challenge.[4]

Financing development relies on three major pillars: (1) more stable and sustainable access to net capital inflows, including aid, (2) the buildup of domestic sources of finance through increased private saving and improved taxation systems, and (3) the generation of stable net foreign revenues through increased exports and diversification of trade.

All three pillars are undermined or enhanced by the degree to which countries (governments and the private sector) use the resulting resources well—a factor that could be labeled cost efficiency.[5] Clearly, if the financial resources that are critical but scarce are not invested effectively, the effect of the same financing on development will be reduced.

How have these three pillars performed in supporting development? A review of the experience indicates that the answer is not so well in general, and that there are sufficient differences among regions to warrant increased attention to the potential for regionalism as a strategy to enhance financing options.

Pillar 1. Foreign Financial Flows: Limited, Volatile, and Procyclical

Table 1.1 presents statistics on both private and official net capital flows since 1970 as a percentage of recipients' GDP. Total external flows have generally been between 0.5 and 3 percent of the GDP of recipient regions—far from sufficient to be relied on as a major source of new development investment or as a substitute for domestic saving. (The regional averages obscure the fact that some countries have received much more; e.g., Uganda, Tanzania, and others in Africa have at times received as much as 5 to 20 percent of their own GDP in official flows, but these are exceptions.)

Table 1.1 also reflects the changes over time in the size of external inflows. The data are divided into four periods corresponding to a period of either exuberance or turbulence in net capital flows to developing countries: the 1970s until the year before the eruption of the Latin American debt crisis; the period from 1982 to 1990; the first half of the 1990s, including 1996, the year before the East Asian crisis; and the period from 1997 to 2002. Financial flows to developing countries rose in the early 1990s, peaking at 1 to 4 percent of their GDP, and have fallen since then;

---

4. Development may be less a function of outside financing of investment in poor countries than of changing the economic incentives people within those countries face (Easterly 2001). Our discussion of financing for development includes sources of domestic financing and is not meant to suggest that financing can happen or make a difference without the right incentives and institutional arrangements.

5. We are grateful to Rudolf Hommes for pointing this out.

Table 1.1 Capital flows to developing countries, 1970–2002 (percent of GDP)

	Mean					Standard deviation				
Region	1970–81	1982–90	1991–96	1997–2002	1970–2001	1970–81	1982–90	1991–96	1997–2002	1970–2001
Total developing countries										
Net private capital flows	n.a.	0.80	3.65	1.08	1.69	n.a.	0.40	0.36	0.79	1.37
Net foreign direct investment	–0.01	0.51	1.63	2.37	0.87	0.27	0.01	0.51	0.28	0.97
Net portfolio investment	0.04	0.25	1.44	–0.13	0.32	0.04	0.14	0.75	0.57	0.67
Other net capital flows	n.a.	0.11	0.77	–1.33	–0.11	n.a.	0.33	0.84	0.52	0.99
Net official flows	0.81	0.97	0.48	0.51	0.74	0.20	0.33	0.33	0.29	0.33
Africa										
Net private capital flows	n.a.	1.26	1.56	1.34	1.37	n.a.	0.99	1.57	0.95	1.12
Net foreign direct investment	–0.01	0.47	0.91	2.66	0.77	0.35	0.11	0.24	1.04	1.07
Net portfolio investment	0.08	0.03	0.54	0.28	0.19	0.16	0.17	0.29	1.49	0.64
Other net capital flows	n.a.	0.83	0.38	–1.52	0.03	n.a.	0.98	1.28	0.71	1.40
Net official flows	1.06	1.41	1.27	1.01	1.20	0.32	0.90	0.97	0.22	0.66
Asia										
Net private capital flows	0.77	1.60	3.93	0.34	1.51	0.42	0.50	1.35	1.41	1.53
Net foreign direct investment	–0.06	0.54	2.48	2.26	0.99	0.30	0.13	0.76	0.28	1.15
Net portfolio investment	0.03	0.15	0.78	–0.35	0.13	0.05	0.15	0.55	0.35	0.44
Other net capital flows	0.49	0.94	0.90	–1.87	0.25	0.39	0.41	0.69	1.50	1.29
Net official flows	0.85	0.73	0.57	0.65	0.73	0.30	0.17	0.37	0.38	0.31

(table continues next page)

Table 1.1 Capital flows to developing countries, 1970–2002 (percent of GDP) (continued)

Region	Mean					Standard deviation				
	1970–81	1982–90	1991–96	1997–2002	1970–2001	1970–81	1982–90	1991–96	1997–2002	1970–2001
Latin America and the Caribbean										
Net private capital flows	3.50	0.24	3.36	2.55	2.38	1.23	1.13	1.08	1.29	1.80
Net foreign direct investment	0.17	0.72	1.36	3.16	1.08	0.48	0.20	0.54	0.69	1.17
Net portfolio investment	0.07	0.02	2.27	0.43	0.52	0.11	0.31	1.506	0.75	1.09
Other net capital flows	2.72	–0.46	–0.17	–1.16	0.56	1.07	0.91	1.404	0.52	1.89
Net official flows	0.58	1.17	0.39	0.39	0.67	0.19	0.68	0.501	0.64	0.58
Middle East										
Net private capital flows	–4.39	0.03	4.70	–0.92	–0.80	3.80	1.73	3.77	2.37	4.39
Net foreign direct investment	–0.15	0.18	0.66	0.62	0.23	0.39	0.15	0.18	0.19	0.43
Net portfolio investment	–0.02	0.92	1.50	–1.25	0.29	0.07	0.65	0.79	0.90	1.09
Other net capital flows	–4.07	–0.92	2.87	–0.25	–1.17	3.67	1.29	3.38	1.95	3.68
Net official flows	0.87	0.81	–0.02	0.22	0.56	0.70	0.42	0.41	0.70	0.67
Transition economies										
Net private capital flows	n.a.	n.a.	1.25	2.45	1.85	n.a.	n.a.	2.630	0.81	1.96
Net foreign direct investment	n.a.	n.a.	1.05	2.86	1.96	n.a.	n.a.	0.579	0.54	1.09
Net portfolio investment	n.a.	n.a.	–0.06	0.35	0.14	n.a.	n.a.	1.119	1.25	1.15
Other net capital flows	n.a.	n.a.	0.24	–0.66	–0.21	n.a.	n.a.	1.778	0.65	1.36
Net official flows	n.a.	n.a.	0.77	0.12	0.45	n.a.	n.a.	0.869	0.81	0.87

n.a. = not available

Source: International Monetary Fund, *World Economic Outlook* database (September 2003).

private flows rose most and then collapsed, from a peak of almost $230 billion in 1996 to only $43 billion in 2001.[6]

For the period as a whole, and for all regions of the developing world, net private flows have been more volatile (as measured by the standard deviation) than net official flows. Among private flows, foreign direct investment (FDI) as a proportion of GDP has increased steadily for developing countries as a group, whereas portfolio flows and other private flows (largely loans from international banks) have been erratic and basically collapsed in the late 1990s.

The evolution of private flows has varied significantly across regions. In Asia, net private flows increased significantly from the 1970s to the mid-1990s, but non-FDI private flows collapsed in 1997. In Latin America and the Middle East, private flows have been erratic throughout the entire period (in Latin America, after peaking in 1981, net international bank lending has been largely negative).[7] Net portfolio flows, however, which were small in the 1970s and the 1980s, increased dramatically in the first half of the 1990s. Indeed, during this latter period, about half of portfolio flows to all developing countries went to Latin America (in dollar terms). In the Middle East, private flows have been erratic throughout; this region has the highest standard deviation for net private capital flows, whether calculated for the entire period or for any of the subperiods. In Africa, net private flows have been much lower in absolute terms than elsewhere (not shown in table 1.1): Even at the peak of portfolio inflows to emerging markets during the first half of the 1990s, Africa only received 3 percent of total net private capital flows. However, net private flows have not been lower than elsewhere as a percentage of Africa's own GDP, and they have not been more volatile.

As a percentage of GDP, official flows were higher than private flows in the 1980s (except in Asia) and then fell in absolute terms in the early 1990s (and also fell in relative terms as private flows rose). Official flows rose, if only modestly, in the period from 1997 to 2002, when private flows fell. In general, official flows have been countercyclical: compensating, but

---

6. Total private flows to developing countries as a whole started to recover in 2003, signaling the possibility that a new cycle of external private financing for these countries had started.

For each of the subperiods analyzed, as well as for the aggregate period under consideration, table 1.1 presents the mean and the standard deviation. Because of the abundance of negative numbers, the standard deviation is a better statistic than the coefficient of variation as a measure of dispersion.

7. An interesting issue is the extent to which lending from foreign banks established in Latin America is (at least partially) making up for the decreased cross-border lending. Participation of foreign banks in Latin America has increased significantly since the late 1990s. By the end of 2001, foreign ownership of bank assets (as a percentage of assets of the banking system) exceeded 50 percent in a number of countries, including Argentina, Mexico, Panama, Peru, and Uruguay.

Table 1.2   Correlation between net capital flows to emerging markets and real GDP growth

	Correlation	
Region	Net private capital flows	Net official capital flows
Africa, 1982–2001	0.36	−0.79
Asia, 1971–2001	0.32	−0.37
Countries in transition, 1991–2001	0.22	0.06
Latin America and the Caribbean, 1971–2001	0.37	−0.35
Middle East and Turkey, including Israel, 1971–2001	0.22	−0.40
Total emerging-market economies, 1982–2001	0.14	−0.23

Note: Capital flows measured as a percentage of GDP. Regional real GDP growth rates are calculated by weighting each country's growth rate by its share of regional GDP (measured in current dollars) for the corresponding year.

Source: International Monetary Fund, *World Economic Outlook* database (September 2002).

only partly, for the volatility of private flows. Table 1.2 illustrates this result by presenting the coefficient of correlation between net capital flows and real GDP growth in the different regions. The statistics show that, with the exception of the transition economies, there is a negative correlation between net official flows and real GDP growth in every region, a correlation that is especially large in Africa. In contrast, the correlation between net private flows and real GDP growth is positive. At times of sharp declines of net private flows, official flows have typically increased significantly, albeit at only a fraction of the decline in private flows (more on this below).

The highly concessional portion of official flows (ODA, official development assistance) has two important statistical characteristics, both of which are shown in table 1.3. With the exception of Africa, ODA is generally less volatile than private net flows, and its volatility has been declining in most of the regions. In addition, its importance as a source of financing differs significantly across regions, and it has generally been much more important for Africa than for Latin America. In 2001, the ratio of ODA to net private flows was only 8 percent in the Latin American and Caribbean region, compared with 61 percent in the Middle East and North Africa, 105 percent in sub-Saharan Africa, and 115 percent in South Asia.

These observations taken together indicate that relying on sustained and predictable availability of foreign private flows is not a sensible approach for developing countries—at least not for the foreseeable future. This by no means implies that countries should not try to improve their access to international capital markets. Indeed our recommendations

Table 1.3 Official development assistance to developing countries, 1970–2001

Region	Official development assistance as percent of net private flows, 2001	Official development assistance as percent of GDP									
		Mean					Standard deviation				
		1970–81	1982–90	1991–96	1997–2001	1970–2001	1970–81	1982–90	1991–96	1997–2001	1970–2001
East Asia and Pacific	19.9	0.86	0.71	0.66	0.44	0.72	0.22	0.12	0.17	0.07	0.22
Latin America and Caribbean	8.4	0.36	0.44	0.40	0.28	0.38	0.10	0.07	0.05	0.03	0.09
Middle East and North Africa	60.7	2.06	1.34	1.58	0.83	1.58	0.48	0.49	0.57	0.13	0.63
South Asia	114.5	1.91	1.60	1.53	0.82	1.58	0.36	0.11	0.46	0.11	0.47
Sub-Saharan Africa	104.9	2.39	4.75	6.04	4.30	4.04	0.41	1.07	0.64	0.14	1.55
Transition economies	25.1	n.a.	0.15	0.93	0.99	0.96	n.a.	0.19	0.18	0.26	0.21
Total	27.5	1.17	1.23	1.10	0.75	1.11	0.08	0.16	0.18	0.06	0.20
Memorandum items:											
China	3.6	0.10	0.43	0.57	0.20	0.37	0.13	0.15	0.16	0.06	0.21
India	35.5	1.15	0.71	0.70	0.36	0.82	0.28	0.14	0.24	0.03	0.35

n.a. = not available

Source: World Bank, *World Development Indicators 2003* (CD-ROM) and *Global Development Finance 2003* (CD-ROM).

include policies and development of instruments to improve access. However, the evidence is increasingly clear that bank lending and the allocation of portfolio funds by international investors to a particular country depend not only on the economic and political conditions of that country but also on international factors. The correlation of bond prices and spreads across countries has been extremely high in the last several decades, not only during global financial crises but also in normal times. Eduardo Fernandez-Arias and Roberto Rigobon (2000) show that the correlations between Mexican and other emerging market bond returns were above 80 percent during the normal period following the 1994 Mexican crisis.[8] This and other evidence indicate that the behavior of asset prices and spreads in emerging markets is partly explained by world aggregate shocks that affect the entire emerging market asset class.[9] Markets do discriminate among countries, with asset prices during crises falling less in those countries perceived as less risky in the precrisis period.[10] Although country-specific fundamentals explain the relative difference in spreads across countries, global factors external to the countries play a key role in explaining their absolute cost of borrowing.

The resulting volatility can be highly detrimental to a country's access to financing for development. For example, uncertainties in the global economy increased significantly in 2002, and many of these uncertainties originated in industrial countries. Important developments included the continuation of slow growth in all industrial regions of the world; the scandals in the corporate sector of the United States, which increased uncertainties about the true profitability of major companies; and the uncertainties generated by a possible armed conflict with Iraq. Investors, facing a riskier environment, shifted the composition of their portfolio toward a greater weight of safer assets. This, of course, implied a shift toward more liquid assets (such as industrial countries' government paper and some selected companies' liabilities with a high credit rating) and away from developing countries' liabilities (as well as industrial countries' junk paper). This increased the cost of international financing for developing countries and, in some cases, closed countries' access to international capital markets.

---

8. The exception was Venezuela, with a correlation of 73 percent.

9. Guillermo Calvo and Enrique Mendoza (1999) argue that certain features of investors' behavior explain the mechanics of contagion; namely, the transmission of an adverse shock to one country to other emerging markets. It is well known that at the time of the Russian default in 1998, leveraged investors had to exit other emerging markets to cover their losses in Russia.

10. Fernandez-Arias and Rigobon (2000) show that the magnitude of increased spreads in individual emerging markets following the Russian crisis corresponded with the initial levels of the spreads. Among Latin American countries, the largest increase in spreads occurred in Venezuela (the country with the highest precrisis spread), and the smallest in Mexico (the country with the lowest precrisis spread).

In addition, of course, there is the possibility that rapidly increasing inflows of private capital, as in the mid-1990s, are speculative and less likely to be cost-efficient, because they contribute to an asset bubble rather than to a highly productive investment, as may have been the case in some countries of East Asia.

Official flows, although they have been countercyclical and ease somewhat the adjustments countries have had to make for the volatility of private flows, are, unfortunately, not entirely reliable. Although they have risen slightly in the most recent period under consideration in this study (1997–2002), they are still universally below their levels of the 1980s (as a percentage of recipient-region GDP), even in Africa and Latin America, where GDP has not risen much. For the poorest countries, there is an additional problem. Although portfolio flows to them are so low that globally induced volatility is not an issue, they are more heavily reliant on grants and concessional loans as a percentage of their GDP than are many emerging markets on private flows. Official flows at the country level are not particularly reliable either: Paul Collier and David Dollar (1999) show that as poor countries undertaking major reforms begin to recover some growth, the official flows on which they are relying to adjust have often declined.[11]

Moreover, as with private inflows, official inflows may not have always contributed positively, or at least not as positively as hoped, to the financing of development. Poor use of official loans in the world's poorest countries clearly contributed to their build-up of unsustainable official debt, finally provoking the internationally agreed-on heavily indebted poor countries' program of debt forgiveness. As implied by the discussion above, the negative correlation between GDP growth and official inflows (table 1.2) reflects in part the greater demand for official help in countries and regions doing less well. At the same time, the large negative correlation for Africa is consistent with statistical evidence that in this region, in which publicly financed investment has been high relative to private investment, overall investment returns have been low (Devarajan, Dollar, and Holmgren 2001).

For the middle-income countries, there is the uncertainty associated with increased questioning of the lending practices of the IMF and other multilateral organizations. Broadly speaking, there are two views. The first argues that the large bail-out packages supplied by the IMF to emerging markets since the Tequila Crisis have created a moral hazard problem. The argument is that private investors tend to overlend to emerging markets in good times based on the expectation that a rescue package from the

---

11. The inefficiencies of the donor system for transferring resources are substantial (Easterly 2002), and between the US and European donors there is a difference in view about such basic financing issues as whether poor countries should be able to borrow at all or be confined to grant financing. Nancy Birdsall and John Williamson (2002) argue in favor of grant financing for the poorest countries with a history of unsustainable public debt to official creditors.

IMF will protect them from potential investment losses in bad times.[12] The second view is that the rapid development of international capital markets and the inflows, at times huge, into developing countries have significantly reduced the efficacy of traditional IMF rescue packages. Relative to the private flows, there are simply not enough funds available at the IMF to do credible old-style bailouts.

Although debate continues, the fact is that multilateral organizations seem to be behaving more cautiously than in the past with respect to supporting countries in difficulty.[13] Moreover, recognition of the moral hazard problem has led the IMF to advance two proposals to increase private sector involvement in crisis resolution: the inclusion of collective action clauses in all sovereign bond contracts, and a proposed sovereign debt restructuring mechanism (SDRM).[14] Although private lenders have indicated their intention to support the wider use of collective action clauses (CACs), they strongly reject the implementation of an SDRM. At the time of this writing, it is unclear how this debate will be resolved. Delays in solving the IMF–private sector debate are costly for developing countries, as they create increased uncertainties about the rules of the game for accessing funds from multilateral organizations as well as from private sources.

Pillar 2. Funding Development Through Private Saving and Taxation

Domestic saving continues to be the largest source of financing for development in developing countries. The Monterrey Financing for Development Initiative explicitly calls for efforts to increase domestic saving. Domestic savings are made up of private and public saving (the difference between tax revenues and public expenditures). We discuss each type of saving in turn.

There is an ongoing and unsettled discussion about the relationship between domestic saving rates and growth. What comes first, saving or

---

12. See the Meltzer Report (IFIAC 2000) for a more extensive discussion of this argument.

13. Some have argued that the IMF's unusually long negotiation process with Argentina in 2002–03 was a case in point, though the subsequent loan to Brazil is a counterexample.

14. Advocates of CACs argue that this is an appropriate way to deal with the holdout or rogue creditor problem, which occurs when a minority of creditors delay crisis resolution until their demands are met, to the detriment of other creditors and the debtor. Proponents of CACs believe that this problem can be solved by binding all bondholders to the will of a supermajority. The SDRM proposal can be better understood by comparing it to bankruptcy courts that currently exist for private-sector companies. By applying to sovereigns' debt negotiations with the private sector some of the principles used in the resolution process of corporations in default, the SDRM aims at insulating governments from adverse court judgments during the process of renegotiating debt contracts and hastening the renegotiation process, advocates claim.

growth? In the 1970s and 1980s, the idea that domestic saving would finance investment and therefore lead to increased growth was the central motivation for the financial liberalization undertaken in many developing countries. The intellectual leadership for these policies came from Ronald McKinnon (1973), who argued that the removal of interest rate ceilings would encourage higher private saving and investment ratios.

However, reality did not follow the theoretical predictions. In a number of developing countries, financial liberalization was followed not by increased saving and growth but, rather, by financial collapse. The issues of delaying financial liberalization until after other liberalizing reforms were completed and of ensuring adequate banking supervision before financial liberalization were then put on the table (Diaz-Alejandro 1985). Evidence mounted indicating that causation runs from growth to saving, and not necessarily from higher saving to higher growth.[15]

That does not mean it is not worth encouraging both private and public saving. Even if there is no direct causality from saving to growth, policies to encourage saving make sense (Plies and Reinhart 1999). For one thing, low (and declining in particular) domestic saving rates contribute to large current account deficits that often lead to currency crises, inhibiting growth.[16] High and stable domestic saving rates also can offset the disruptive consequences of volatile international capital flows.

It does mean that in the case of private saving, governments' short-term and direct policy instruments are relatively limited. The only possible exception comes from evidence that with the institution of a fully funded private pension scheme in Chile, private saving rose (without completely offsetting declines in public saving). However, few developing countries today can finance the fiscal cost of the transition to such a system, which requires support for current pensioners coming from general revenues rather than from the contributions of current workers. Differences across regions in average private saving illustrate that other policy instruments for encouraging private saving are indirect at best.

Table 1.4 presents the evolution from the mid-1960s to the mid-1990s of gross private saving as a ratio of gross private disposable income[17] for a sample of industrial countries and for developing countries grouped by regions, based on Loayza et al. (1998).[18] Private saving ratios in East Asia,

---

15. See, for example, the papers by Carroll and Weil (1993) and Gavin, Hausmann, and Talvi (1997).

16. As noted by a number of observers, low and decreasing domestic saving rates were an important factor leading to the Tequila Crisis in 1994.

17. The subperiods in table 1.4 do not correspond to those in tables 1.1 and 1.3 because such as classification was not available for the private savings ratios.

18. See Loayza et al. (1998) for the countries included in every region and for methodological details.

Table 1.4   Gross private saving/gross private disposable income
            (percent)

Region	1965–73	1974–84	1985–94	1965–94
Africa				
Average	19.5	11.2	10.7	11.6
Standard deviation	1.9	11.5	9.2	10.3
East Asia				
Average	21.4	27.3	28.6	26.8
Standard deviation	4.3	5.9	8.9	7.4
Industrial countries				
Average	24.6	23.3	23.2	23.6
Standard deviation	5.2	4.9	4.8	5.0
Latin America				
Average	16.4	15.4	10.9	14.1
Standard deviation	7.4	6.6	7.4	7.4
Middle East				
Average	10.9	20.2	19.7	18.4
Standard deviation	3.9	16.4	10.4	13.4
South Asia				
Average	14.4	18.8	23.3	19.5
Standard deviation	5.3	5.0	4.6	5.9

Source: Loayza et al. (1998).

where economies were growing, increased consistently during the period under study, reaching levels comparable to those of industrial countries, albeit with a higher degree of volatility. Private saving ratios in South Asian countries (in which there also was growth, although it was less rapid than in East Asia) showed an increasing trend as well. In sharp contrast, gross private saving rates in Africa and Latin America, in which economic growth has been negligible, have been low—half the level of those rates achieved in Asian countries—and declined throughout the period from the mid-1960s to the mid-1990s. In Middle Eastern countries, after significantly increasing from the mid-1960s to the mid-1980s, private saving ratios declined in the 1990s as the price of oil declined.

The differences in average growth rates across regions are not the only explanation of regional differences in saving rates: Differences in financial sector depth (domestic capital markets and confidence of small savers) also explain some of the gap in private saving ratios between Latin America and Asia.[19] Demographic differences also matter. Loayza et al. (1998) show that young-age dependency ratios (population younger than 15 years old as a percentage of working-age population) have a negative effect on private saving rates.[20]

---

19. See, for example, Edwards (1995).

20. See also Kelley and Schmidt (1995, 2001) on the effects of demographic changes on savings, investment, and growth in East Asia compared with Latin America and other regions.

In principle, increasing public saving is a much more direct and accessible policy instrument than increasing private savings: Public saving is merely the difference between government revenues and government spending. We concentrate on the revenue side (i.e., on governments' ability to raise adequate revenues through taxes) and focus on taxation performance rather than on the behavior of overall public saving because a given public saving ratio is consistent with an infinite combination of levels of expenditures and revenues. Developmental efforts require some minimum level of expenditure on the provision of public goods, however, especially in the social areas. Although we would not want to seem to minimize the importance of fiscal discipline in the sense of spending and borrowing no more than the expected revenue stream affords, and of spending resources well, the fact is that a critical challenge facing most developing countries is that of developing the capacity to raise sufficient tax revenues to provide the level of public goods needed to advance the development process, whether directly or through sustainable public borrowing. Adequate tax revenue greatly simplifies for governments the challenge of financing countercyclical expenditures during economic downturns and of avoiding significant fiscal imbalances that, by weakening macroeconomic stability, would debilitate the sustainability of the development efforts.

Problems facing developing countries in establishing an adequate tax system have been studied extensively.[21] The most common difficulties include, first, a large share of the agricultural and informal sectors in many countries, which limits the collection capacity of personal income taxes and other modern taxes used in industrial countries; second, deficiencies in the institutions in charge of tax administration; and third, the severe limitations in the generation of reliable tax statistics, which constrain policymakers' efforts to assess the potential effect of specific tax reforms. In addition, concentration of political power in the richest percentiles of the population partly explains the resistance in certain countries to efficiently use personal income and property taxes.

Table 1.5a shows a comparison of tax revenue ratios to GDP in industrial countries and in developing countries by regions. Data for each region are an unweighted average for a sample of countries using the most recent data available from the IMF Government Finance Statistics Yearbook.[22] On average, industrial countries' ratios of tax revenues to GDP

---

21. See, for example, Tanzi and Zee (2000).

22. The industrial countries group includes France, Germany, the United Kingdom, the United States, and Sweden. Southeast Asia includes Indonesia, Korea, the Philippines, Thailand, and Singapore. The South Asia group is formed by India, Pakistan, and Sri Lanka. The Middle East incorporates Bahrain, Egypt, Iran, Israel, Jordan, Morocco, Syria, and Tunisia. The Latin American and the Caribbean group includes Argentina, Bolivia, Brazil, Chile, Colombia, Costa Rica, Dominican Republic, El Salvador, Mexico, Panama,

Table 1.5a Government tax revenue
(percent of GDP)

Region	Percent
Africa	15.9
East Asia	16.1
Industrialized countries	39.4
Latin America and the Caribbean	17.0
Middle East	17.6
South Asia	12.7
Transition economies	29.1

Note: Data reported are unweighted averages of the latest available in the period 1997–2001.

Sources: International Monetary Fund, *International Financial Statistics* (February 2004), International Monetary Fund, *Government Finance Statistics Yearbook* (2002), and World Bank, *World Development Indicators 2003* (CD-ROM).

are about twice the level of those of all the developing regions, with the exception of the transition economies.[23] The positive correlation between tax ratios and development is no surprise. Countries with higher levels of income and development also have the capacity to raise more taxes.[24]

Table 1.5b presents the most important components of tax structures around the world. Again, there are crucial differences between the tax systems in industrial countries and those in developing countries. First, developing-country regions are much more reliant on consumption taxes compared with income taxes, although their overall tax take, even for consumption taxation, is lower than in the developed countries. Even

Peru, Uruguay, and Venezuela. Africa includes Cote d'Ivoire, Ghana, Kenya, Mauritius, Sierra Leone, Zambia, and Zimbabwe. Finally, the group of transition economies includes Bulgaria, the Czech Republic, Kazakhstan, Poland, Russia, and Ukraine.

The averages in tables 1.5a and 1.5b are unweighted because we are only including a sample of countries in every region and not the entire group of countries. However, the analysis does not change if the statistics are weighted. The most important differences in table 5a would be that the ratio for industrialized countries would decline to the low 30s because of the large share of the United States (in terms of GDP), and that the ratio for Latin America would increase to the low 20s because of the importance of Brazil in the sample.

23. Exceptional cases among developing countries with ratios close to those in industrial countries include Brazil (29 percent) and Israel (39 percent).

24. See, for example, Easterly and Rebelo (1993). There is no theory on the *optimal* level of taxation for a given degree of economic development, indicating that developing countries do best to focus on the appropriateness of their tax structures (see Tanzi and Zee 2000). An adequate design of tax structures and institutions will minimize distortions while increasing revenue collection.

Table 1.5b Composition of tax revenue (percent of GDP)

| Region | Income taxes[a] | | | Consumption taxes | | Property tax | International trade tax | Social Security tax |
	Total	Individual	Corporate	Total	Of which: Value added tax or sales			
Africa	4.24	1.47	1.27	6.40	2.56	0.27	4.58	0.40
East Asia	6.09	2.53	2.44	6.47	2.85	0.56	1.15	0.81
Industrialized countries	14.04	9.68	2.57	9.80	6.63	2.42	0.05	11.68
Latin America and the Caribbean	3.92	0.81	2.21	7.78	4.05	0.70	1.98	2.72
Middle East	4.97	1.57	2.46	6.13	4.04	0.37	3.53	1.52
South Asia	2.94	0.86	1.79	4.30	3.46	0.26	1.98	0.00
Transition economies	7.80	3.54	n.a.	10.04	n.a.	0.69	0.70	9.12

n.a. = not available

a. Sum of individual and corporate tax may not equal total because some tax revenue is not allocated between the two categories.

Note: Data reported are unweighted averages of the latest available information in the period 1997–2001 (when available).

Sources: International Monetary Fund, *International Financial Statistics* (February 2004) and International Monetary Fund, *Government Finance Statistics Yearbook* (2002).

where consumption taxes emphasize the value added tax, as in Latin America, collection rates are much lower than the statutory rates because of the exclusion of many final goods and services.[25]

Second, in industrial countries the lion's share of revenues raised by income taxes comes from personal taxes, whereas in most developing countries, the corporate income tax is more important. The reliance of developing countries on some forms of corporate taxation makes the countries vulnerable to the increasing cross-border mobility of capital.[26] Large, multinational firms can reduce their tax burden by simply relocating their mobile capital. Problems in collecting personal income taxes explain the relatively higher reliance of developing countries on consumption taxes (and the increasing popularity of value added tax in some regions). In Latin America, for example, revenues from personal income taxes as a percentage of GDP are the lowest in the world because high personal exemption levels leave a large number of potential taxpayers out of the tax net, and because there is a significant degree of tax evasion. Issues on taxation in open economies as well as some specific recommendations for developing countries are presented in appendix 1.1 at the end of this chapter.

Third, the tax ratio on international trade is higher in developing countries. In Africa and the Middle East, revenues from taxes on international trade are more than 20 percent of total tax revenues. Even in East Asia they are much more important than in the developed countries, representing 7 percent of total tax revenues compared with less than 0.1 percent of this revenue in developed countries.

There are also notable differences across developing countries in tax structure. Tax systems of transition economies most closely resemble those of industrial countries. The overall tax ratio and the revenues from social security taxes as a percentage of GDP are close to those in industrial countries, and the reliance of these countries on taxes on international trade is very small. As noted earlier, Africa and the Middle East are heavily dependent on trade taxes, whereas Latin America has eschewed trade taxes and relies heavily on consumption and payroll taxes.

---

25. In Latin America, reforms to tax systems were significant, especially in the first half of the 1990s, with a marked emphasis on implementation of the value added tax, a form of taxation that has been favored by multilateral organizations because, when designed as a broad tax on consumption, it does not distort the relative prices of products transacted between producers. See Ebrill et al. (2001) for a comprehensive discussion of the implementation of value added tax in developing countries. Problems in collecting other categories of taxes may create an incentive to rely on the more easily collected value added tax. The danger, of course, is overreliance on this form of taxation. See Lora (2001) for a summary of tax reforms in Latin America. Also, on issues of taxation in Latin America, see Shome (1999).

26. Even the OECD countries face this problem—especially those within the European community.

The real message from these international comparisons is that regional differences are significant when it comes to finding alternative sources of finance for development. Divergences in the design and effectiveness of tax systems are joined by regional differences in access to international capital markets and by behavior of private saving rates.

Pillar 3. Generating Resources Through Higher Export Ratios and Trade Diversification

Moving ahead in the development path involves the acquisition of a large number of import products. Imports of goods and services essential for growth and development in turn require foreign exchange. In countries with no restrictions on the convertibility of domestic currency into foreign currency, the demand for foreign currency, if large enough, can lead to significant changes to the exchange rate in a flexible exchange rate regime or to important losses of foreign exchange reserves—both scenarios having negative effects on the real economy. Countries that have some intervention in the foreign exchange markets cannot avoid these problems completely, or must resort to interest rate increases that also have real costs.

Net changes in foreign exchange flows can only be avoided if imports are fully financed with proceeds from exports or from net international capital flows. The volatility of net capital flows discussed above does not serve well the purpose of sustained acquisition of necessary imports. Indeed, a typical feature of adjustment in developing countries following a significant decline in capital inflows is their resorting to big declines in imports as the only way to generate necessary current account surpluses. Improvement in export ratios, therefore, is the only way to complement (and offset) the fickle behavior of net capital flows.[27]

Export-promoting policies need not involve increased intervention by government in the economy. In many cases, a reduction in barriers to trade, most notably reduced import tariffs, will increase exports. Because imports are an important input in production, a decrease in tariffs (especially on capital and intermediate goods) is equivalent to a reduction in costs and is, therefore, an improvement in international competitiveness. A more open and competitive economy involves higher ratios of both exports and imports to GDP.

However, tariffs and import and export quotas are not the only barriers to trade that are associated with borders separating nations; in many developing countries, after more than a decade of trade liberalization,

---

27. Emphasis on exports as a motor of growth in many developing countries responds precisely to the perception that the large inflows of capital observed in the first half of the 1990s will not be repeated in the foreseeable future.

they may not even be the major barriers. Other important factors in some regions and subregions are lack of transportation infrastructure across borders and bureaucratic or even corrupt customs arrangements; these factors matter most for small countries with many neighbors that have limited access to the sea (e.g., many countries in sub-Saharan Africa and some, like Bolivia and Paraguay, in Latin America).[28] Also important in raising the costs of trade can be differences in languages, cultures, and domestic regulations.[29] Examples of costs to investors in this category are the collection of information particular to a country's legal system, additional expense related to lawyers' services, hiring staff knowledgeable in the local language, and adapting products to the particular customs of the country.[30]

The task of dealing with these trade barriers (imposed by developing countries themselves or by industrial-country trade partners) is an enormous one. It involves much more than the reduction of tariffs and of nontariff barriers. It often involves institutional changes (e.g., in customs arrangements) and new investments in infrastructure that make demands on resources and on administrative capacity as well as institute policy changes.

For some developing countries whose exports are highly concentrated in a few commodities, the issue is not only or mainly to increase their exports but, rather, to diversify them. Dependence on commodity exports is problematic both because of the secular decline in world prices and because of their price volatility, implying (for countries dependent on them) substantial vulnerability to terms-of-trade shocks. Diversification of exports would be encouraged through better access to more trade partners. For other countries, the main issue is overall expansion of exports. Brazil, for example, has the lowest commodity dependence ratio in Latin America, but it has a low overall trade ratio. This low ratio,

---

28. See Gallup and Sachs (1999), and Radelet and Sachs (1998) for the negative effects of the wrong geography, independent of trade policy and institutions. In a comment on chapter 2, Willem Buiter notes that landlocked countries are particularly disadvantaged when trade is restricted, referring specifically to central Asia.

29. James Anderson and Eric van Wincoop (2001) classify some of these as non–rent generating, in comparison to tariffs.

30. Failure to adapt products to local tastes is not easy to distinguish from imposed barriers. Mexico City's consumption of Mexican beer, Modelo, outweighs by far the consumption of US beer even when tariffs on beer between the two countries were eliminated in 2002. Does this consumption pattern reflect the particular taste of Mexicans? Not according to the *Wall Street Journal*, which reported tie-ups (that would be illegal in the United States) that prevent competition by US beers. Likewise, in January 2003, the US court of appeals ruled an indefinite postponement of cross-border trucking, effectively preventing Mexican trucks from operating on US highways on the basis that further analysis of the environmental and safety impacts were needed. Fortunately, this latter case was resolved in 2004 in favor of Mexico.

Table 1.6 Indicator of trade openness (ratio of exports plus imports of goods and services to GDP)

Region	1970–79	1980–89	1990–99	2000–01[a]	Change from early 1970s to early 2000s	Change from first to last year
East Asia and Pacific	32.5	45.4	60.9	77.2	44.6	52.1
Latin America and Caribbean	22.6	26.0	29.5	35.5	13.0[b]	16.3
Middle East and North Africa	77.5	62.6	63.3	69.5	−18.1[b]	−19.9
South Asia	15.8	20.2	27.1	32.1	16.3	21.2
Sub-Saharan Africa	53.7	54.4	56.2	63.0	9.3	16.0
Transition economies	n.a.	45.8	63.5	75.0	29.2[c]	19.0

n.a. = not available

a. For Latin America and the Caribbean and Middle East and North Africa, average for 2000–01 only.
b. For Latin America and the Caribbean and Middle East and North Africa, change from the 1970s to 2001 only.
c. For transition economies, change from the 1980s to 2002.

Source: World Bank, *World Development Indicators 2003* (CD-ROM).

combined with Brazil's dependence on foreign inflows, makes it all too vulnerable to adverse external shocks.

How have developing-country regions performed in terms of the volume of increased overall trade and export diversification? Table 1.6 shows for each region the ratio of exports plus imports of goods and services to GDP (the trade ratio), one indicator of trade outcomes, for the 1970s, 1980s, 1990s, and early 2000s, and the changes over the entire period. Table 1.7 shows the countries' dependence on commodity exports.[31] These two tables need to be analyzed together to understand the nature of the challenge for different regions in increasing and diversifying their exports.

The East Asian and Pacific region has seen the largest increase in its trade ratio (by 52 percentage points between 1970 and 2002), with it reaching a relatively high level by the early 2000s. That increase is associated with a large decline in the region's dependence on commodity exports (as its manufacturing exports grew). Commodity exports as percentage of total merchandize exports in East Asia declined to 20 percent in the early 2000s, falling to the lowest current level among the developing-country regions (an average of 20 percent in the early 2000s). The high

---

31. The ratios in table 1.6 were calculated by adding the value of exports and imports of all countries in every region and then dividing that aggregate by the total GDP of countries in the region. A similar methodology was used in table 1.7.

Table 1.7 Commodities exports (percent of merchandise exports)

	1970–79	1980–89	1990–99	2000–01[a]	Change from early 1970s to early 2000s	Change from first to last year
East Asia and Pacific	61.1	47.2	22.8	20.0	−41.1	−48.2
Latin America and Caribbean	79.6	74.0	56.2	51.5	−28.1	−32.7
Middle East and North Africa	94.9	88.5	83.2	86.3	−8.6	−7.6
South Asia	49.8	41.3	23.9	21.9	−27.8[b]	−29.9
Sub-Saharan Africa	81.2	87.1	67.5	67.1	−14.2[b]	−14.1
Transition economies	n.a.	n.a.	45.6	44.6	n.a.	−3.1

n.a. = not available

a. 2000 for South Asia and sub-Saharan Africa.
b. For South Asia and sub-Saharan Africa, change from 1970s to 2000 only.

Source: World Bank, *World Development Indicators 2003* (CD-ROM).

trade ratio in the Middle East reflects its high dependence on oil exports. It is the region with the highest dependence on commodity exports overall, making it especially vulnerable to fluctuations in the price of oil.

Latin America and South Asia have relatively low trade ratios. Between the two, Latin America is still much more dependent on commodity exports—indeed, it remained more reliant on these exports in the 1990s and early 2000s than South Asia was in the 1970s. Africa has had relatively high trade ratios for decades, but these ratios have clearly reflected its concentration in commodities, on which the region remains highly dependent. The low amount of intraregional trade in sub-Saharan Africa (8 percent of all trade, compared with almost 50 percent in Asia; Birdsall 2004, table 3) reflects poor cross-border infrastructure and other problems as well as trade barriers; the resulting difficulty in achieving specialization and economies of scale, given the small size of many economies, reinforces the difficulty of reducing commodity dependence by diversifying into manufacturing. Finally, the transition economies have seen healthy increases in their trade ratios during the 1990s and early 2000s.

Implications of the Evidence on Sources of Financing for Development

Two conclusions emerge from this analysis. First, net capital inflows are too volatile to be counted on—even taking into account official sources. Increases in domestic sources of finance, through increased private saving, more efficient and effective taxation systems, and increased exports (particularly noncommodities), are therefore essential if development needs are to be financed predictably and sustainably.[32]

Second, differences in the relevant indicators of domestic financing sources and capacity—including private saving, tax revenue capacity, and export volumes and diversity—are substantial across regions. There is diversity within regions as well (e.g., in private saving rates across countries), but there are also substantial commonalities within regions in tax structure, in measures of trade and commodity dependence, and in access to external private capital. Those commonalities indicate that there is some logic in complementing country policies with more regionally based strategies for financing development.

Open and Radical Regionalism: Benefits and Strategies

We here discuss the benefits of open and radical regionalism and argue that this kind of regionalism is a good strategy for strengthening countries' sources of financing for development. By open regionalism, we mean regionalism viewed as a step toward helping countries to integrate further into the global economy. Devlin and Castro (in this volume) conclude that the regionalism of the 1990s has been essentially open. Similarly, Barry Eichengreen and Jeffrey Frankel (1995, 89) conclude that regionalism "has been used as a device for overcoming entrenched resistance to multilateral liberalization and for building coalitions favoring liberalization over wider areas."[33] Open regionalism may have been easier to manage during a period of global growth; still, this approach needs to be maintained and strengthened going forward, if a spaghetti-like framework of multiple regional (and bilateral) trade agreements is not to undermine an optimal open multilateral trading system (see, e.g., Bergsten 1997).

By radical regionalism, we refer to the idea that cooperative approaches within regions in the development of regional public goods can compensate for the failures of markets (IDB 2002). Because of various market imperfections, including externalities and information asymmetries, certain goods and services needed for development will not necessarily be provided by the markets. Concerted agreements among countries in a

---

32. Ironically, as domestic sources of finance improve, terms of access to international capital markets would also likely improve; international creditors and investors would become more confident in obtaining a positive return on their investment as a country diversifies its sources of finance to service the external debt on a timely basis.

33. It is important to emphasize that by no means do we want to dismiss the importance of global efforts, such as those undertaken by the WTO or by proposals of multilateral organizations, to promote international dialogue at the global level in key areas. A welcome example is the proposal for an International Tax Dialogue jointly proposed by the IMF, Organization for Economic Cooperation and Development, and World Bank on March 13, 2002.

region in a variety of areas, not only trade, can facilitate the provision of these goods and services.

We discuss the benefits of regionalism and the implications for greater emphasis on regionalism as a strategy in four areas: trade, infrastructure and economic and social institutions, arrangements to limit financial vulnerability, and negotiating strategies for adapting to a global system.[34] Willem Buiter, in his comment on chapter 2, notes that regionalism is the first-best solution to the problem that arises when the externality in public good provision is strictly regional in scope. This is usually the case for infrastructure and for certain economic and social institutions. For trade and for monetary arrangements to limit financial vulnerability, however, a global solution is best (the latter is true because, as Buiter notes, across regions, participants can benefit from the likelihood that economic shocks are less likely to be positively correlated). At the same time, we argue that regionalism, even when second-best, may also have benefits when it is an alternative to a first-best but unattainable global solution. It may also have benefits if, as an economic arrangement, it strengthens healthy political ties (as many would argue is the case with respect to the European Union). It is in that spirit that we outline the benefits of regionalism.

Regional Trade

Regional trade agreements directly enhance financing capacity to the extent they increase and diversify trade among partners (referring to pillar 3). When they include an industrialized country (as does the North American Free Trade Agreement [NAFTA], e.g., and as would the Free Trade Area of the Americas), they also increase access to foreign investment flows (referring to pillar 1). In chapter 2, Devlin and Castro discuss the benefits to member countries of recent regional trade agreements. For example, the Asia Pacific Economic Cooperation (APEC) forum launched in 1993 has led to a large increase in APEC intratrade, as well as a significant increase in overall exports by many member countries. This is the result of an important reduction in the level of protection, with average tariffs among APEC members having been halved between 1988 and 1998.

Latin America and the Caribbean provide clear evidence of the benefits of regional trade integration. In this region, more than half of noncommodity exports go to intraregional markets. Thus, regional integration is providing an impetus for export diversification into products with larger value added. Moreover, Robert Devlin and Antoni Estevadeordal (2001) show that these trends are occurring with no significant evidence of trade diversion.

---

34. We do not discuss the benefits of labor mobility.

Mexico's gains from NAFTA exemplify to a large extent the potential benefits to be gained from regional trade agreements. Not only have Mexico's annual exports more than tripled since 1993, but Mexico's export composition has also changed dramatically from a structure dominated by oil to one in which noncommodity exports with high value added have been increasing systematically. Moreover, Mexico's access to sustainable external sources of finance has improved significantly as FDI flows have accompanied the impressive growth of Mexico's total exports.

Countries that were candidates (and those that still are) for becoming members of the European Union have experienced important benefits from the treaty between EU countries and eligible countries from central and Eastern Europe. In particular, these countries have benefited from virtually free access for their industrial exports since 1995. Trade between the European Union and eligible candidates increased by 300 percent in the eight years from 1993 to 2001. Moreover, FDI between the partner countries in the treaty has systematically increased, even during the economic slowdown of the early 2000s and during the overall global fall in total FDI from 2000 to 2001.

Infrastructure and Economic and Social Institutions

Transborder infrastructure, programs to contain contagious diseases, watershed management, and management of such regional bads as environmental spillovers are all examples of regional public goods. They all refer to the provision of goods and services that are essential for development but that are not provided by markets or by single nations. Although these examples initially need, rather than generate, financing resources, they indirectly enhance the future availability of financial resources for development. In addition, they create the appropriate environment for foreign direct investment. In many cases they increase trading options and, by reducing costs, make members more competitive in global as well as regional markets.

In chapter 3, Marco Ferroni discusses extensively the concept of regional public goods. In a nutshell, pure regional public goods are those services or resources whose benefits are shared by countries in a region and that satisfy two conditions. The first is that one country's consumption of the services or resources does not subtract from the amount available to other countries. The second is that no country in the region can be excluded from the benefits. An example is investment in agricultural technology that is specific to a region or subregion because of that area's geographic characteristics.[35] Most of what we refer to as regional public

---

35. Jeffrey Sachs (2000) has argued that production technology in tropical regions has lagged behind temperate zone technology in the areas of agriculture and health. His recommendations call for concerted efforts to develop technologies specific to the needs of the tropical economies.

goods are not pure public goods in the strict sense, as they combine national and transnational benefits. Efforts to deal with shared natural resources, such as the Nile River Basin Initiative or the Mekong River Commission, and with transborder roads and other transportation infrastructure that have excludable properties are examples of regional public goods.

Exploiting the benefits from regional public goods requires a cooperative strategy on the part of at least two countries. Indeed, because regional efforts are constrained by the difficulty of coordination, or collective action, among countries, any outcome of regional cooperation can be thought of as a regional public good.

In recent years, there has been considerable attention in the development community to the problem of suboptimal investment in global public goods (see, e.g., Ferroni and Mody 2002; Kaul, Le Goulven, and Schnupf 2002; World Bank 2001). Although there is no way to make systematic comparisons, we suspect that the level of underinvestment in regional public goods within developing country regions is even greater. At least investment in global public goods brings clear benefits to the developed countries; thus, the latter nations took the lead in developing the Montreal Protocol (agreeing on reductions in ozone-depleting emissions) and are now managing the initiative to reduce global financial contagion (e.g., through development of international banking standards; see the chapter by Rojas-Suarez in this volume for a perspective from the developing countries on the Basle II initiative). In contrast, there has been extraordinarily little investment in, for example, transborder transportation in sub-Saharan Africa—to the point that it is still easier to travel from west to east Africa by flying through Europe than directly. The benefits to Africa's small, landlocked countries of a better transportation infrastructure would probably be very high.[36] The same would be true for regional electricity grids (now being developed in Central America) and for regional arrangements to reduce customs delays by harmonizing customs procedures.

In short, the level of underinvestment up to now implies a long list of investments with potentially high returns. Many of these opportunities would attract private investors if countries were to establish with their neighbors the necessary regional frameworks that would promise predictability, guarantee property rights, and so forth.

Regional Arrangements to Limit Financial Vulnerability

A major problem facing developing countries is the volatility of international capital flows. Regional arrangements can play a role in dealing

---

37. Birdsall (2004) suggests that for this reason the donors as a group ought to assess more systematically the potential benefits of supporting cross-border regional investments.

with this difficulty. There are two kinds of arrangements: regional financial integration, and regional financial cooperation to support a country or countries within the region that are facing liquidity problems as a result of loss of access to the international capital markets.

Financial integration agreements usually involve eliminating restrictions to cross-border financial operations by institutions from countries within the region. These arrangements, therefore, contribute to the increased availability of sustainable capital flows (pillar 1) and the development of financial markets (enhancing pillar 2). After the East Asian crisis in the late 1990s, countries in that region started initiatives to harmonize and standardize their bond markets. As reported by a number of analysts, the crisis motivated regional financial cooperation because of the region's desire to diversify their sources of finance beyond those available in the US and European capital markets.[37] Identifying impediments to the development of the government bond market at the local level (such as inappropriate legal and clearing systems) has been the first step. Thus, integration efforts have given impetus for reform at the domestic level.

In Latin America, the move toward financial integration has taken both an informal and a formal path. The informal process has manifested itself through the large and increasing participation of foreign banks, mostly from developed countries. This indicates a de facto integration with developed countries, rather than regional integration. The formal process has taken the form of formal regional agreements. Mexico is likely to benefit from NAFTA provisions aimed at allowing the operation of financial institutions among the three countries in the group and at avoiding discriminatory treatment of financial institutions. For the most part, however, among developing countries, progress has been quite limited, largely being restricted to efforts by Caribbean countries to develop a regional stock market (Barbados, Jamaica, and Trinidad and Tobago) and to the effort in Central America for the harmonization of capital markets.

The second kind of regional financial agreements aims at establishing a regional financing arrangement to supplement existing international facilities. This kind of initiative attempts to somehow relax the immediate constraints associated with limited and highly volatile access to net

---

37. In the view of a number of analysts of the Asian crisis, the lack of a well-developed regional bonds market played a role in the effects and magnitude of the crisis. The argument is that, in the absence of regional bond markets, a large portion of the huge stock of international reserves was invested in US dollar– and European currency–denominated assets. These investments were recycled back to the region in the form of short-term dollar–denominated debt through local banks (because there was no developed domestic bond market). The resulting currency and maturity mismatches in the context of managed exchange rates created severe fragilities in the Asian financial systems. See Rhee (2000).

international flows, both private and public.[38] A good example is the Chiang Mai Initiative in Asia, which consists of a network of bilateral swap agreements, including those between China and Japan. Through an agreed surveillance process in which countries assess each other's performance, the initiative also tries to minimize contagion effects in the region. In his comment on chapter 5 Roberto Zahler also cites the Association of South East Asian Nations' (ASEAN) pilot macroeconomic surveillance and monitoring schemes; the Arab Monetary Fund's provision of liquidity for intraregional trade; the Latin American Reserve Fund, which complements the IMF in providing liquidity financing during crises (e.g., following the currency crisis in Ecuador, the Latin American Reserve Fund lent about $400 million to the Ecuadorian government in 1999 to support its balance of payments; this loan, which constitutes the largest amount of funds disbursed by the Latin American Reserve Fund, has been amortized on a timely basis); and the operations of subregional development banks such as the Andean Development Corporation and the Arab Investment Guarantee Fund.

Regional Negotiating Strategies in a Global Economic System

The design and implementation of the rules of the game in today's global economic system do not necessarily reflect the priorities of developing countries. Nancy Birdsall (2003) refers to the reality of asymmetry in the way global rules are set, resulting from the greater power and resources of the richer economies.[39] In the current environment, in which industrial countries have in place a number of trade restrictions adversely affecting developing countries, developing countries are better positioned to negotiate the rules of the game in trade through regional blocs than by isolated efforts. The smaller economic size of developing countries weakens their ability to negotiate the rules of the global system, except to the extent with which they cooperate with each other. Their failure to get a good deal in the Uruguay Round can be compared with their initial success (on a few issues, such as acknowledgment of their right to use compulsory licensing to acquire medicines in the case of clear public health needs) in the initial meetings of the current Doha Trade Round, when several large developing countries agreed on a common negotiating strategy.

An example of how a regional strategy could strengthen developing

---

38. Buiter, in his comment on chapter 2, argues that regional IMFs and bilateral swap agreements are only acceptable as a fourth- or fifth-best approach—although they are still better than nothing at all.

39. Thus Oxfam (2002) titled its analysis of the global trading system "Rigged Rules and Double Standards." See also Birdsall and Clemens (2003) on the resulting responsibilities of the rich countries given their commitments to work with poor countries for achievement of the Millennium Development Goals.

countries' negotiating capacity in trade agreements comes from Latin America. Until its recent weakening (with Argentina's financial collapse, and before that with the Brazilian devaluation), the existence of the Southern Cone Common Market (Mercosur) and the possibility that it would be extended to include Chile, Bolivia, and the members of the Andean group in Latin America created a position of strength for Brazil and its Mercosur partners in discussions of the Free Trade Area of the Americas with the United States. Although at the time of this writing it seems more difficult, and recognizing that Latin American countries are far from homogenous and that their objectives are not always aligned, there would still be benefits to the region of developing a common negotiating strategy on issues such as agricultural subsidies to counter with strength the domestic political pressures in the United States that might otherwise dominate the final agreement.

Sustaining a common regional negotiating position is not easy, however. It requires that all governments adhere to the open portion of open regionalism. The Andean Group initially failed to work because members wanted to keep their markets closed. In the early 1990s, the fact of the agreement helped overcome entrenched protectionism. More recently, however, some member governments, including Venezuela under Chavez, have returned to nationalism, undercutting the benefits of the subregional agreement.[40] The risk has been heightened by the recent trade agreement between the United States and Colombia and Peru. Separate agreements are difficult to resist for individual countries, but they risk undermining their ability to sustain a common Latin American position in a negotiation with the United States.

A good example outside of the trade area of the use of a regional strategy to strengthen access to financing for development is the New Partnership for Africa's Development (NEPAD). African governments agreed on a common framework emphasizing their own peer review of country commitments to economic and political reforms in return for a commitment from donors to provide development finance. NEPAD represents an approach to design and monitoring of country policies at the regional level as a mechanism to better lock in predictable donor financing.

Role of RDBs in Guiding Regionalism and Enhancing the Sources of Financing for Development

Effective regionalism is no mean feat. It requires overcoming difficult coordination problems among the countries concerned. This is obvious in

---

40. The IDB and the Andean Development Corporation have not used conditionality or other visible initiatives at the country level to prevent the reversions to trade barriers that could lead to the dissolution of the Andean agreement.

the case of open regional trade agreements, which require not just agreed border arrangements but also deep integration in the sense of mutually agreed-on regulatory, safety, and other standards.[41] However, in contrast to the comprehensive regional integration of the European Union, most regional integration efforts in developing countries do not envisage the creation of supranational institutions to deal with collective action problems. To some analysts, the absence of supranational institutions able to enforce policy decisions aimed at ensuring the continuous improvement of the integration arrangements is an important weakness. For example, Robert Pastor (2001, 5) argues that a major shortcoming of the NAFTA charter is that it assumes that the social, economic, and political consequences of dismantling trade and investment barriers will be trivial: "NAFTA . . . overlooked the concept of externalities . . . that markets generate unintended but costly social, environmental, and political consequences."[42]

The combination of collective action problems in regionalism efforts of developing countries and the absence of supranational institutions indicates how important the RDBs can be in supporting regional strategies. There are at least four critical roles of the RDBs in their support of regional strategies for financing development.

First and most obvious is that they provide a coordination mechanism for member countries to plan and finance the provision of regional transborder infrastructure and other regional public goods requiring large initial investments. The potential coordination role of the RDBs has been dramatically underutilized because they have not had a simple financing mechanism for such regional goods; their principal instrument is a loan to an individual country that must carry the borrower's guarantee. Such country-based loans raise the problem of *ex ante* definition of each country's expected benefits from an investment, and thus each country's appropriate liability. (Even in the case of the highly concessional soft windows of the banks, for which borrower guarantees are not relevant, there is the need to allocate repayment of principal.) The only straightforward instrument the RDBs have for financing regional goods is, therefore, their very limited grant facilities (table 1.8). It would make sense for their members to use more of their net income to infuse their grant facilities with more resources if they are to realize their full potential as instruments of regionalism.

Still, such projects as the Central American electricity grid and the initiative to develop the Peru-Ecuador border region as part of the peace

---

41. Nancy Birdsall and Robert Lawrence (1999) discuss the public good nature of such deep integration at the regional level, and the resultant benefits for developing countries.

42. See Rojas-Suarez (2002) for a discussion of supplementary economic and financial policies that might be needed to ensure the sustainability of a Free Trade Area of the Americas in the absence of supranational institutions with the capacity to enforce policy agreements.

Table 1.8 Average annual loan disbursements and grant approvals of multilateral development banks, 1995–2002[a]

Bank	Loans (millions of dollars)	Of which: Regional (percent of total)	Grants (millions of dollars)	Of which: Regional (percent of total)
African Development Bank	1,319	1.42	49	16.48
Asian Development Bank	4,761	0.20	162	19.52
European Bank for Reconstruction and Development	2,206	n.a.	112	23.83
Inter-American Development Bank	6,124	1.24	87	34.36
World Bank	20,255	n.a.	n.a.	n.a.

n.a. = not available

a. Or years available.

Notes: Inter-American Development Bank figures are for authorized loans; Asian Development Bank figures are for loans excluding equity investment; African Development Bank figures include loans and grants; European Bank for Reconstruction and Development figures are gross disbursements; and World Bank figures are the sum of IBRD and IDA disbursements for foreign and local expenditures, and include HIPC. Grant figures are approved grants for technical cooperation.

Sources: Annual reports of the Inter-American Development Bank, Asian Development Bank, European Bank for Reconstruction and Development, and World Bank, and statistical indicators of the African Development Bank.

agreement between the two countries (both projects organized under the umbrella of the IDB and financed in part through the limited IDB grant funds) and the Asian Development Bank's (ADB) plan to improve regional gas transmission in the central Asian republics provide examples of the tremendous potential—so far largely unrealized—for the RDBs to support regional goods and, through these, to help catalyze the increased trade and increased attractiveness for foreign investment that constitute more sustainable financing sources for development.

Second, the RDBs provide technical support to regions in support of negotiating trade agreements both among developing countries in a developing region and between groups of developing countries and developed countries. For example, the IDB, along with the Organization of American States, has provided and helped finance the Secretariat for the Free Trade Area of the Americas planning. Moreover, the ADB has made resources available to support APEC's World Trade Organization capacity-building initiative through its technical assistance program.

Third, RDBs have the ability to provide a regional public good essential for development: the transmission and utilization of region-specific knowledge. That ability positions them to help countries within their respective regions design specific policies most appropriate to countries' economic needs and political constraints. The regional differences in financing sources and institutions that can further development lend support to the need for policy design with region-specific features. In chapter 4, Liliana Rojas-Suarez points to the problems faced by developing countries in adopting and implementing international standards set by global multilateral institutions, such as the IMF and the World Bank, for strengthening financial systems.[43] Showing that a too-rapid implementation of some of the financial standards may bring unwanted side effects to some countries, Rojas-Suarez calls for the design of transitional country- and region-specific policies that, in the short run, may diverge from the international standards but that, in the long run, would contribute to achieving them. Although recognizing that responsibility for policy decisions rests ultimately with the country themselves, the author makes a case for a key role for RDBs: Because the RDBs have extensive experience in dealing with the particular economic and financial features of their regions, they are well equipped to help countries in identifying constraints to the effective implementation of the standards. RDBs can also exploit synergies in designing common solutions applicable to several countries within the region.

Fourth, to the extent that developing countries are better represented in their respective RDBs than in the World Bank and the IMF, the RDBs provide a greater sense of ownership to developing countries of domestic economic and institutional reforms. Judicial and legal reforms, strengthening of the rule of law and property rights, rationalizing tax systems, improving banking supervision, and so forth are all critical for increasing export competitiveness and attracting foreign investment. The RDBs can provide a mechanism for transmitting positive policy contagion across countries within a region, especially to the extent that RDB loans are a mechanism for supporting positive policy change.[44] The African Development Bank, for example, can play a central role in support of the NEPAD process mentioned above. Ownership by developing country members of the RDBs also invites their contributing, through research and other efforts, to improving the workings of the international financial system, taking into account the difficulties that problems in the system pose for the developing countries, given their less deep financial markets and their greater vulnerability to global crises.

Similarly, the RDBs also can play a strong role in representing their developing country members in discussions of reform of the international financial system, through research and other efforts.

---

43. Other global standards-setting bodies include the Basel Committee on Banking Supervision and the Financial Stability Forum.

44. Birdsall (2004) discusses the effects of greater ownership by borrowers of the IDB, where borrowers control 50 percent of the votes as well as the leadership.

Additional examples of how RDBs can enhance each of the three pillars for financing development follow.

Role of RDBs in Enhancing Sustainable Access to International Capital Markets

Although RDBs are direct providers of net capital flows to developing countries and are, therefore, part of the statistics presented in table 1.1, a key challenge for these institutions is the design and development of financial products that improve the sustainability of net capital flows to countries in their region. In chapter 5, Manuel Hinds advances specific policy recommendations in this regard. Two of the proposed recommendations are the creation of a series of instruments aimed at enhancing debt issued by their member countries through eliminating asymmetry of information, and liquidity loans aimed at ameliorating the effects of contagion on financially healthy countries.[45]

There remains much work to be done in this area, and there is no consensus on what kind of instruments could serve the countries' needs while at the same time protecting the international credit standing of the corresponding RDB. Enhancing a country's access to international capital markets through the issue of RDB guaranteed debt is a case in point. Although some analysts strongly support the use of these instruments, others caution RDBs about the potential risks to the institutions. After the default by Argentina, the downgrade by Standard and Poors in October 2002 of three bonds issued by Argentina, Colombia, and Thailand backed by partial guarantees from the World Bank has only increased skepticism among those who oppose an extensive use of this instrument. Although the credit rating did not affect the creditworthiness of the World Bank itself, a number of analysts have argued that the downgrade damaged its credibility as perceived by bondholders and credit rating agencies. There is even more controversy over the idea of the RDBs supplementing the IMF's financial resources in dealing with liquidity crises. In discussing Hinds's chapter, Roberto Zahler puts emphasis instead on the role of RDBs in prevention, calling for them to design vulnerability indicators and early warning systems and to help the IMF in the design of debt workouts (where the RDBs' possibly greater knowledge of the local political economy might contribute to quicker and more sustainable resolution of difficult allocation of losses among taxpayers, depositors, and local and foreign creditors).

---

45. Hinds also suggests that financial integration could be further developed within regions. Certainly, increasing regional cooperation among banking supervisors and regulators would be useful. Some of Hinds's other suggestions, for example, that the RDBs require borrowers to obtain market credit ratings, are criticized by Zahler in his commentary.

The RDBs can play a significant role in promoting initiatives and reforms to improve the environment for sustainable foreign flows. The provision of regional goods such as the coordination of transport infrastructure among neighboring countries or the collective efforts to fight infectious diseases, needs the support of RDBs. As discussed above, provision of these regional public goods improves the overall investment climate and therefore helps attract foreign direct investment. In addition, RDBs can effectively support needed reforms (albeit to different degrees in the different regions) to the judiciary systems, the establishment of adequate property rights, and sound bankruptcy laws. Because countries within a region or subregion often share common institutional arrangements and laws as well as similar market practices, RDBs can exploit important synergies in designing and implementing common reforms to countries within a region.

RDBs' Contribution to Increased Private Saving Ratios and Improved Taxation Systems

RDBs are in a good position to help countries identify and prioritize reforms needed to improve their private saving ratios. Countries in Latin America have shared similar experiences during the eruption and resolution of financial crises. The IDB is, therefore, well aware of the fragilities that characterize the Latin American financial systems and can effectively and promptly support policies to strengthen financial systems in this region. In Africa, the African Development Bank could be a critical force in developing a regional consensus for encouraging reduced fertility, eventually supporting higher private saving by increasing the ratio of workers to children—a critical contributor to the saving and investment surge that began in East Asia three decades ago.[46]

Turning to the taxation systems in developing countries, here again we have a strong case justifying the adoption of regional policies with the support of RDBs. Take, for example, the high reliance on international trade taxes in Africa and the Middle East. The challenge for these regions is the improvement of other forms of taxation, such as consumption taxes, and the strengthening of tax administration systems to decrease levels of evasion. Only under those circumstances can governments in these regions reduce their dependence on the highly distortionary taxes on international trade.

In the transition economies, reforms need to be directed mostly at the creation (in some cases) or strengthening (in other cases) of modern tax institutions. Discrimination in the application of taxes across enterprises (including with the purpose of preventing firms from failing) still remains

---

46. See the essays in Birdsall and Sinding (2001).

in a number of countries.[47] The achievement of accession to the European Union is undoubtedly the greatest incentive for the potential candidates in this region to reform their tax systems. This is certainly one of the clearly stated objectives of the European Bank for Reconstruction and Development in supporting countries in this region.

RDBs' Role in Augmenting Trade-Related Resources

For the reasons advanced above related to the intrinsic knowledge of RDBs about the peculiarities of countries in their region, these institutions have the capacity to help countries identify areas of needed domestic reform (elimination of distortionary tariffs, exemptions, or other trade barriers, for example) that would enhance subregional and regional integration efforts. Helping countries to understand the benefits and limitations involved in every stage of trade liberalization, as well as enhancing their capacity to negotiate trade agreements, could provide a major contribution toward a sustainable global integration. In a nutshell, open regionalism can be enhanced by RDBs.

Final Remark

The discussion in this introductory chapter has provided but a taste of the rich analysis that the reader will find in the rest of the chapters in this book. Throughout, experts on the subject and their commentators discuss at length the different facets of regionalism and advance specific proposals and policy recommendations to strengthen the role that RDBs can play in enhancing the sources of financing for development. It is our hope that their contributions will motivate a more open and more radical regionalism throughout the developing world.

References

Anderson, James E., and Eric van Wincoop. 2001. *Borders, Trade, and Welfare.* NBER Working Paper 8515. Cambridge, MA: National Bureau of Economic Research.

Baldwin, Richard, and Paul Krugman. 2002. *Agglomeration, Integration and Tax Harmonization.* NBER Working Paper 9290. Cambridge, MA: National Bureau of Economic Research.

Bergsten, C. Fred. 1997. *Open Regionalism.* Institute for International Economics Working Paper 97-3. Washington: Institute for International Economics.

Bhagwati, Jagdish. 1992. *Regionalism and Multilateralism: An Overview.* Paper presented at the World Bank and CEPR Conference on New Dimensions in Regional Integration, (April 2–3), Washington.

---

47. See Tanzi and Tsiboures (2000) for a comprehensive discussion of the progress on fiscal reforms in the transition economies.

Birdsall, Nancy. 2003. *Global Economic Governance and Representation of Developing Countries: Some Issues and the IDB Example.* Center for Global Development Working Paper 22. Washington: Center for Global Development.

Birdsall, Nancy. 2004. *Underfunded Regionalism: A Donor Opportunity?* Washington: Center for Global Development.

Birdsall, Nancy, and Michael Clemens. 2003. *From Promise to Performance: How Rich Countries Can Help Poor Countries Help Themselves.* Brief volume 2, no. 1. Washington: Center for Global Development.

Birdsall, Nancy, and Robert Z. Lawrence. 1999. Deep Integration and Trade Agreements: Good for Developing Countries? In *Global Public Goods: International Cooperation in the 21st Century*, ed., Inge Kaul, Isabelle Grunberg, and Marc A. Stern. UNDP, Oxford University Press.

Birdsall, Nancy, and S. W. Sinding. 2001. How and Why Population Matters: New Findings, New Issues. In *Population Matters: Demographic Change, Economic Growth, and Poverty in the Developing World*, ed., Nancy Birdsall, A. C. Kelley, and S. W. Sinding. New York: Oxford University Press.

Birdsall, Nancy, and John Williamson, with Brian Deese. 2002. *Delivering on Debt Relief: From IMF Gold to a New Aid Architecture.* Washington: Center for Global Development and Institute for International Economics.

Calvo, Guillermo, and Enrique Mendoza. 1999. Globalization, Contagion, and the Volatility of Capital Flows. In *Capital Inflows to Emerging Markets*, ed., Sebastian Edwards. Cambridge, MA: National Bureau of Economic Research.

Carroll, C. D., and D. N. Weil. 1993. *Saving and Growth: A Reinterpretation.* Carnegie-Rochester Conference Series on Public Policy 40: 133–93. North-Holland.

Collier, Paul, and David Dollar. 1999. *Aid Allocation and Poverty Reduction.* World Bank Working Paper 2041. Washington: World Bank.

Devarajan, Shanta, David Dollar, and Torgny Holmgren, eds. 2001. *Aid and Reform in Africa.* Washington: World Bank.

Devlin, Robert, and A. Estevadeordal. 2001. What's New in the New Regionalism in the Americas. In *Regional Integration in Latin American and the Caribbean*, ed., Victor Bulmer-Thomas. Institute of Latin American Studies. University of London, School of Advanced Study, London.

Diamond, P. A., and J. Mirrlees. 1971. Optimal Taxation and Public Production, I: Production Efficiency (II: Tax Rules). *American Economic Review* 61, no. 8-27: 261–78.

Diaz-Alejandro, Carlos. 1985. Good-bye Financial Repression, Hello Financial Crash. *Journal of Development Economics* 19 (September/October): 1–24.

Easterly, William. 2001. *The Elusive Quest for Growth: Economists' Adventures and Misadventures in the Tropics.* Cambridge, MA: The MIT Press.

Easterly, William. 2002. *The Cartel of Good Intentions: Markets vs. Bureaucracy in Foreign Aid.* Center for Global Development Working Paper 4. Washington: Center for Global Development.

Easterly, William, and Sergio Rebelo. 1993. Fiscal Policy and Economic Growth: An Empirical Investigation, *Journal of Monetary Economics* 32, no. 3: 417–58.

Ebrill, Liam, Michael Keen, Jean-Paul Bodin, and Victoria Summers. 2001. *The Modern VAT.* Washington: International Monetary Fund.

Edwards, Sebastian. 1995. *Why are Saving Rates So Different Across Countries? An International Comparative Analysis.* NBER Working Paper 5097. Cambridge, MA: National Bureau of Economic Research.

Eichengreen, Barry, and Jeffrey Frankel. 1995. Economic Regionalism: Evidence from Two 20th Century Episodes. *North American Journal of Economics and Finance* 6, no. 2: 89–106.

Fernandez-Arias, Eduardo, and Roberto Rigobon. 2000. Financial Contagion in Emerging Markets. In *Wanted: World Financial Stability*, ed., Eduardo Fernandez-Arias and Ricardo Hausmann. Washington: Inter-American Development Bank.

Ferroni, Marco, and Ashoka Mody, eds. 2002. *International Public Goods: Incentives,*

Measurement, and Financing. Washington: Kluwer Academic Publishers and the International Bank for Reconstruction and Development, the World Bank.

Gallup, John Luke, and Jeffrey Sachs. 1999. *Geography and Economic Development.* CAER II Discussion Paper 39. Cambridge, MA: Harvard Institute for International Development.

Gavin, Michael, Ricardo Hausmann, and Ernesto Talvi. 1977. *Saving Behavior in Latin America: Overview and Policy Issues.* IDB Working Paper 346. Washington: Inter-American Development Bank.

Gropp, Reint, and Kristina Kostial. 2001. FDI and Corporate Tax Revenue: Tax Harmonization or Competition? *Finance and Development* 38, no. 2.

IDB (Inter-American Development Bank). 2002. *Beyond Borders: The New Regionalism in Latin America.* Washington: Inter-American Development Bank.

IFIAC (International Financial Institutions Advisory Commission). 2000. *International Financial Institutions Reform.* Washington: IFIAC, US Congress (March).

Kaul, Inge, Katell Le Goulven, and Mirjam Schnupf. 2002. *Global Public Goods Financing: New Tools for New Challenges.* New York: Office of Development Studies, United Nations Development Programme.

Kelley, Allen, and Robert M. Schmidt. 1995. Aggregate Population and Economic Growth Correlations: The Role of the Components of Demographic Change. *Demography* 32, no. 4: 543–55.

Kelley, Allen, and Robert M. Schmidt. 2001. Economic and Demographic Change: A Synthesis of Models, Findings and Perspectives. In *Population Matters: Demographic Change, Economic Growth and Poverty in the Developing World,* ed. Nancy Birdsall, A. C. Kelley, and S. W. Sinding. New York: Oxford University Press, 67-105.

Loayza, Norman, Humberto Lopez, Klaus Schmidt-Hebbel, and Luis Serven. 1998. *Saving in the World: Stylized Facts.* World Bank, Washington. Photocopy.

Lora, Eduardo. 2001. *Structural Reforms in Latin America: What Has Been Reformed and How to Measure It.* Inter-American Development Bank, Working paper 466. Washington: Inter-American Development Bank.

McKinnon, Ronald. 1973. *Money and Capital in Economic Development.* Washington: Brookings Institution.

Ocampo, José Antonio. 2001. Past, Present, and Future of Regional Integration. In *Integration and Trade* 5, no. 13. Washington: Inter-American Development Bank.

Oxfam. 2002. Rigged Rules and Double Standards: Trade, Globalization and the Fight against Poverty. www.maketradefair.com (accessed in August 2003).

Pastor, Robert. 2001. *Toward a North American Community: Lessons from the Old World to the New.* Washington: Institute for International Economics.

Plies, William, and Carmen Reinhart. 1999. Saving in Latin America and Lessons from Europe. In *Accounting for Saving,* compiled by Carmen Reinhart. Washington: Inter-American Development Bank.

Radelet, Steven, and Jeffrey Sachs. 1998. *Shipping Costs, Manufactured Exports, and Economic Growth.* Paper presented at the 1998 American Economics Association meeting, January, Chicago.

Rhee, S. Ghon. 2000. *Regionalized Bond Markets: Are the Region's Markets Ready?* Paper prepared for the Workshop on Asian Development Forum on Strengthening Regional Financial Architecture, Singapore, June 7–8.

Rojas-Suarez, Liliana. 2002. *Toward a Sustainable FTAA: Does Latin America Meet the Necessary Financial Preconditions?* Institute for International Economics Working Paper 02-4. Washington: Institute for International Economics.

Sachs, Jeffrey D. 2000. *Tropical Underdevelopment.* Center for International Development, Harvard University, Working paper 57. Cambridge, MA: Harvard University.

Shome, Parthasarathi. 1999. *Taxation in Latin America: Structural Trends and Impact of Administration.* IMF Working Paper WP/99/19. Washington: International Monetary Fund.

Tanzi, Vito, and George Tsiboures. 2000. *Fiscal Reform over Ten Years on Transition.* IMF Working Paper WP/00/113. Washington: International Monetary Fund.

Tanzi, Vito, and Howell H. Zee. 2000. *Tax Policy for Emerging Markets: Developing Countries*. IMF Working Paper WP/00/35. Washington: International Monetary Fund.

United Nations. 2001. *Report of the High-Level Panel on Financing for Development*. New York: United Nations General Assembly.

Wilson, J. 1999. Theories of Tax Competition. *National Tax Journal* 52, no. 2: 269–304.

World Bank. 2001. *Global Development Finance 2001: Building Coalitions for Effective Development Finance*. Washington: World Bank.

Appendix 1.1
Lessons from Taxation in Open Economies

The increasing mobility of capital has given rise to a new literature on taxation in open economies. One branch of theoretical analysis predicts two outcomes. The first is that in their efforts at retaining foreign direct investment, countries will engage in a race to the bottom; that is, countries will engage in tax competition that drives corporate tax rates to levels below what is optimal from a social perspective. Evidence of tax competition within OECD countries is presented by Reint Gropp and Kristina Kostial (2001) who show that between 1988 and 1997, the OECD average statutory corporate tax rate declined from 44 percent to 36 percent while the dispersion around the average also declined significantly. The second impact on taxation resulting from increasing capital mobility is that to offset the losses in taxation revenues from corporations, countries would redistribute the tax burden from mobile capital onto less mobile factors, especially labor. This may result in more regressive tax systems.[48] Supporters of this analysis recommend the harmonization of capital tax rates between countries or regions potentially subject to engage in a suboptimal tax competition.

A second branch of the literature argues that countries significantly differ in other respects that are more relevant than tax systems for corporations, so that the emphasis on corporate tax rates as a determinant to net inflows of foreign direct investment should not be overstated.[49]

Although the issue of competition versus harmonization of corporate tax rates remains unresolved even in more developed countries, several policy recommendations that are consistent with alternative theoretical analysis can be advanced for developing countries. The first is that countries should agree to national treatment of capital; that is, foreign investors should be treated no less favorably than domestic investors. As the 2001 United Nations' *Report of the High-Level Panel on Financing for Development* (the so-called Zedillo Report, p. 46) indicated, "national treatment

---

48. A review of the literature on tax competition is contained in Wilson (1999). The theoretical analysis regarding the difficulties to tax corporations' income in small open economies derives from Diamond and Mirrlees (1971).

49. For example, Baldwin and Krugman (2002) argue that wealthy countries are in a better position than less developed countries to offer capital favorable external economies such as an established base of infrastructure or accumulated experience. These benefits allow some countries to levy relatively high tax rates without the danger of losing mobile capital. Indeed, when dividing EU countries into two categories—the wealthiest and the less advanced nations—Baldwin and Krugman did not find that the average corporate tax rate between the two subgroups followed a race to the bottom. Instead, since the mid-1980s, tax rates of the less wealthy countries have been converging upward, toward those rates prevailing in the richest countries of the European Union.

does not mean special treatment: foreign investors should not be exempted from domestic laws governing corporate and individual behavior, nor should the authority or domestic courts, tribunals and regulatory authorities over foreign investors and their enterprises be curtailed. . . . The wrong way (to attract foreign direct investment) is to hand out tax concessions or erode domestic social or environmental standards."

A second policy recommendation is that focusing excessively on the matter of corporate taxation as a way to attract international capital may distract from reforms in other areas, such as improved bankruptcy laws, efficient judicial systems, and enforcement of the rule of law and contracts, that might be more important to attract and retain foreign direct investment. A third recommendation is that given the long list of problems facing developing countries in optimizing their tax structure, modifications to the corporate tax system should not be made in a vacuum but with consideration for all the other components of the tax structure.

2

Regional Banks and Regionalism: A New Frontier for Development Financing

ROBERT DEVLIN and LUCIO CASTRO

The 1990s witnessed the parallel forces of globalization and regionalization strongly at work. Although seemingly contradictory, these forces are, in fact, complementary dimensions of market development. This chapter focuses on regionalism and, in particular, on policy-driven regional co-operation. We give special attention to recent advances and challenges in two crucial aspects of regionalism: regional trade and financial co-operation. We also explore how regional development banks (RDBs) are supporting regional initiatives, and we identify some emerging issues with which these banks should be preparing to deal.

Regional Integration and Development

Concept of Regional Integration

Regional integration occurs naturally, albeit very unevenly, during the course of development of private markets.[1] This natural market integration is characterized by a progressive convergence of economic and social parameters between localities and regions and by increasing degrees of interdependence.

Robert Devlin is deputy manager of the Integration and Regional Programs Department of the Inter-American Development Bank. Lucio Castro is a senior economist at Maxwell Stamp Plc. The authors thank Antoni Estevadeordal, Gary Hufbauer, and Jaime Zabludovsky for their helpful comments. The views expressed here are the authors' and not necessarily those of the Inter-American Development Bank.

1. This section draws substantially on Devlin, Estevadeordal, and Krivonos (2002).

Regional integration can also be driven by policy-induced regional cooperation or regionalism. Formal policy-induced integration can emerge in the economic, social, or political sphere. Many developing countries share a particularly extensive postwar experience with economic integration, the most typical starting point of which has been the creation of free trade areas or customs unions (often with the objective of developing these areas into a common market or community).

Two or more countries in a region can also cooperate without pretension of regional integration (Balassa 1961). This more functional regional cooperation involves an adjustment of policies and activities to achieve outcomes that the parties prefer to the status quo. Mutually beneficial functional regional cooperation is possible in practically any field of public policy, from security matters to environmental concerns, disaster management, or epidemiological issues. Although functional regional cooperation can and does occur independent of formal integration processes, it also can constitute a parallel track to such a process or, through time, contribute to its emergence.

Reciprocal preferential trade agreements are very often the point of departure for formal regional integration, for several reasons. First, trade usually attracts support from the relatively well-organized and well-financed private business communities. Second, unlike many other economic arrangements, the mutual benefits of trade agreements and the distribution of those benefits can be reasonably assessed ex ante by participants and can be monitored and enforced ex post, because they usually contain very precise legal language and because the institutions for negotiating and administering such agreements are usually already in place. Third, trade agreements such as free trade areas can be designed in ways that initially involve little concession of national sovereignty, and thus can accommodate nationalistic sentiments. Fourth, trade agreements among members of the World Trade Organization (WTO) are subject to the multilateral rules and procedures of that organization.

In contrast, regional agreements in areas outside of trade tend to be difficult to negotiate, in part because of the very nature of the issues to be negotiated. Whereas preferential trade arrangements are concerned with the removal of distorting policies, integration in other economic areas, as well as in the social and political fields, often requires the introduction of new policies, which can be more difficult to deal with because they impinge on sovereignty. Moreover, installed institutional cross-border capacities for these areas are often less well developed than those for trade. Finally, a critical mass of regional trade among partners acts as a support structure on which other areas of regional cooperation can be built.

Indeed, growing and mutually beneficial economic interdependence among countries in a region typically induces demands for further economic cooperation to exploit more fully the revealed advantages of a maturing regional market. Moreover, demands for noneconomic and even political cooperation arise from the social externalities generated by closer economic ties. In effect, the centripetal forces of trade among partners can be an effective catalyst for deeper formal integration, whether planned or not. An excellent contemporary example is western Europe, where growing interdependence through trade has served to drive forward a political agenda, among certain partners at least, of very deep integration and broad-based cooperation. In effect, the opening of regional markets has served to widen the scope of cooperation, or, has led to "integration by stealth" (García and Glocker 2000).

Policy-induced financial integration is complex and usually lags the integration of goods markets. It involves the liberalization or harmonization of money and capital markets to facilitate payments and provide a primary source for medium- to long-term securities and debt instruments, which are essential for investment in the regional market. In the broadest sense, it includes all capital market institutions, such as commercial banks, private financial institutions, investment funds, and insurance companies (United Nations Economic Commission for Africa 2001).[2]

New Regionalism

The 1990s witnessed what some have called the New Regionalism (Ethier 1998), led by trade agreements that had as their objective the creation of free trade areas or common markets.[3] The important defining difference between the New Regionalism and earlier postwar efforts at regional integration was the policy environment. The policy framework encompassing the old regionalism of the postwar period in developing countries involved an inward-looking, protectionist, state-led import substitution strategy, often by authoritarian regimes. In contrast, the New Regionalism occurs within a framework of policy reform that promotes open and competitive market-based economies in a modern, democratic institutional setting. Indeed, the New Regionalism is an extension of that very process.

Perhaps the most dramatic change in the character of regional integration efforts, however, was the gradual shift during the 1990s from the traditional intraregional (South–South) focus toward a growing interest in interregional (North–South) agreements, which link developing countries

---

2. Financial integration also can be driven by market forces. Foreign direct investment and the internationalization of financial systems, in particular the banking sector, might generate a noninstitutionalized financial integration among different economies. As an example, during the 1990s in Latin American and the Caribbean the increasing participation of foreign banks and investment funds drove a de facto integration of financial markets across the region (Zahler and Budnevich 1998).

3. This section draws substantially on Devlin and Estevadeordal (2001).

commercially with industrialized countries in reciprocal free trade, often in conjunction with ambitious functional cooperation programs. This is something that would have been politically inconceivable before the new policy framework was adopted. Examples of this trend are Mexico's participation in the North American Free Trade Agreement (NAFTA); Canada's free trade agreements with Costa Rica and Chile; Chile's negotiations toward a free trade area with the United States; the European Union's free trade and cooperation agreements with Mexico, Chile, and South Africa and its ongoing negotiations with the Southern Cone Common Market (Mercosur), Chile, and the countries of the Caribbean Community (Caricom); the Western Hemisphere summit process and negotiations toward a Free Trade Area of the Americas (FTAA), and the Asia-Pacific Economic Cooperation forum and Singapore's recent free trade agreement with Japan.

Objectives

Developing countries' interest in pursuing regional integration agreements (RIAs) involves more than securing stable access to markets. The broader motive is to strengthen structural reform and the capacity to participate in globalization. This motive is seen when examining some of the specific objectives of the new regional integration.

■ The clearest link to the structural reform process is the enhancement of countries' commitments to trade liberalization, which has been a central feature of many developing countries' development strategy. In effect, regional economic integration has become the third tier of a three-tier process, with the first two tiers being unilateral and multilateral opening. Moreover, regional opening is facilitated by political economy considerations: full reciprocity, binding rules-based commitments, and the possibility of signaling liberalizing commitments to the private sector, especially when it is not feasible to pursue unilateral or multilateral opening. The three tiers have worked in tandem to reinforce each other (see Mercosur's Brazil and Argentina in figure 2.1). Regional opening goes beyond what can be achieved through the unilateral and multilateral approaches, lowers average levels of protection, and increases competition. Meanwhile, the commitment to unilateral and multilateral opening gives credibility to these commitments to liberalize more ambitiously at the regional level.[4]

■ Regional trade agreements (especially those with deep objectives) or the so-called second-generation free trade agreements (which go beyond

4. In contrast, in Latin America during the 1960s it was the strong overall commitment to high levels of protection that eroded the credibility of programs to liberalize regionally (Devlin and Estevadeordal 2001).

Figure 2.1 Argentina and Brazil: Tariffs to partner countries

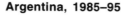

Argentina, 1985–95

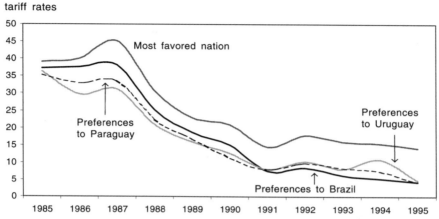

Brazil, 1985–95

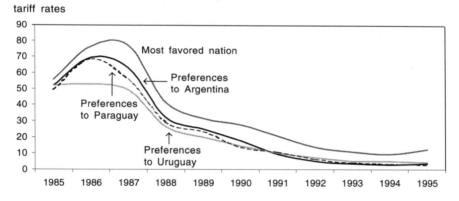

Source: Estevadeordal, Goto, and Saez (2000).

traditional market access in goods) encourage institutional modernization directly through the disciplines they introduce and indirectly through the increased demands brought about through regional competition.

- Regional agreements establish disciplines within a framework of legal rights and obligations and, hence, lock-in commitments, making them more difficult to retract than unilateral pledges (Fernández 1997).

- Reciprocal opening, guarantees of market access, trade preferences, and the like provide new opportunities for export growth and diversification.

Regional markets also serve as an outlet for an important array of products such as textiles, dairy products, meat, and processed foods, which confront very high levels of international protection.

- The New Regionalism is designed to create trade, but regional integration builds on longer-term strategic considerations that arise from imperfect and incomplete markets at home and abroad that handicap both the spread of efficiency gains in certain sectors and the development of new production patterns with progressively higher degrees of value added (Devlin and Ffrench-Davis 1999). That is to say, dynamic economic transformation effects are sought through the catalyst provided by access to a secure, enlarged market; more specific information flows; and defined market competition and identifiable export opportunities, all of which can induce investment, greater specialization (through economies of scale), product differentiation, increased productivity, competitiveness, employment, and growth. In the process, regional integration also can contribute to completing markets in labor, finance, and technology.

- As W. Ethier (1998) has pointed out, developing countries worldwide now compete to attract foreign direct investment (FDI), recognizing its potential contribution in the areas of export networks, technological and know-how spillovers, and institutional modernization. A regional agreement, by creating a larger, liberalized, rules-based regional market, can help member countries compete for—and attract—FDI (Blomstrom and Kokko 1997). Moreover, because FDI tends to cluster geographically, initial success in this area can lead to even more success.

- A group of like-minded countries can use a regional scheme to, among other things, establish a security network for fragile democracies, promote disarmament and peace among neighbors, and enhance bargaining power in international geopolitical forum.

- The New Regionalism also is reflected in an increased interest in functional regional cooperation in the economic, social, and political arenas to deal with externalities arising from increasing interdependencies in regional and world markets.

Finally, developing countries are showing an increasing interest in North–South agreements because they perceive that a regional agreement anchored by an industrialized country whose policies are credible will magnify the benefits just outlined.

Potential Costs

For developing countries undergoing policy reform, RIAs are part of the reform process; like any other structural reform, they require adjustments, which impose costs on the participating countries.[5] These costs should be minimized where possible. Some of the costs that typically emerge are the following:

- Preferences and rules of origin in regional trade agreements can divert trade away from nonmember countries even when such trade is more efficient (Bhagwati and Panagariya 1996; Yeats 1996). Some trade diversion is inevitable in preferential arrangements, and it imposes costs on domestic consumers and on countries outside the arrangement. These costs must be weighed against the amount of trade created and against the potential for this trade diversion to evolve into cost-reducing and welfare-enhancing dynamic transformation effects (Corden 1972; Ffrench-Davis 1980). Some analysts point out that North–South RIAs present fewer risks of trade diversion than do South–South arrangements (Venables, forthcoming).

- When there are serious asymmetries in average tariff levels between partners to an economic integration agreement, the loss of tariff revenue in the high-tariff country can have a serious redistributive impact between partners (Panagariya 1996). Part of what would have been realized as tariff revenue on imports from the partner country before the agreement is transferred to the partner's producers as tariffs are eliminated.

- In the absence of corrective mechanisms, the benefits of regional integration are often asymmetrically distributed among partners, with some partners receiving the bulk of the benefits while others are dependent on uncertain spillovers (Puga and Venables 1997).

Regional integration also presents risks for third parties.

- An explosion of economic integration agreements, with preferences granted to participants, can create a "spaghetti bowl" of differing trade and investment rules that reduce transparency and raise administrative costs in world trade (Wonnacott and Wonnacott 1995).

- Although enlarged regional markets and expanded preferences can attract FDI, they can also divert FDI from locations where it would be more efficient (Winters 1997).

- The emergence of agreements can create a "gang effect," leaving other countries little option but to join the agreement (Winters 2001).

- Regional integration can distract attention from, and hence weaken, the multilateral system (Winters 2001).

---

5. This section draws substantially on Devlin and Ffrench-Davis (1999).

An RIA is not an end in itself, but an instrument to achieve an objective. Hence, the only way to determine whether an agreement makes sense for the participating countries and the rest of the world is to evaluate the benefits and weigh them against the costs. Unfortunately, empirical evaluation is inherently difficult because of serious gaps in data availability, the complex causality of dynamic productive transformation effects (from which one expects the greatest benefits), and the methodological difficulties in generating plausible conclusions from broad counterfactual analysis.

Trends in Regional Integration

Regional Integration in Africa

Regional integration has been an element of countries' development strategies in Africa for most of the postwar period.[6] In part as a result of decolonization, the number of regional integration initiatives boomed in the 1960s. Today, as reflected in the treaty establishing the African Economic Community, integration remains a key strategy for overcoming Africa's problems of poverty and inefficient scale and for promoting economic growth. However, most of the regional groupings created in the 1960s no longer exist, and the record of contemporary agreements has been, according to the United Nations, unsatisfactory at best.[7]

The current integration landscape of the region includes a wide array of RIAs of varying design, scope, and objectives. Five subregional integration arrangements together encompass all of the countries of Africa:

- the Arab Maghreb Union, whose five members (Algeria, Libya, Mauritania, Morocco, and Tunisia) include all of North Africa except Egypt;

- the Common Market of Eastern and Southern Africa (COMESA), which includes all but one of the countries of eastern Africa, as well as parts of southern Africa (Angola, Botswana, Burundi, the Comoros, the Democratic Republic of the Congo, Djibouti, Egypt, Eritrea, Ethiopia, Kenya, Madagascar, Malawi, Mauritius, Namibia, Rwanda, Seychelles, South Africa, Sudan, Swaziland, Tanzania, Uganda, Zambia, and Zimbabwe);

- the Economic Community of Central African States, whose 11 members encompass all of Central Africa (Angola, Burundi, Cameroon, the Central African Republic, Chad, the Republic of Congo, the Democratic

6. This section is based on United Nations Economic Commission for Africa (2001).

7. Many of integration arrangements in Africa seem to share the shortcomings of the Latin American Integration Association: Preferences have been only partial and not universal, and they have lacked permanency.

Republic of the Congo, Equatorial Guinea, Gabon, Rwanda, and São Tomé and Principe);

- the Economic Community of West African States (ECOWAS), which covers all of west Africa (Benin, Burkina Faso, Cape Verde, The Gambia, Ghana, Guinea, Guinea-Bissau, Côte d'Ivoire, Liberia, Mali, Mauritania, Niger, Nigeria, Senegal, Sierra Leone, and Togo); and

- the Southern African Development Community (SADC), whose 14 members encompass all of Southern Africa (Angola, Botswana, the Democratic Republic of the Congo, Lesotho, Malawi, Mauritius, Mozambique, Namibia, South Africa, Seychelles, Swaziland, Tanzania, Zambia, and Zimbabwe).

In addition, there are eight other RIAs in Africa, some of which are subsets of these five larger RIAs. The smaller groups include the Central African Economic and Monetary Community, a group of six countries from the Economic Community of Central African States; the Great Lakes River Basin, consisting of three members of Economic Community of Central African States; the East African Community of COMESA, whose members are Kenya and Uganda and SADC member Tanzania; the Indian Ocean Commission, a grouping of five countries, four of which are in COMESA, with the fifth (Réunion) a dependency of France. Other RIAs are the Intergovernmental Authority for Development, which embraces seven countries in the Horn of Africa and the northern part of East Africa; the Mano River Union, consisting of three of the member countries of ECOWAS; the West Africa Economic and Monetary Union, encompassing eight members of ECOWAS; and the Southern African Customs Union, consisting of five member countries of SADC and the East African Community, which includes Tanzania (a member of SADC) and two members of COMESA (Uganda and Kenya).

Trade

Despite decades of market integration policies and experimentation, levels of intra-African trade remain extremely low. On average, trade within African regional agreements has reached only around 10 percent of the members' total trade in the last decade. As table 2.1 indicates, the East African Community surpasses the other African RIAs in the proportion of members' total trade that is within the regional arrangement. Africa's most sluggish performers on this measure are the Indian Ocean Commission, the Interstate Committee for Drought Control in the Sahel, and the Nile Basin Initiative. The pattern and direction of commerce remain largely oriented toward Western trading partners, mostly in Europe. The average African country sends about 43 percent of its exports to the European Union and only about 10 percent to other countries in the region (IMF 2001).

Table 2.1 Africa: Trade within regional agreements as a share of total trade, 1989–98 (percent)

Agreement[a]	1989	1990	1991	1992	1993	1994	1995	1996	1997	1998	1999	Average 1995–98
All Africa	6.64	7.58	7.45	7.88	8.26	8.97	9.74	10.36	10.66	10.06	10.20	10.21
CEMAC	n.a.	n.a.	n.a.	n.a.	0.78	1.91	2.57	1.79	n.a.	n.a.	n.a.	n.a.
EAC	n.a.	n.a.	n.a.	n.a.	n.a.	34.69	18.06	24.55	10.74	19.97	19.27	18.33
ECOWAS	n.a.	n.a.	n.a.	n.a.	n.a.	n.a.	17.83	10.46	7.50	7.09	4.09	10.72
WAEMU	n.a.	n.a.	n.a.	n.a.	n.a.	n.a.	3.47	8.59	19.83	12.59	11.99	11.12
SADC	n.a.	45.10	47.78	1.70	2.94	4.74	8.31	4.67	3.84	3.05	3.20	4.97
CBI-RIFF	n.a.	6.63	4.93	2.38	3.18	10.65	7.38	10.80	5.28	11.08	10.73	8.64
CILSS	n.a.	n.a.	n.a.	n.a.	n.a.	n.a.	1.76	0.75	2.96	5.32	1.52	2.70
ECCAS	n.a.	n.a.	n.a.	n.a.	0.92	2.13	2.82	1.86	n.a.	n.a.	n.a.	n.a.
NBI	n.a.	n.a.	n.a.	0.62	n.a.	3.58	4.79	4.35	2.16	3.94	3.59	3.81
GAD	n.a.	n.a.	n.a.	0.52	n.a.	33.70	11.80	18.80	3.49	14.86	31.96	12.24
IOC	n.a.	0.85	0.34	1.15	1.51	0.87	1.17	1.35	1.63	1.76	1.33	1.48
MRU	n.a.	n.a.	n.a.	n.a.	n.a.	n.a.	0.14	0.06	0.04	n.a.	n.a.	n.a.
COMESA	n.a.	6.55	4.87	2.01	3.12	4.25	4.68	4.25	2.54	3.95	3.43	3.86

n.a. = not available

a. See the text for the full names of the agreements. Data for the Southern African Customs Union are not available.

Notes: Figures are calculated as intraregional imports multiplied by two and divided by the sum of total exports and total imports. Intraregional imports are multiplied by two because of unavailability of sufficient data on exports. Nomenclature: Harmonized System, Rev. 6 1992–96.

Source: United Nations Economic Commission for Africa (2001).

Some other key features of Africa's intraregional trade are worth noting (Yeats 1998):

- The relative importance of intraregional trade changes frequently because of unstable political conditions, volatile commodity prices, and natural disasters. The extreme instability of trade has harmed the prospects for industrialization and growth derived from intra-African commerce.

- Intraregional trade is also highly concentrated within subregional groups; almost no trade takes place between east and west Africa or between south and north Africa. These patterns indicate that transportation and cultural barriers are important obstacles to intra-African trade.

- Intraregional trade is driven by a few primary commodities: petroleum alone accounts for about one-third of this trade, and cotton, live animals, maize, and cocoa add a further 18 percent. In contrast, African trade in machinery and transport equipment accounts for less than 4 percent of intraregional trade.

- Almost no intraindustry trade occurs among African countries or between Africa and the industrialized countries.

A main factor underlying the deceptive history of African trade integration is that the elimination of barriers to intraregional trade has been, in most of the RIAs, slow and incomplete. As an example, the average rate of actual tariff reduction in COMESA by the end of 2000 was only 66.5 percent of the agreed tariff reduction plan. Moreover, the overall restrictiveness of African trade regimes remains high. The simple average of most favored nation (MFN) tariffs in 2000 was 19 percent in sub-Saharan Africa, compared with 12 percent in Asia and 12 percent in Latin America. In addition, nontariff barriers in the region have been pervasive. Africa also displays a real spaghetti bowl of regional arrangements, with multiple and overlapping memberships. Eleven African countries are members of at least two regional agreements. Yet at the same time, the integration has not generated much trade, diversification, or intraindustry specialization.

In addition, many African governments rely heavily on tariffs and other trade taxes for revenue and therefore are reluctant to pursue further trade liberalization. These are the typical difficulties associated with RIAs among small economies, where losses from eliminating tariff revenue offset gains from greater trade volume (Schiff 1996). Moreover, all the RIAs in the region, with the exception of the agreement between the European Union and South Africa, are South–South arrangements.

Finally, apart from these trade-related factors, recurrent domestic political and economic disturbances have seriously hampered trade among African countries.

Financial and Monetary Cooperation

Although several African agreements have made provisions for macroeconomic policy harmonization and other similar measures, Africa's prevailing economic conditions have made implementation an extremely complex and difficult task. High international indebtedness, largely underdeveloped financial markets, and large budget deficits are common to most of the African economies. These difficulties are only aggravated by the fact that these economies are at different levels of development and liberalization. Only one African stock exchange is regional in scope: the Regional Exchange Market of Transferable Securities, based in Abidjan, Côte d'Ivoire.

The record of African regional arrangements in terms of financial integration has been mixed. Full monetary and financial integration has been achieved in the two monetary unions (Central African Economic and Monetary Community and West Africa Economic and Monetary Union), as this was part of their structure from the outset. Monetary and financial harmonization has also been achieved in the SADC countries through official links between the Reserve Bank of South Africa and the monetary authorities of the other members. Other regional groupings, such as COMESA and ECOWAS, have established criteria for macroeconomic harmonization with a view to achieving economic and financial union. They also have established clearinghouses and RDBs. COMESA, in particular, has developed guidelines for harmonization of procedures in the capital and money markets. However, it is clear that most of the countries involved in the implementation of convergence criteria are still far from achieving some of the targets. As an example, almost half of COMESA's members were unable to meet their inflation and external debt targets. Other regional arrangements have a similarly poor record. The rest have not yet established such convergence criteria.

Regional Integration in Asia

RIAs in Asia are fewer and less deep than in other regions. Most Asian RIAs are partial preferential trade agreements or, at best, free trade areas. There is no example of a customs or monetary union. Political differences, economic disparities, and a past plagued by conflict and war have historically hampered regional cooperation. In East Asia, in particular, intraregional trade has traditionally advanced through market-led integration, not as a consequence of regional liberalization (Hosono 2001).

However, in part as a response to the worldwide wave of RIAs and the negative effect of a common financial crisis, efforts toward regional economic cooperation had received new impetus by the late 1990s. Two East Asian RIAs have dominated integration efforts in Asia during the last decade: the Asia Pacific Economic Cooperation (APEC) forum and the Association of South East Asian Nations (ASEAN). APEC belongs to the new wave of interregional, North–South RIAs. In other parts of Asia, regional integration initiatives have been far less successful. For example, the South Asian Association for Regional Cooperation has been seriously hampered from the start by the Indo-Pakistani conflict and by competition among country members' exports.

Trade

ASEAN today comprises all of the countries of Southeast Asia: Brunei Darussalam, Cambodia, Indonesia, the Lao People's Democratic Republic, Malaysia, Myanmar, the Philippines, Singapore, Thailand, and Vietnam. Although it was created more than 30 years ago, in 1967, only since the 1990s has this preferential trade agreement started to show some results on the trade liberalization front. Today ASEAN is considered the most important and promising RIA in Asia.

The ASEAN Free Trade Area was established in January 1992 during the fourth ASEAN summit meeting held in Singapore. The original goal was to reduce tariff rates on intra-ASEAN trade to less than 5 percent within 15 years, beginning in January 1993, through the adoption of a common effective preferential tariff scheme. In September 1994 the planned tariff liberalization was accelerated by shortening the initial period from 15 years to 10. Vietnam, which joined ASEAN in 1995 and ASEAN Free Trade Area in 1996, was granted a 10-year implementation period, ending in 2006.

Driven by these renewed liberalization efforts, intra-ASEAN trade reached significant levels over the 1990s (table 2.2). On average, intraregional trade represented around 21 percent of the total trade of ASEAN members between 1993 and 2000. The importance of the region in ASEAN's total trade varies across countries, from 35 percent in the case of Brunei Darussalam to 13 percent in the Philippines.

Members' extra-ASEAN trade is mostly with industrialized countries, in particular the United States and Japan. In fact, according to ASEAN (2001), trade with the United States represented around 18 percent of total ASEAN trade in 1993–2000. The importance of the US market as a destination also varies greatly within the group, from only around 7 percent of total trade in Brunei Darussalam to around 25 percent in Malaysia. Japan and the European Union closely follow the United States as ASEAN trade partners, with around 17 percent and 14 percent of total trade, respectively. Among nonmember developing countries, China has recently acquired an increasing share of ASEAN trade, from around 2 percent in 1993 to around 8 percent in 2000 (ASEAN 2001).

The APEC initiative was launched in 1993 with the goal of promoting the free exchange of goods, services, and investment among its members

Table 2.2   Asia: Trade within regional agreements as a share of total trade (percent)

Agreement	1970	1980	1985	1990	1995	1996	1997	1998	1999
APEC	57.8	57.9	67.7	68.3	71.9	72.1	71.8	69.7	71.9
ASEAN	22.9	18.7	19.8	19.8	25.4	25.4	25.0	21.7	22.2
SAARC	3.2	4.8	4.5	3.2	4.4	4.3	4.0	5.3	4.7

APEC = *Asia Pacific Economic Cooperation*. Members include Australia, Brunei Darussalam, Canada, Chile, People's Republic of China, Hong Kong, Indonesia, Japan, Republic of Korea, Malaysia, Mexico, New Zealand, Papua New Guinea, Peru, Philippines, Russia, Singapore, Taiwan, Thailand, United States, and Vietnam.

ASEAN = *Association of South East Asian Nations*. Members include Brunei Darussalam, Cambodia, Indonesia, Lao People's Democratic Republic, Malaysia, Myanmar, Philippines, Singapore, Thailand, and Vietnam.

SAARC = *South Asian Association for Regional Cooperation*. Members include Bangladesh, Bhutan, India, Maldives, Nepal, Pakistan, and Sri Lanka.

Notes: Figures are calculated as intraregional imports multiplied by two and divided by the sum of total exports and total imports. Intraregional imports are multiplied by two because of unavailability of sufficient data on exports.

Source: World Bank (2001).

as a tool for sustainable economic growth and development. Free trade was placed on the APEC agenda in 1994, with the very ambitious objective of achieving free trade throughout the region by 2010 for the industrial-country members and by 2020 for the developing ones. In 1995 the Osaka Action Agenda established a practical mechanism for achieving that goal: the Individual Action Plans. The mechanism is quite unique for an RIA in that the Individual Action Plans are voluntary agreements for unilateral MFN—not preferential—liberalization in both trade and investment. The main criticisms have been that Individual Action Plans do not provide liberalization beyond existing WTO disciplines or already-determined domestic liberalization schedules (Aggarwal and Morrison 1999; Bergsten 1997a, 1997b).

When combined with national unilateral programs, the regional liberalization effort within APEC has resulted in an important reduction in protection. In fact, the average unweighted tariffs among APEC members were reduced by more than half between 1988 and 1998, from 15.4 percent to 7.6 percent (Lee 1999).[8] APEC intratrade increased explosively through the first part of the 1990s but was hindered by the financial crisis of 1997–98. Moreover, progress at trade liberalization has been scant

8. This figure must be interpreted with care, however, because the average is affected by extra-APEC commitments such as the Canada–US FTA, NAFTA, and Uruguay Round liberalizations. Thanks to Jaime Zabludovsky for this observation.

in certain sectors—in particular, such sensitive industries as fishing and wood (Feinberg 2000).

At each year's ministerial meeting, APEC defines and funds work programs for three committees, one subcommittee, 10 working groups, and other APEC forums. The committees are the Committee on Trade and Investment, the Economic Committee, and the Budget and Management Committee. The Committee on Trade and Investment aims to develop an APEC perspective on trade and investment issues and to pursue liberalization and facilitation initiatives. It is responsible for implementation of the Osaka Action Agenda, including work on tariffs, nontariff measures, services, deregulation, dispute mediation, implementation of WTO obligations, investment, customs procedures, standards and conformance, mobility of businesspeople, intellectual property rights, competition policy, government procurement, and rules of origin. The core activity of the Committee on Trade and Investment is implementation and enhancement of the collective action plans, which are the main vehicle for advancing APEC's agenda on trade and investment facilitation. The main function of the Economic Committee is to analyze economic trends and issues in support of APEC's trade and investment liberalization and economic and technical cooperation agendas.

In South Asia, attempts have also been made to encourage regional trade under the aegis of the South Asian Association for Regional Cooperation, established in 1985. In 1993 a South Asian Preferential Trade Agreement was drawn up, providing for bilateral reductions in tariff and nontariff barriers on specified commodities on a reciprocal basis, but with special provisions given to the least-developed countries. The ultimate but failed goal of the South Asian Preferential Trade Agreement was to achieve by 2001 a South Asian Free Trade Area based on multilateral tariff reductions. As the Center for Strategic and International Studies (1999) has noted, "although tariff concessions have not been negligible, they have been introduced on items that represent no more than 1 percent of the total" trade of this regional grouping. In sum, the achievements of the South Asian Association for Regional Cooperation and the South Asian Preferential Trade Agreement in terms of trade liberalization have been very modest indeed.

Finally, a new North–South RIA emerged recently in Asia when Japan signed its first free trade agreement, with Singapore. Another such agreement may be forthcoming if a Chinese proposal for a pan-Asian free trade area prospers. These new RIAs belong to a recent wave of new bilateral free trade areas and subregional arrangements across the region, particularly among the East Asian countries (Hosono 2001). At least 20 new preferential initiatives already are at various stages of negotiation, planning, and study.[9]

---

9. See Scollay and Gilbert (2001) for a list of these initiatives.

Financial and Monetary Cooperation

The financial crisis that affected the entire region in 1997–98 has propelled monetary and financial regional cooperation initiatives among the Asian countries. In the immediate aftermath of the crisis, several proposals to strengthen cooperation in those areas were advanced.[10] These efforts have been focused on three issues.

■ Three initiatives have been taken in the area comprising information exchange and surveillance. First, the Manila Framework Group was established in November 1997. It meets annually with deputies from the central banks and finance ministries from 14 countries, and with representatives of international and regional financial organizations, to provide surveillance reports. Second, the ASEAN Surveillance Process was established in 1998 to monitor policymaking in economic and social issues. The process includes provisions for capacity building and institutional strengthening. Finally, the ASEAN+3 (Japan, China, and Korea) Surveillance Process was formalized in November 1999. The ASEAN Secretary General and finance ministers of 13 countries meet twice a year to engage in policy coordination. Within the framework of the ASEAN+3, some actions have been taken to monitor private capital flows and to establish a regional early warning system.

■ Resource provision mechanisms to strengthen cooperation were also an area of focus. Although countries in the region strongly resisted the original Japanese proposal to establish a $100 billion Asian Monetary Fund, the experience and consequences of the 1997 financial crisis brought new impetus to the idea of a regional stabilization fund. In May 2000, the ASEAN+3 launched the Chiang Mai Initiative (CMI). The CMI has been considered a potential first step toward the implementation of a Framework for Regional Monetary Stabilization (Sussangkarn 2000a) along the lines of the initial idea for an Asian Monetary Fund. The CMI's main goal is to establish a regional financing arrangement to supplement existing international facilities. Some progress has been made within the CMI framework. An ASEAN swap arrangement was set up, covering all ASEAN members and encompassing funds of around $1 billion. In addition, a network of bilateral swaps and repurchase agreements was created, including also China, Japan, and South Korea. The bilateral swaps and repurchase agreements' main goal is to provide short-term liquidity assistance in the form of dollar-denominated swaps. Seven bilateral swaps and repurchase agreements are now in place, out of a possible 30. However, the amounts involved are small compared with total cross-border capital flows. Finally, there

---

10. This section draws in large part on ADB (2002).

are also provisions within the CMI framework to establish repurchase agreements to provide liquidity through securities trade, among other initiatives (Sussangkarn 2000a, 2000b).

- Progress in the area of regional exchange rate agreements has been slower than in the previous two areas. Efforts have been focused more on conducting detailed studies on implementing concrete steps toward macroeconomic and exchange rate policy harmonization. For example, an ASEAN Task Force on Currency and Exchange Rate Mechanisms was established in March 2001. Other regional projects are exploring the potential for monetary and financial cooperation within the region. The Kobe Research Project is an initiative of Asian and European finance ministers to promote monetary cooperation in East Asia. Studies in the project are concerned with a variety of topics including information exchange, surveillance, and regional financing facilities as well as regional exchange rate arrangements and coordination mechanisms. The projects' ultimate goal is development of a road map for ASEAN+3 cooperation in this area.

- The primary emphasis of the countries is on financial and monetary cooperation: Some have expressed interest in initiating action toward a common currency, but if the European experience is any indication, this is a long-term proposition.

Other Cooperation

ASEAN and APEC are involved in an extensive array of other regional cooperation programs (table 2.3).

Regional Integration in Latin America and the Caribbean

Trade

Since 1990, the countries of Latin America and the Caribbean have launched close to 30 free trade areas or customs unions aiming at building a common market or economic community (table 2.4). Initially these agreements were intraregional, but beginning with Mexico's entry into a free trade agreement with the United States and Canada, there has since emerged a wave of interest in North–South agreements.

The major intraregional blocs are the following:

- Mercosur, with Argentina, Brazil, Paraguay, and Uruguay as members and with Chile and Bolivia as free trade associates

- The Central American Common Market (CACM), whose members are Costa Rica, El Salvador, Guatemala, Honduras, and Nicaragua

Table 2.3 Asia: Forms of regional cooperation within regional agreements

	Trade-related	Economic	Nontrade cooperation				Other
			Political	Social and cultural	Environment	Human resources and science and technology	
Asia Pacific Economic Cooperation forum	Deregulation, dispute mediation, implementation of World Trade Organization obligations, customs procedures, standards and conformance, intellectual property rights, competition policy, government procurement, and rules of origin	Macroeconomic policy, financial stability, structural reforms, economic infrastructure, business facilitation, financial systems, free movement of investments, mobility of businesspeople, capital markets, energy, tourism, fisheries, transportation, telecommunications, small and medium-size enterprises, agriculture, rural infrastructure, food production, and biotechnology	Political dialogue through ministerial meetings	Social safety, social development, and gender integration	Environmental protection and marine resource conservation	Industrial science and technology, human resources development, knowledge and skills development, information and communications technology, and electronic commerce	Emergency preparedness

Association of South East Asian Nations			Political and security cooperation	Human and social development, poverty reduction, women and youth issues, cultural cooperation	Environment	Science and technology, human resources development, information and communication technology and electronic commerce	Combating the abuse of and traffic in narcotics and drugs and transnational crime
	Customs, dispute settlement, standards, and conformance	Macroeconomic and financial stability; freeing movement of capital; investment facilitation; industrial development; infra-structure; food, agriculture, and rural development; forestry; mining; energy; energy; tourism; transport; and communication					

Source: Devlin, Estevadeordal, and Krivonos (2002).

Table 2.4 Bilateral and plurilateral preferential trade agreements involving countries in the Americas

Agreement	Entry into force
First-generation agreements	
Chile-Mexico (Latin American Integration Association model)	1992
Chile-Venezuela	1993
Bolivia-Chile	1993
Colombia-Chile	1994
Chile-Ecuador	1995
Chile-Mercosur	1996
Bolivia-Mercosur	1997
Chile-Peru	1998
Second-generation agreements	
Central American Common Market (CACM)[a]	1960
Andean Community (AC)[a]	1969
Caribbean Community (Caricom)[a]	1973
Southern Cone Common Market (Mercosur)	1991
United States–Canada	1992
North American Free Trade Agreement (NAFTA)	1994
Costa Rica-Mexico	1995
Group of Three (G-3)[b]	1995
Bolivia-Mexico	1995
Canada-Chile	1997
Mexico-Nicaragua	1998
Chile-Mexico	1999
Mexico-Israel	2000
Mexico-EFTA	2000
CACM–Dominican Republic	2001
Caricom–Dominican Republic	2001
CACM-Chile[c]	2001
Mexico–El Salvador-Guatemala-Honduras	2001
Mexico–European Union Association Agreement	2001
Costa Rica–Canada[d]	2001
Chile–European Union Association Agreement[c]	2002
Costa Rica–Trinidad and Tobago[d]	2002
El Salvador–Panama[d]	2002
Chile–European Union	2002

a. Relaunched in the 1990s.
b. Colombia, Mexico, and Venezuela.
c. Pending full legislative approval.
d. Awaiting ratification.

Sources: IDB (2000) and authors' compilation.

- The Andean Community, consisting of Venezuela, Colombia, Ecuador, Peru, and Bolivia

- Caricom, consisting of Antigua and Barbuda, the Bahamas, Barbados, Belize, Dominica, Grenada, Guyana, Haiti, Jamaica, St. Kitts and Nevis, St. Lucia, St. Vincent and the Grenadines, Suriname, Trinidad and Tobago, and Montserrat

- NAFTA, whose members are Canada, Mexico, and the United States.

The CACM, the Andean Community, and Caricom have their origins in early postwar initiatives, and they underwent renewal in the 1990s. Mercosur and NAFTA were launched in the 1990s. With the exception of NAFTA, which is an ambitious, second-generation free trade area, all have the objective of establishing common markets or economic communities.

The change in the global policy framework in the region has contributed to a fundamental change in the modalities and instruments of regional integration. Liberalization of the regional market paralleled a dramatic reduction in third-party external protection, as average MFN tariffs declined from an average of more than 40 percent in the mid-1980s to 12 percent in the mid-1990s. Moreover, the traditional laborious positive lists for regional trade liberalization (a positive list is one in which only those goods listed were subject to trade preferences) were abandoned for more automatic schedules that liberalize the bulk of trade within 10 years, generally with a very limited negative list (Devlin and Estevadeordal 2001). Meanwhile, free trade objectives began to go beyond traditional liberalization of goods to incorporate new issues such as services, investment, government procurement, and intellectual property.

Table 2.5 shows that, as these agreements emerged, intraregional trade grew considerably faster than extraregional trade, creating commercial and economic interdependencies among many of the countries for the first time in their history. Nevertheless, the United States remains the major market for most countries in the region, with the European Union's importance increasing the further south one goes (see table 2.6). Asia is an important market only for a few countries, especially Chile.

Certain characteristics of intraregional trade are worth noting:

- The opening process during the 1990s brought a flood of imports to the region. Had intraregional trade not grown as fast as it did, balance of payments problems and pressures for protection might have emerged (IDB 2000).

- More than half of Latin America and the Caribbean's exports of manufactures not based on natural resources go to intraregional markets (IDB 1998). Hence, regional integration is serving as a basis for diversification into products with greater value added.

Table 2.5. Latin America: exports within regional agreements as a share of total exports (percent)

Agreement	1970	1980	1985	1990	1995	1996	1997	1998	1999
Southern Cone Common Market	9.4	11.6	5.5	8.9	20.3	22.7	27.8	25.0	20.5
Andean Community	1.8	3.8	3.2	4.1	12.0	10.3	11.8	13.9	9.3
Caribbean Community	4.2	5.3	6.3	8.1	4.6	13.3	14.4	17.3	15.3
Central American Common Market	26.0	24.4	14.4	15.4	21.7	22.0	18.1	15.6	11.6
North American Free Trade Agreement	36.0	33.6	43.9	41.4	46.2	47.6	49.1	51.7	54.6
Group of Three[a]	1.1	1.8	1.3	2.0	3.2	2.4	2.8	2.7	1.8

a. Colombia, Mexico, and Venezuela.

Source: World Bank (2001).

■ Outside of NAFTA there is very little trade between the major subregions.

■ The array of agreements does create something of a spaghetti bowl, although this is slightly mitigated by the common frameworks that encase many of the agreements: the NAFTA framework around the Mexican bilaterals and the Latin American Integration Association framework around the South American agreements.

■ Available empirical studies suggest no evidence of systematic trade diversion (Devlin and Estevadeordal 2001), but limited evidence indicates that regional markets have provided some sectors with opportunities for efficiency gains. Indeed, interindustry trade appears to be a significant dimension of intraregional trade (Institute for the Integration of Latin America and the Caribbean (INTAL) 2000, Taccone and Nogueira 2001, Echavarria 1998, Giordano 2001).

■ Except in NAFTA, liberalization of services trade in the region has seen little progress. However, the extensive network of Mexican bilateral agreements does include liberalization of services—usually in the form of standstills—subject to important exceptions.

■ The four major intraregional groupings (Mercosur, CACM, Caricom, and the Andean Community) all have the objective of deep integration and were launched with the formation of a customs union. All provide for relatively free circulation of goods, but the common external tariff is in varying degrees of incompleteness, and tariff revenue is still in the national domain. The most advanced customs union project

Table 2.6   Latin America: Trade with the United States and the European Union as share of total, 2001 (percent)

Country	Exports	Imports	Total trade
Trade with the United States			
Honduras	88.7	73.1	80.7
Mexico	88.7	73.1	80.7
Costa Rica	49.1	50.9	50.0
Venezuela	52.4	37.6	47.5
Colombia	49.8	40.2	45.3
Guatemala	36.0	39.6	38.3
Ecuador	36.4	26.0	32.0
Nicaragua	37.9	24.2	27.9
Peru	27.4	23.4	25.3
Bolivia	24.0	22.0	22.9
Brazil	23.9	23.1	23.5
El Salvador	23.7	34.2	31.5
Chile	16.5	19.8	19.1
Argentina	11.8	18.7	15.2
Uruguay	7.8	9.7	9.0
Paraguay	3.9	7.2	6.2
Trade with the European Union			
Brazil	25.0	25.9	25.5
Chile	24.6	20.6	22.6
Argentina	16.2	21.6	18.7
Costa Rica	24.8	11.4	18.1
Uruguay	15.3	18.5	17.3
Peru	16.4	15.1	15.7
Colombia	13.6	17.0	15.3
Ecuador	14.4	14.0	14.2
Paraguay	16.0	8.6	10.8
Venezuela	6.4	17.5	10.6
Bolivia	9.5	9.8	9.7
Guatemala	6.5	8.9	7.9
El Salvador	6.1	8.3	7.7
Mexico	4.0	10.1	7.1
Nicaragua	9.3	4.6	6.3
Honduras	6.5	4.2	5.2

Source: Data from Inter-American Development Bank, Integration and Regional Programs Department, 2001.

is the Andean Community, whereas Mercosur's common external tariff is in serious disarray.

■ The old nemesis of macroeconomic instability has upset some of the integration processes of the 1990s. This instability reflects incompleteness, or policy inconsistencies, in the structural reform process and shortcomings in the international financial architecture.

- Unilateral action, as opposed to rules-based dispute settlement and compensation, was a characteristic of the old postwar integration and, except in NAFTA-inspired agreements, remains a problem in the New Regionalism.

Other dimensions of the Latin American and Caribbean experience are worth noting:

- Mercosur, the Andean Community, and the Caricom countries began in the 1990s to jointly negotiate trade agreements with third parties. Mercosur and the Andean Community partners also have worked together to stave off threats to democracy in their subregions.

- With the exception of Mexico in NAFTA (see below), FDI into Latin America and the Caribbean has been primarily attracted by national dynamics, especially privatizations (ECLAC 1998). The precise effect of regional integration remains to be determined, but clearly it has been secondary.[11]

- Integration schemes in Latin America and the Caribbean generally have weak institutions and personnel and unstable budgetary support.

- Notwithstanding countries' propensity for unilateral action, and without any hard empirical proof, we suspect that regional schemes and collective peer pressure, particularly where there is some form of customs union discipline, have restrained backtracking on liberalizing commitments.

- Mexico's experience with NAFTA has pointed to some potential advantages of North–South agreements and has certainly influenced other countries' interest in this type of strategy. Since 1993, Mexico's annual goods exports have more than tripled, to more than $100 billion—more than 85 percent of which go to NAFTA partners. Mexico's exports also display strong structural change, evolving from petroleum to machines, including growing intraindustry trade with NAFTA partners (Perry 2001). Trade diversion does not seem to be an issue (Krueger 1999, 2000), and risks may have been further reduced by Mexico's free trade agreement with the European Union. Annual FDI flows jumped from 1 percent of GDP in 1987–93 to 3 percent in the post-NAFTA period, despite little privatization in the latter period (López Córdova 2001). There was some fear that the agreement would divert FDI to Mexico from the Caribbean Basin, but this was mitigated by the United States granting the area NAFTA parity. Redistribution of

---

11. The Inter-American Development Bank Institute for the Integration of Latin America and the Caribbean (IDB-INTAL) is currently supporting studies in this area.

tariff revenue does seem to have occurred (Panagariya 1999), although this may be interpreted as payment of dues for more secure entry into the North American market. Lock-in effects are evident, as NAFTA partners have been spared from some Mexican MFN tariff increases. However, the effects of NAFTA in Mexico have been asymmetrically distributed in favor of the northern part of the country (Perry 2001).

■ The FTAA process has advanced steadily since its launch in 1995, and it is on track.[12] Even though negotiations toward the FTAA are not scheduled to finish until 2005, the process already has generated a number of very positive externalities for the region, in terms of capacity building, and for the rest of the world in the areas of transparency and customs facilitation (Iglesias 1999).

■ Regionalism has not diminished interest in the multilateral system. Latin American and Caribbean countries were active in the Doha discussions, and some were quite instrumental in the launch of a new round of multilateral trade talks. Chile almost became the site of the last WTO ministerial, and Mexico will be the site of the next one. Moreover, some trade initiatives such as the FTAA and the Mercosur-EU free trade area will depend on WTO negotiations to complete their agendas.

Monetary and Financial Cooperation

Advances in formal processes toward monetary and financial cooperation have been very limited. With the exception of NAFTA, there has been little progress in regional financial services liberalization beyond the approval of protocols. The major subregional agreements, all of which set the goal of a common market or something more profound, are in incipient stages of macroeconomic coordination and monetary cooperation, even though levels of economic interdependence among certain partners are quite significant and there are risks of contagion in relations with international capital markets. Caricom and the CACM have a regional mechanism to monitor macroeconomic and monetary convergence indicators. Meanwhile, Mercosur (including its free trade associates, Bolivia and Chile) and the Andean Community have established formal targets for fiscal deficits, external public debt, and inflation, The governments in Mercosur also have committed themselves to a review process, should a partner fail to comply with the targets. The small islands of the Association of Eastern Caribbean States (part of Caricom) have a long-functioning common currency and central bank.

---

12. For a detailed analysis see Schott (2001).

Other areas of financial cooperation include subregional development banks in Central America (the Central American Bank for Economic Integration), the Andean area (the Andean Development Corporation), and Caricom (the Caribbean Development Bank), as well as a Latin American Reserve Fund, which provides forms of balance of payments support to the Andean Community countries.[13] Meanwhile, the Latin American Integration Association has a reciprocal payments system to finance trade among its members. The system, designed to overcome foreign exchange obstacles to trade, recently facilitated a $1.7 billion payment from Brazil to Argentina. More extensive monetary cooperation is hindered by the fact that no country in the region has a hard currency or an abundance of reserves.

Other Cooperation

An interesting development is the emergence of important intersubregional and interregional functional cooperation. The 12 South American countries have joined together in a South American Regional Infrastructure Initiative to coordinate and finance environmentally sustainable and development-oriented regional infrastructure projects. Mexico and the Central American countries, including Panama, have joined together in the Puebla-Panama Plan, a comprehensive initiative to cooperate in the development of regional infrastructure and tourism and to pursue functional cooperation in the preservation of the environment, in natural disaster control, and in human resource development.

The four major subregions all have functional cooperation mechanisms in the economic, social, and political areas. The network of mechanisms is quite extensive in Caricom and the CACM, but these mechanisms are of highly varying intensity and effectiveness.

Ambitious North–South functional regional cooperation initiatives have also become prominent: the Western Hemisphere summit process, the EU-Latin American and Caribbean initiatives, and APEC each involve more than 20 areas of functional regional cooperation among participating countries (tables 2.7 and 2.8 present examples of cooperation in the hemisphere and with the European Union; see table 2.3 for APEC).

Frontier of Regional Integration: Future Challenges

Notwithstanding the encouraging instrumental focus of the New Regionalism and some important advances in the 1990s, at the beginning of the 21st century, many developing countries find themselves facing major

---

13. The Andean Development Corporation and the Reserve Fund have recently extended membership to countries outside the Andean subregion.

Table 2.7 Areas of action identified at the 1994 Miami Summit

Preserving democracy	Economic integration and free trade	Eradicating poverty	Sustainable development
Protecting human rights	Free Trade Area of Americas	Universal access to education	Sustainable energy use
Invigorating community participation	Capital markets development and liberalization	Equitable access to basic health services	Partnership for biodiversity
Promoting cultural values	Hemispheric infrastructure	Strengthening role of women in society	Partnership for pollution prevention
Combating corruption	Energy cooperation	Encouraging microenterprise and small business	
Combating illegal drugs and crime	Telecommunications and information infrastructure	Creation of an emerging development corps	
Eliminating threat of terrorism	Cooperation in science and technology		
Building mutual confidence	Tourism		

Source: Devlin (2002).

challenges in trade and regional integration. These challenges will define the rules of the game in commercial, economic, and even political relations with their neighbors and with the rest of the world over the coming decades. In addition, growing externalities resulting from regional and international market integration have raised demands for cooperation in areas outside of trade. Confronting these challenges successfully will create many opportunities for enhanced economic growth, development, and poverty reduction; failure to confront them will have significant economic and political repercussions.

The challenges are formidable in both scope and depth. This is best expressed by reviewing the multiple fronts on which countries are undertaking initiatives.

Table 2.8 Areas of negotiation within the Southern Cone Common Market–European Union Interregional Association Agreement

Political dialogue	Economic cooperation	Social and cultural cooperation	Financial and technical cooperation	Trade cooperation
Peace and stability	Industrial cooperation	Social cooperation	Public administration modernization	Market access (broadly deferred)
Confidence- and security-building measures	Technical regulations and conformity assessment	Education and training	Interinstitutional cooperation	Services
Protection of human rights, democracy, and rule of law	Services	Social dialogue	Cooperation on regional integration	Intellectual property
Sustainable development	Investment promotion	Drugs and organized crime		Investment
Action on drug traffic, arms traffic, organized crime and terrorism	Macroeconomic policy	Cultural cooperation		Government procurement
	Scientific and technological cooperation			Competition
	Energy cooperation			Dispute settlement
	Transport			
	Telecommunications			
	Agriculture			
	Fisheries			
	Customs procedures			
	Statistics			
	Environment			
	Consumer protection			
	Date protection			

Source: Devlin (2002).

Strategic Fronts

South–South Integration Initiatives

Many South–South RIAs and their member countries are working to preserve their hard-won gains in regional trade liberalization in the face of protectionist pressures at home that arise from domestic economic and political problems and from a world economic slowdown. Macroeconomic and political instability in domestic economies is a major enemy of regional integration—above all in the early stages—as it turns attention away from collective objectives to more narrow domestic problems (Machinea 2002). Many RIAs are struggling to consolidate common external tariffs on the road to developing real customs unions. These unions promise, among other things, to facilitate trade and complete a necessary stage for achieving the goal of a common market or community.[14] Credibility regarding the rule of regional law is another fundamental challenge because without it, investment in the regional market will be below potential and skewed to the larger market members at the expense of balance, equity, and ultimately, the stability of the pact itself. Then there is the need to greatly strengthen the regional institutions, their personnel and finances, and local counterparts to support these objectives. Finally, political sensitivities concerning the potential benefits of regional integration must be raised in regions such as Asia that have a limited tradition in the practice of regionalism (ADB 2002).

All these are the basic foundations for economic integration with which many RIAs are still grappling. However, superimposing itself on these fundamental challenges is an emerging agenda for deepening integration, which is becoming increasingly relevant for harvesting the full benefits of existing commitments and increasing the socioeconomic returns from regional integration. This future road to regional integration is much more challenging because it involves complex multisectoral and multidisciplinary efforts at regional cooperation, with increased institutional and political demands:

- Overcoming the limited coordination in the development of regional infrastructure as well as border development is essential for the competitiveness of the regional market and for maximizing the benefits and distributing them more equitably among the population.[15]

---

14. The benefits of a customs union are clear, but the institutional hurdles are formidable and include creating a common customs and tariff collection and distribution system, along with a regional authority capable of administering it.

15. Border development is an important but often overlooked strategic component of regional integration. Borders often encompass a miniature subregion whose development is truncated by a national divide that houses dysfunctional regulatory asymmetries and creates coordination problems between authorities on each side. This is unfortunate because border areas are primary corridors for regional trade and often represent serious pockets of poverty. (See Pardo [2001] on the example of the Andean area.)

- Eliminating nontariff barriers and dysfunctional regulatory asymmetries in regional markets will significantly enhance the development effects of integration, but these are very difficult measures to pursue because they impinge directly on domestic policy.

- Although regional integration is designed to attract FDI, unless there is harmonization of fiscal incentives, costly investment promotion wars can sour collective commitments.

- Advances in financial services integration are especially important for the development of regional capital markets. However, financial markets, even more than goods markets, can be an important transmission mechanism for external shocks, or contagion, among a region's economies. Therefore, financial integration demands a set of essential preconditions or requirements (Machinea 2002, Zahler 2001, Zahler and Budnevich 1998). Especially important is strengthening and eventually harmonizing financial regulation. This process should include convergence to world-class disciplines with similar capital and liquidity requirements among partners, as well as minimization of time mismatches between assets and liabilities, as a way to constrain short-term borrowing by banks (Machinea 2002).

- Cooperating in the area of macroeconomic policy also is difficult but is increasingly necessary where partners have attained a significant degree of economic interdependence through trade, investment, and risk of financial contagion. One of the major threats to regional integration is macroeconomic instability in partner countries. Macroeconomic stability is a national responsibility, but it can be encouraged through collective commitments. Developing relevant convergence targets (e.g., on inflation, fiscal deficits, external debt, and current account deficits) and corresponding collective databases, realistic systems to provide surveillance, and incentives for compliance all are new areas of work. Regional payments systems for trade and balance of payments cooperation can also contribute to stability (Machinea 2002).

- Although currency unions are usually considered appropriate only within regions that constitute optimal currency areas, experience also shows that such unions can endogenously drive integration. Hence, perfecting these unions where they exist, or building a strategic road map for eventual currency union, can also have a place in RIAs with deep objectives.

Functional cooperation, which may or may not be embedded in a formal South–South RIA, is a growing area of interest in the world of the New Regionalism and should not be overlooked. In view of the integrating forces of the world economy and the externalities that functional cooperation can create among countries, such cooperation can be expected to be a growth industry even among countries without formal integration objectives. An especially ripe area in volatile developing economies is functional cooperation in the macrofinance and monetary areas.

North–South Initiatives

As already mentioned, developing countries have shown an increasing disposition to link up with industrialized-country markets in free trade areas. They are doing this to, among other things, secure access to major export markets, anchor their economies, and attract FDI, as well as to import institutional modernization. Indeed, to focus just on market access, economic models indicate that agreements such as the FTAA or the EU-Mercosur arrangement would provide significant export and growth opportunities to the participating countries (Monteagudo and Watanuki 2001). However, compared with South–South RIAs, trade liberalization in these agreements has much stronger implications for competition, redundant capital and labor, and fiscal revenue losses; they also invariably push the envelope on some second-generation trade issues as well as on politically sensitive areas such as labor and environmental standards.

Another complex dimension of these agreements is that they often set up a comprehensive, multidisciplinary agenda of functional cooperation parallel to the agreement itself. In principle, this is an extremely useful complement given the strong asymmetry in levels of development. However, as already mentioned, the international community has much less experience with functional cooperation than with trade negotiations. Successful regional cooperation requires an effective architecture involving clear objectives, work programs, and defined outputs; monitoring and follow-up, as well as effective mechanisms of evaluation; and adequate financial and technical support. All of these requirements have proved elusive in many cases, eroding the credibility of the trade and cooperation nexus that the initiatives promised to construct (Devlin 2002; Devlin, Estevadeordal, and Krivonos 2002).

Multilateral Initiatives

RIAs among WTO members are subject to that organization's multilateral rules, and those rules attempt to enhance regionalism's articulation with the rest of the world. The Doha meeting launched a new round in the WTO, one that is ambitious in scope and content. It also includes negotiations on regional issues, which is the third front that must be attended to.

Another complexity, one that is cross-cutting in nature, is that many of these initiatives have their own strong raison d'être and are vital complements, making it strategically difficult to focus on one at the expense of the other. Because regional agreements go beyond WTO disciplines and apply to a limited group of like-minded countries, they are a separate product from that of the multilateral system, which involves more than 140 countries. Yet the two processes have strong positive synergies. For instance, the new WTO round will help regional initiatives like the FTAA and the various negotiations between the European Union and the Latin American and Caribbean countries to complete certain items on their agendas. An example is reduction of distortions in agricultural trade, which would be difficult or impossible to accomplish without negotiations at the multilateral level. Moreover, because the WTO is the baseline for regionalism, further strengthening of the multilateral system and its rules spills over to create stronger regional arrangements. In turn, as was witnessed in the NAFTA negotiations, ambitious regional agendas can be catalysts for advancing the scope and depth of multilateral negotiations. Indeed, innovations in regional negotiations often serve as a laboratory for the multilateral system.

Just as regionalism and the multilateral system are not substitutes for each other, neither are many of the regional agreements. For example, the FTAA is a major opportunity for Latin America and the Caribbean, but it is not a substitute for deepening subregional integration. The subregional schemes have deeper common market objectives and are driven by more than business. Indeed, a subregional agreement can attend to local interests and opportunities in a way that a hemispheric, business-only hypermarket such as the FTAA could not easily replicate. Moreover, moving beyond free trade to a common market would allow member countries to combine their factors of production more effectively so as to compete in the FTAA. Likewise, the FTAA and the EU negotiations complement each other as each offers vital market access and involves a unique trade-cooperation nexus with major market and political partners.

The multiple initiatives emerging out of the New Regionalism pose several challenges to the participating countries, in preparing for the negotiations themselves, in implementing the agreements that emerge, and in adjusting both at the macroeconomic and at the sectoral level.

Good and sustainable agreements require good negotiations. As developing countries pursue multiple agreements with industrialized countries, many of them find themselves in an asymmetric position in terms of negotiating capacity, with fewer skilled negotiators to cover a broad agenda of complex issues as well as poorer access to information and support services of a logistical and technical nature. Moreover, because these governments operate in democratic settings, there are urgent demands to develop formal mechanisms of consultation with civil society during the course of negotiations. Given that many countries are negotiating in subregional blocs, meeting all these demands can require an unprecedented degree of intergovernmental coordination. In Latin America and the Caribbean, for example, many trade ministries operate in an institutional milieu more reflective of an era when trade was not so central to the region's development strategy, and when those trade negotiations that did take place were with neighbors of roughly similar capacity.

It is one thing to negotiate an agreement and another to implement it. Developing countries have displayed institutional weaknesses in implementing agreements at both the regional and the multilateral level. The new issues of the multilateral system go beyond such traditional areas as tariff reduction to affect domestic policy, legislation, and institutions. A country's failure to effectively implement disciplines to which it has agreed can lead to underexploitation of opportunities, to trade and investment disputes, and even to political problems. Countries have also experienced difficulties in implementing intraregional agreements in those areas that go beyond trade in goods, and this has stalled agendas and caused a loss of momentum—and sometimes even backtracking. If countries are to successfully implement the agreements they have signed, they need to augment the national resources available for this purpose, strengthen regional institutions and their national counterparts, and train personnel.

Finally, integration agreements create demands for economic adjustment in developing countries. These adjustments are magnified when the agreement involves large industrialized countries, because the countries' very different levels of development bring about marked changes in competition and relative prices. Countries need to make macroeconomic adjustments, such as efficient substitution of other sources of fiscal income for forgone tariff revenue, and to protect against surges of capital inflows and overvaluation of their currencies to maintain macroeconomic stability and competitiveness. At the microeconomic level, firms and sectors need a supportive environment in which to compete, and labor markets need social protection networks and retraining opportunities.[16] All these adjustments, of course, complicate the ongoing structural adjustment process, which, as mentioned earlier, is in many cases very incomplete and already the cause of serious vulnerability on the external front.

Role of the RDBs

Regional integration and functional cooperation are a type of impure public good (Sandler 1992). In a pure market environment, the production of regional public goods is inherently difficult, and not enough goods are produced from the standpoint of public welfare. This happens because, from an individual or even a national point of view, the prospective benefits are largely nonexclusive and indivisible, and are thus not

---

16. Schott (2001) analyzes readiness and adjustment issues for the Latin America and Caribbean countries' prospective entry into an FTAA.

fully internalized. Moreover, problems of coordination or collective action arise from informational asymmetries and political and institutional limitations on the certainty of commitments (Devlin, Estevadeordal, and Krivonos 2002).

It is this public goods dimension of regional integration and functional cooperation that makes the support of regional institutions, such as RDBs, so vital. Despite their name, RDBs traditionally have had a national rather than a regional focus for their financial and nonfinancial products.

The Inter-American Development Bank has had a mandate to support regional integration since its inception in 1959. Its Eighth Replenishment, in 1995, restated regional integration as a primary objective, and such integration is one of the four support pillars of the bank's new corporate strategy. The bank has always had a unit at its Washington headquarters, and since 1995, an entire department has been dedicated to issues of regional integration. That unit has had the task of preparing regional programming (regional support strategies) for the bank and has been markedly reinforced since 1995. Since 1965, the bank has also had an institute in Buenos Aires (INTAL) dedicated to supporting training, research, and more recently, regional technical cooperation projects. Notwithstanding its special attention to regionalism, however, the bank's activity is overwhelmingly nationally oriented. Loans for regionalism are about 2 percent of nearly $8 billion in authorizations, and nonreimbursable funds for regional technical cooperation are about $12 million annually.[17]

During the 1990s the bank's support of subregional integration strategically centered on consolidating market access issues, an essential first step in the formation of regional markets, and supporting functional cooperation in diverse areas of the structural reform agenda. Country lending has also been supportive, especially in the areas of infrastructure and structural reform. The bank's Multilateral Investment Fund has had extensive programs supporting convergence toward modern regulatory frameworks.

Since the mid-1990s, the bank has developed a new niche in its support of regional cooperation. With the emergence of the hemispheric summit process in 1995, governments requested that the bank provide technical and financial support to this process. In the case of the FTAA, this was carried out along with the Organization of American States and the UN Economic Commission for Latin America and the Caribbean (the three institutions have a tripartite committee). The novelty is that not only did the bank contribute resources through a traditional regional technical co-

---

17. The first figure understates the true amount because it does not include national loans that facilitate integration, such as lending for road building. In the mid-1990s, available annual funding for regional technical cooperation was $50 million. These resources fell off sharply after the debt relief program for the heavily indebted poor countries was launched in 1996.

operation project, but it also directly executed the projects out of headquarters and complemented that effort with direct expert staff support. The bank's FTAA team, working in the context of the tripartite committee, has provided direct technical support to the negotiators as well as to the FTAA's temporary administrative secretariat (which it helps finance). These services have leveled the playing field by ensuring homogeneous support to governments with very different institutional capacities, and it has contributed to the remarkably steady pace of progress since the launch of negotiations in 1995. When the bank received requests from member governments to support the South American Regional Infrastructure Initiative and the Puebla-Panama Plan, it drew on its FTAA experience to provide somewhat similar modalities of support services. For example, it collaborated with the Andean Development Corporation and the Financial Fund for the Development of the River Plate Basin in the former, and with the Economic Commission for Latin America and the Caribbean and the Central American Bank for Economic Integration in the latter. By establishing priorities for support of functional cooperation programs in the hemispheric summit process (IDB 2001), the bank also indirectly signaled the need for advances in functional cooperation programs.

Among other innovations are the following:

- the establishment of a special loan facility to allow for wholesale modernization of national trade-related ministries

- an agreement with the WTO Secretariat to finance its training courses throughout the region

- establishment of regional policy dialogues in key areas,[18] whereby high-level policymakers meet twice a year at bank headquarters to deliberate on national and regional issues, with the bank covering the cost of technical and logistical support

- a program of high-profile visiting scholars at the bank to explore policy responses to many of the challenges listed above

- support for evaluation of the effects of trade liberalization and for outreach to civil society

- special attention to border development issues and identification of projects

- creation of a Japan Program designed to strengthen ties with Asia.

---

18. Trade and Integration, Macroeconomic Policy, Poverty and Social Protection Networks, Education and Human Resources, Transparency and Public Policy Management, and Management of National Disasters and Environment.

The ADB is a multilateral development finance institution, established in 1966, for Asia and the Pacific. Its mandate is to promote regional cooperation, and its charter provides that the ADB shall give priority to regional, subregional, and national programs and projects that contribute most effectively to harmonious economic growth in the region. The ADB's Long-Term Strategic Framework for 2001–15 identifies support for regional cooperation and integration for development as one of three cross-cutting themes that will both broaden and deepen the core areas of the ADB's intervention.

The ADB's support for regional cooperation and integration for development addresses several objectives: it supports the development of the ADB's developing member countries through cooperation, it provides wider development options through greater access to resources and markets, it addresses shared problems that stretch across borders, and it takes advantage of opportunities for sharing knowledge and information.

The ADB supports a number of broad-based regional and subregional cooperation initiatives to accelerate the development of participating countries. The Greater Mekong Subregion initiative is the most prominent example. The ADB has also led regional cooperation efforts in South Asia and the Central Asian republics. Under its policy of supporting regional cooperation, the ADB has provided considerable support through regional technical assistance and complementary project investment in national infrastructure to promote and realize cooperation among its developing member countries. Funding for regional technical cooperation is about $12 billion annually. Recently, a unit of ADB initiated a process of regional economic monitoring to complement economic and financial surveillance at the national and the global levels. This unit also supports the ASEAN Surveillance Process. A number of the macroeconomic and monetary cooperation initiatives outlined earlier in this chapter also received ADB support.

Promotion of economic cooperation and regional integration has been an integral part of the activities and goals of the African Development Bank (AfDB) since its inception in 1964.[19] Recently, the AfDB strengthened this commitment in its strategic operational document called "A Re-Invigorated Bank: An Agenda for Moving Forward," which emphasizes regional integration as one of the focal points of the institution. In pursuit of this renewed mandate, the AfDB has collaborated with other regional and international institutions, financed regional integration studies, and supported financing for regional projects and programs. In cooperation with other institutions, the AfDB has supported the creation of a joint secretariat to coordinate its development efforts and initiatives with those of the UN Economic Commission for Africa and the Organization

---

19. This description of activities is based on the African Development Bank and African Development Fund policy (2000).

of African Unity. In addition, the AfDB has financed several studies aimed at facilitating regional integration. One of the most important of these has been the Cross Border Initiative. Together with the World Bank, the International Monetary Fund, and the European Union, the AfDB is creating a program aimed at promoting trade liberalization and investment and encouraging policy harmonization among 14 participating countries in Eastern and Southern Africa and the Indian Ocean. The AfDB has also played a key role in the establishment of regional institutions such as the Shelter Afrique, the Africa Project Development Facility, and the African Management Services Company, among others. The AfDB also established the Association of African Finance Associations to foster cooperation among national financial institutions on a regional basis, and it has assisted in the development of regional infrastructure projects.

Conclusion

Since the early 1990s, there has been an important renewal of integration processes in developing countries. Even areas such as East Asia, which traditionally have not shown great interest in formal regional integration, have recently pursued important collective initiatives. Moreover, this New Regionalism generally is being approached in a manner that promotes structural reform and a more effective integration of member countries into a globalizing world economy.

The Latin American and Caribbean region seems to be the most advanced at moving these processes forward. Africa has many initiatives under way, but the results have so far been unsatisfactory. Asia, meanwhile, has surged forward with ambitious initiatives and appears to be the most advanced in financial and monetary cooperation. How far such cooperation can go without deeper reciprocal commitments to free trade remains to be seen, although indications are that this may advance as well.

Although overall progress is encouraging, many of the fundamental first steps toward regional integration exhibit serious shortcomings at a time when growing interdependence in regional and world economies has created demands for more complex forms of regional cooperation; for example, in the monetary and financial areas. The new North–South initiatives such as the FTAA are placing great demands on countries because of the complexity of the issues, the magnitude of the external opening that will be demanded, and the fragility of many of the participating economies in a period of slow world economic growth and restrictions on access to private credit for emerging markets. Furthermore, since November 2001, the comprehensive Doha negotiation has been added to every country's trade agenda.

In many cases the regional, North–South, and Doha agendas all have their raison d'être and exhibit positive synergies, making it difficult, if not impossible, to pick and choose among them. This ambitious agenda will clearly tax countries' capacities in negotiation and implementation and require important adjustments at the macroeconomic and microeconomic levels.

How prepared are the RDBs to support countries in these efforts? A starting point in this preparation is effective support of the structural reform process and of macroeconomic stability. Fluid market structures and stable economies are essential components to sustained processes of integration, whether with the world or with regions. After many years of structural reforms, there have been enough recent bouts of economic instability in Latin America, Asia, and Africa to indicate that the banks need to reflect on their programs and prescriptions for policy mix. Included in this review is how well national programs are preparing counties to assume their regional obligations, particularly of the North–South type, which often put a premium on pioneering trade related disciplines (and labor and environmental issues), as well as challenge institutional capacities in the regulatory area, including prudential regulation in financial markets.

In supporting national policy and its regional dimensions, the banks must develop their own vision of the functional role of regional integration and cooperation and must identify priority areas of support. Given the very large spectrum of potential areas of support, an effective internal institutional exercise of regional programming is essential to identify current and approaching critical gaps in integration processes at both the national and the regional levels, as well to mobilize support projects that draw on the complete spectrum of financial and nonfinancial services of the bank. Regional programming also should address these gaps in an efficient sequence and, to the extent possible, husband resources by maximizing synergies among proposed projects.

Regional integration is still a "boutique" activity in national policy circles. Given this fact, coupled with the strong national orientation of regional bank programs and the incentive structure that this can build into the day-to-day activities of bank staff, it probably is useful to have a specialized department or division with a mandate of proactively driving forward the institution's support of regional integration and cooperation. This unit should help develop an institutional vision of regional integration and should work closely with other units in charge of country programs to help them identify activities for the national pipeline that are consistent with the objectives of the member states' regional obligations.

Regional banks generally have policy dialogues with their member countries either as a special exercise or as a part of the development of the national financing pipeline. Given the regional public goods nature of integration, in some ways regional policy must be nurtured even more carefully than national policy, where self interest is more evident. Hence, policy dialogues also should be established on regional issues both with individual countries and in the collective forums of the regional agreement. The public goods nature of regional integration also indicates that there is a strong potential role for nonreimbursable resources to grease the wheels of collective initiatives at critical junctures of their development. Unfortunately, the availability of this type of financing has not grown in relation to the increasing demand for regional public goods, and indeed, in some cases it has declined sharply (e.g., in the Inter-American Development Bank).

Regional banks can encourage regional integration and cooperation by signaling that resources in support of collective endeavors are additional to the national pipeline, and perhaps the banks can even make these additional resources conditional to compliance with existing regional obligations or with more comprehensive regional agreements where the collective rates of return are high.

The limited availability of nonreimbursable resources for regional integration indicates that the banks should more aggressively use their prestige to coordinate all donors in their respective geographical areas of influence in matters of regional integration, functional cooperation, and trade capacity building. Likewise, the situation also indicates that the banks should develop regional lending instruments and encourage development of regional obligors to assume reimbursable financing for collective goals. Nonfinancial services such as the regional policy dialogues mentioned above and research and policy seminars are also important for support of regional integration.

In addition regional banks must improve their own and their member countries' capacity to evaluate the effects of regional integration, particularly the so-called dynamic effects (where the big numbers are expected to be) and the nontraditional political economy effects (which can be an important policy tool). Evaluation of the effect of regional integration, although very difficult, is extremely important because a regional initiative may not make sense, and even those initiatives that do can go awry because of flawed policy or implementation. Likewise, the banks must improve the evaluation of their support programs—a difficult task at the national level, but one even more so at the regional level, where externalities are especially strong.

Finally, regional banks should seek to work with each other and with other international organizations to promote healthy regionalism. Regional banks could meet regularly to exchange best practices in this area. In view of the fact that more than 50 percent of world trade passes through a regional agreement, the World Trade Organization (WTO) should work closely with regional banks to support compliance with WTO rules and to help countries further develop the policies with regard to regional integration. A closer relationship with the IMF on regional matters also would be useful, so that this latter institution could be more sensitive in the design of its national programs in relation to the obligations derived from, as well as possibilities for, regional integration and cooperation. One pioneering area in this regard is macroeconomic coordination and monetary cooperation among partners of a politically and economically relevant regional agreement.

References

ADB (Asian Development Bank). 2002. *Monetary and Financial Cooperation in Asia*. Manila: Asian Development Bank.

African Development Bank and African Development Fund. 2000. *Economic Cooperation and Regional Integration Policy*. Abidjan: African Development Bank.

Aggarwal, V., and C. Morrison. 1999. *APEC as an International Institution*. Paper presented at the 25th Meeting of Pacific Trade and Development (PAFTAD), Osaka, June 16–18.

ASEAN (Association of South East Asian Nations). 2001. Asian Trade Data. www.aseansec.org (accessed January 2002).

Balassa, Bela. 1961. *The Theory of Economic Integration*. Homewood, IL: Irwin.

Bergsten, C. Fred. 1997a. APEC in 1997: Prospects and Possible Strategies. In *Whither APEC? The Progress to Date and Agenda for the Future*, ed. C. Fred Bergsten. Special Report 9. Washington: Institute for International Economics.

Bergsten, C. Fred. 1997b. Open Regionalism. In *Whither APEC? The Progress to Date and Agenda for the Future*, ed. C. Fred Bergsten. Special Report 9. Washington: Institute for International Economics.

Bhagwati, Jagdish, and A. Panagariya. 1996. *Preferential Trading Areas and Multilateralism*. Washington: Economic Development Institute, World Bank.

Blomstrom, M., and A. Kokko. 1997. *Regional Integration and Foreign Direct Investment*. Washington: International Trade Division, World Bank.

Center for Strategic and International Studies. 1999. South Asia: Regional Trade Integration: Modest Progress. *South Asia Monitor* 9 (May). www.csis.org/saprog/sam9.html (accessed April 22).

Corden, W. Max. 1972. Economies of Scale and the Theory of Customs Unions. *Journal of Political Economy* 80: 465–75.

Devlin, Robert. 2002. The FTAA and the EU-Mercosur Free Trade Process: Reciprocal Lessons? In *Towards an Agreement between Europe and Mercosur*, ed. Paolo Giordano et al. Paris: Chair Mercosur, Université de Sciences-Po.

Devlin, Robert, and A. Estevadeordal. 2001. What's New in the New Regionalism in the Americas. In *Regional Integration in Latin America and the Caribbean*, ed. Victor Bulmer-Thomas. London: Institute of Latin American Studies.

Devlin, Robert, A. Estevadeordal, and K. Krivonos. 2002. The Trade and Cooperation Nexus: How Does the Mercosur–EU Process Measure Up? In *An Integrated Approach to the European Union-Mercosur Association*, ed. Paolo Giordano. Paris: Chair Mercosur, Université de Sciences-Po.

Devlin, Robert, and R. Ffrench-Davis. 1999. Towards an Evaluation of Regional Integration in Latin America in the 1990s. *The World Economy* 22(2): 261–90.

Echavarria, J. J. 1998. Trade Flows in the Andean Countries: Unilateral Liberalization or Trade Preferences. In *Trade: Towards Open Regionalism*. Washington: World Bank.

ECLAC (Economic Commission for Latin America and the Caribbean). 1998. *La Inversión Extranjera*. Santiago: Economic Commission for Latin America and the Caribbean.

Estevadeordal, A., J. Goto, and R. Saez. 2000. *The New Regionalism in the Americas: The Case of Mercosur*. INTAL-IDB Working Paper 5. Washington: Department of Integration and Regional Programs, Inter-American Development Bank.

Ethier, W. 1998. The New Regionalism. *The Economic Journal* 108, no. 449 (July): 1149–61.

Feinberg, R. 2000. Comparative Analysis of Regional Integration in a Non-identical Twins Case: APEC and FTAA. *Integration and Trade* 10. Buenos Aires: IDB-INTAL.

Fernández, R. 1997. *Returns to Regionalism: An Evaluation of Non-Traditional Gains from RTAs.* Working Paper 5970. Cambridge, MA: National Bureau of Economic Research.

Ffrench-Davis, R. 1980. Distorsiones del Mercado y Teoría de Uniones Aduaneras. *Integración Latinoamericana*, no. 45/46 (April, May).

García, Herrero, and G. Glocker. 2000. *Options for Latin America in a Globalized World: A Regional Monetary Union versus Dollarization.* Frankfurt: European Central Bank.

Giordano, P. 2001. *Economie Politique de l'Integration Regionale dans le Mercosur.* Paris: Presses de Sciences-Po.

Hosono, A. 2001. Economic Integration in Asia and the Pacific: Experiences and New Initiatives. *Integration and Trade* 13. Buenos Aires: IDB-INTAL.

IDB (Inter-American Development Bank). 1998. *Periodic Note.* Washington: Integration and Regional Programs Department, Inter-American Development Bank.

IDB (Inter-American Development Bank). 2000. *Periodic Note.* Washington: Integration and Regional Programs Department, Inter-American Development Bank.

IDB (Inter-American Development Bank). 2001. *Cumbre de las Américas: La Agenda del BID.* Washington: Inter-American Development Bank.

Iglesias, Enrique. 1999. Statement at the Fifth Free Trade Area of the Americas Trade Ministerial Meeting, Toronto (November).

IMF (International Monetary Fund). 2001. *Direction of Trade.* Washington: International Monetary Fund.

INTAL (Institute for the Integration of Latin America and the Caribbean). 2000. *El Impacto Sectorial del Proceso de Integración Subregional en la Comunidad Andina: Sector Lácteo y Sector Textil.* Buenos Aires: IDB-INTAL.

Krueger, Anne O. 1999. *Trade Creation and Trade Diversion under NAFTA.* Working Paper 7429. Cambridge, MA: National Bureau of Economic Research.

Krueger, Anne O. 2000. NAFTA's Effects: A Preliminary Assessment. *The World Economy* 23(6): 761–75.

Lee, H. 1999. *An Assessment of APEC's Progress Towards the Bogor Goals: A Political Economy Approach to Tariff Reductions.* KIEP Working Paper 99-19. Seoul: Korea Institute for International Economic Policy.

López Córdova, E. 2001. *Nafta and the Mexican Economy: Analytical Issues and Lessons for the FTAA.* INTAL-ITD-STA Occasional Paper 9. Washington: Department of Integration and Regional Programs, Inter-American Development Bank.

Machinea, J. 2002. *Macroeconomic Policy Coordination in Mercosur.* Washington: Integration and Regional Programs Department, Inter-American Development Bank.

Monteagudo, J., and M. Watanuki. 2001. *Regional Trade Agreements for Mercosur: The FTAA and the FTA with the European Union.* Washington: Integration and Regional Programs Department, Inter-American Development Bank.

Panagariya, A. 1996. The Free Trade Area of the Americas: Good for Latin America? *The World Economy* 19(9): 485–515.

Panagariya, A. 1999. The Regionalism Debate: An Overview. *The World Economy* 22(4): 455–76.

Pardo, M. 2001. *Estudio Integral de Fronteras Intra-Andina/Plan Andino de Cooperación Transfronteriza.* Washington: Integration and Regional Programs Department, Inter-American Development Bank.

Perry, G. 2001. Mexican Competitiveness: Are the Rankings Informative? Washington: World Bank (February).

Puga, D., and A. Venables. 1997. *Trading Arrangements and Industrial Development.* Washington: International Trade Division, World Bank.

Sandler, Todd. 1992. *Collective Action.* Ann Arbor: University of Michigan Press.

Schiff, M. 1996. *Small Is Beautiful. Preferential Trade Agreements and the Impact of Country*

Size, Market Share, Efficiency, and Trade Policy. Washington: International Trade Division, World Bank.

Schott, Jeffrey. 2001. *Prospects for Free Trade in the Americas.* Washington: Institute for International Economics.

Scollay, R., and John G. Gilbert. 2000. *New Subregional Trading Arrangements in the Asia Pacific.* POLICY ANALYSES IN INTERNATIONAL ECONOMICS 63. Washington: Institute for International Economics.

Sussangkarn, C. 2000a. *East Asian Monetary Cooperation.* Paper presented at the Seventh Conference on Asia-Pacific Cooperation in the Global Context: Regionalism and Globalism, Hakone, Japan (September 29–October 1).

Sussangkarn, C. 2000b. A Framework for Regional Monetary Stabilization. *NIRA Review* (Autumn): 16–20.

Taccone, J., and U. Nogueira, eds. 2001. *Mercosur Report.* Buenos Aires: IDB-INTAL.

United Nations Economic Commission for Africa. 2001. *Annual Report on Integration in Africa (ARIA): Synthesis of Findings and Way Forward.* New York: United Nations.

Venables, A. Forthcoming. Regionalism and Economic Development. In *New Frontiers in Development: Policies and Institutions for Trade and Regional Integration,* Robert Devlin and A. Estevadeordal, eds. Washington: Inter-American Development Bank.

Winters, L. Alan. 1997. *Assessing Regional Integration Arrangements.* Washington: International Trade Division, World Bank.

Winters, L. Alan. 2001. *Regionalism and Multilateralism in the Twenty First Century.* Washington: Integration and Regional Programs Department, Inter-American Development Bank.

Wonnacott, P., and R. Wonnacott. 1995. Liberalization in the Western Hemisphere: New Challenges in the Design of a Free Trade Agreement. *North American Journal of Economics and Finance* 6, no. 2: 107–19.

World Bank. 2001. *World Development Indicators.* Washington: World Bank.

Yeats, A. 1996. *Does Mercosur's Trade Performance Justify Concerns About the Effects: Yes!* Washington: International Trade Division, World Bank.

Yeats, A. 1998. *What Can Be Expected from African Regional Trade Arrangements?* Washington: World Bank.

Zahler, R. 2001. Strategies for Monetary Cooperation/Union. *Integration and Trade* 13. Buenos Aires: IDB-INTAL.

Zahler, R. and C. Budnevich. 1998. *Integración Financiera y Coordinación Macroeconómica en el MERCOSUR.* Paper presented at the Seminario Internacional Coordinación de Políticas Macroeconómicas en el Mercosur. Hacia una Moneda Unica, organized by the Fundación Gobierno y Sociedad and the Secretaria de Planeamiento Estratégico de la Presidencia de la Nación, Buenos Aires.

Comment

ENRIQUE IGLESIAS

Discussion of the role of regional development banks has always been with us. Before the Inter-American Development Bank (IDB), the first of these institutions, was created in 1959, one of the issues on which strong opinions were voiced was why a regional development bank was needed when the World Bank already existed to serve the needs of development. Perhaps a bit of the history of the IDB will prove enlightening about the specific contribution of these institutions.

The initiative for the IDB can actually be said to date from 1889, many years before the Bretton Woods conference. In that year, the Congress of the United States instructed the president to convene a meeting of the ministers of trade of all the countries of the Americas. At that time, there were 19 countries in the hemisphere. The ministers came and stayed for four months, and in the end they decided on three things. First, they decided to put in place a free trade area of the Americas—that initiative is still pending. Second, they decided to establish a common currency based on silver—an initiative that did not prosper. Finally, they decided to create a hemispheric bank. Many of the Latin American countries at that time had been independent for 70 years, and it took 70 more years to see the creation of the bank. It is interesting to note that even 100 years ago these ministers realized that a regional bank could play an active role in the development of the region.

It is also interesting to notice how, throughout its history, the IDB has been able to work very closely with other institutions. Indeed, it continues to work on a daily basis in a very cooperative manner with the

Enrique Iglesias is the president of the Inter-American Development Bank.

International Monetary Fund (IMF) and the World Bank, and it has benefited greatly from this cooperation with them.

What, then, is the comparative advantage of the IDB and the other regional banks, and where does it fit in among the other international financial institutions? On the basis of my 14 years of experience as head of the IDB, I believe there are three very special characteristics about the IDB and its sister institutions.

The first is the feeling of ownership on the part of the borrowing members. The countries of the Latin American and Caribbean region feel very keenly that the bank is their institution. This sense of ownership has important implications for what the bank can do at the level of specific programs and policies.

The second special feature is the access that this ownership gives us to all kinds of stakeholders. We have a very direct dialogue not only with national and local governments but also with trade unions, with civil society, with legislatures, and with the judiciaries of the countries in our region. This sort of dialogue builds a network of communication, which we count among our most important assets.

Finally, the bank is widely accepted in a variety of regional initiatives that contribute to a range of regional objectives. These include not only integration schemes but also political bodies.

Together, these three special assets constitute our comparative advantage, which of course is complementary to what happens at the world level. What can we draw from these three basic components of comparative advantage? First of all, of course, we provide financing. I have always believed that financing in our institution is and will become less and less important than the nonfinancial services that the bank provides, however. The more we see the private sector playing an active role in our region, which consists mostly of middle-income countries, the more our nonfinancial services will become relevant as part of the assistance we offer our countries.

One specific advantage is our capacity, based on the close connections I just mentioned, to engage in a dialogue with national governments on very important issues. As an example, when a new government takes office in one of IDB's borrowing member countries, the bank tries to meet with the new president and the economic team, to give the new administration a sense of how we see the country and its problems. Our visits tend to be very well accepted, and we see this as a nonfinancial service.

This acceptance is especially important when it comes to dealing with the delicate matters of governance. Institutions from outside the region might not find it so easy to gain access to members of a country's judicial system, to intrude on parliaments, or to work with indigenous groups. This capacity to deal with specific areas of extreme sensitivity in some countries tends to be a simpler matter for us than for other institutions.

Another area that also highlights our comparative advantage has been our active involvement in lending to microenterprises. Thirty years ago the IDB started to work with civil society in the financing of microenterprises. In the last 10 years alone the bank has done approximately $100 million worth of lending to such businesses, of which there are now literally hundreds of thousands.

Another area of advantage is economic integration. Latin America has a long history of integration efforts. Indeed, in this respect Latin America is ahead of other regions, and the IDB is ahead of other institutions, simply because the bank was born out of this movement toward integration and cooperation.

The chance to further that integration is very important for the bank, and it became even more important in the 1990s, when integration became part of the global process of economic reform and part of the region's access to the world market. Under that umbrella, the IDB became deeply involved in the process of economic reform as a means of accelerating integration and entering world markets.

Part of this effort is opening the door to support for countries in their external economic reforms, to help them become integrated with the world and with the region. The IDB is engaged in outreach efforts, to make people aware of the benefits of integration with the rest of the world and to support governments in their efforts at capacity building.

One other area that remains only a possibility for us is monetary complementarity in the region. There is tremendous potential there, and it is something we can eventually achieve. In that area, too, the IDB has a specific comparative advantage.

Clearly the IDB has a comparative advantage in the area of physical infrastructure. In Central America, we are on the brink of achieving what has been a dream since the 1970s; namely, the integration of the energy grid. We have approved the first loan for a project in which all the Central American countries will link with Mexico in one grid that stretches from Panama to Mexico. At the same time, we are working with the Andean Development Corporation and Fondo Financiero para el Desarrollo de la Cuenca del Plata (Fonplata) on similar initiatives in South America.

Regional public goods are yet another important area in which the bank's comparative advantage is evident. The development of border areas provides an example: We are working to bring development to borders that have long been turbulent—such as that between Ecuador and Peru or those between some of the countries in Central America. We are also working with countries that have suffered natural disasters. These are areas in which we try to identify where we can make a worthwhile contribution for the good of the region.

Finally, the matter of financial crisis forms a backdrop to much of our discussion in such a forum as this one, and Latin America certainly has seen some dramatic crises in recent years. These crises present a serious challenge to many of our efforts toward development. With respect to crisis prevention, I believe that the IDB and the other regional banks should be able to do something; for example, by helping build effective supervisory and regulatory systems in the financial domain. Together with the World Bank and the IMF, IDB is doing that.

When a crisis erupts and countries must be rescued, however, it is quite clear that the IDB is not the IMF—this is not its role. The IMF has a specific responsibility in promoting macroeconomic adjustment—it is the leader in that area—but there is certainly a role for the regional development banks to play in limiting the social repercussions of a crisis, which are often very serious.

Comment

C. FRED BERGSTEN

Regionalism will probably create the most profound changes in the international economic architecture that we will see over the next five to 10 years. The regional scene will witness more sweeping developments than all the reforms now being discussed in the International Monetary Fund (IMF), the World Bank, and probably even the World Trade Organization (WTO) and the trading system.

This is clearest in the area of trade, as the chapter by Devlin and Castro points out very nicely, and a great deal on this issue has also been published at the Institute for International Economics. There has been, of course, a veritable explosion of regional and subregional trade agreements. Indeed, that is where the action has been in the global trading system over the last decade and where it will remain in the future. Well over 200 bilateral and subregional free trade agreements have been notified to the WTO just within the last decade.

Some of these are what one might call megaregional arrangements. One is the Free Trade Area of the Americas (FTAA), which will surely come to fruition within a decade, following discussions toward such an agreement that have lasted for over a century. Another is the EU–Southern Cone Common Market agreement, which, its shortcomings notwithstanding, will pull together two of the largest existing trade groupings in the world. In Asia, there have been discussions of a possible Association of South East Nations+3 (ASEAN+3) or some other regional arrangement

C. Fred Bergsten is the director of the Institute for International Economics.

that would amount to an East Asian free trade area. In fact, such an arrangement would lead to a tripolar world economic structure if it occurred. Overarching even that possibility is the Asia Pacific Economic Cooperation forum, which despite little progress of late, still claims to be dedicated toward its goal of free trade throughout both sides of the Pacific Ocean by 2010 or 2020. If even a fraction of all this integration takes place, and I suspect it will, we will see an enormous change in the international economic architecture, because all of these regional, subregional, megaregional, and cross-regional agreements will have profound implications for the world economy.

The action is taking place not only on the trade side but in the monetary domain as well. In Asia, although we have not yet seen the development of an Asian Monetary Fund, as was first proposed in 1997 and rejected in that form, we have seen the creation of something that begins to look very much like what the global monetary system looked like over 30 or 40 years ago. The Asians have created a network of bilateral swap agreements: the Chiang Mai Initiative (CMI). Although it presently amounts to only $30 billion, this arrangement includes swap agreements between Japan and China: the world's two largest holders of financial reserves. It includes cross-cutting swap agreements between all of the northeast Asian creditor countries and Singapore, on the one hand, and the southeast Asian debtor countries on the other. It thus very much resembles the Group of Ten of the 1960s, when the group was first getting under way. The CMI includes a form of peer review, a multilateral surveillance process in which the participating countries are beginning to scrutinize each other's economies and are taking steps to avoid neighborhood contagion effects and the like. Over a period of five to 10 years, this framework will likely evolve into a very important player in the international financial system, whether it is ever actually called an Asian Monetary Fund or not.

One motive for these new initiatives, on both the trade and the financial side, is exactly what Enrique Iglesias has described: ownership. We all know that in Asia, for example, there has been deep resentment of the way the IMF and the United States handled the 1997–98 crisis. Although it is seldom enunciated in quite these terms, there is a strongly held view in the region that it should never again be subjected to the tender mercies of Washington. The next time a crisis hits, the Asian countries want to have institutions of their own that can respond, at least in part. Notwithstanding the huge questions this raises about global versus regional public goods and about the coordination or lack thereof between global and regional institutions, there is a strong sentiment in all the world's regions for moving in this direction.

One of the inspirations for such a move is precisely the regional development banks. Development finance is the one functional area in which all the regions have already been operating for 20 to 40 years. When

Asians talk about an Asian Monetary Fund, they point out, to each other at least, that they have had for decades now an Asian Development Bank (ADB), which has been accepted and recognized as a valuable part of the global network of development banks, working with and sometimes competing with the World Bank. Why not do the same thing in the international financial area? In his comment, Enrique Iglesias also expressed the desire—one that has been felt in this hemisphere for many decades—to do something similar in Latin America and the Caribbean.

The regional development banks thus provide much of the institutional inspiration for new proposals in the monetary and other domains. Theirs is one area in which regionalism has demonstrably worked over an extended period and in which relations between regional and global institutions have, in fact, been put in place. When we ask what role is appropriate for the regional development banks in what Devlin and Castro call the New Regionalism, therefore, it is hugely important that we take note of what has already happened in the past. In particular, we should look at how the regional banks have worked with the World Bank in developing expertise, new innovations, and new lending programs and patterns in their own area of the world.

However, the question then becomes, what can the regional banks offer to the New Regionalism both in the areas of trade and finance and perhaps elsewhere? The two most important contributions have already been mentioned. The first is intellectual leadership, to help the individual countries of each region develop their thinking on all these issues. The second and related contribution is technical assistance—capacity building—to support the efforts of the countries to work out these new regional developments in ways that are mutually sensible, as well as sensible in terms of the global mechanisms that we now have in place.

One can already cite a couple of examples in which this is being done. The Inter-American Development Bank has been playing an enormously important role in the development of the FTAA, in developing ideas, analyzing the effects of trade liberalization, and helping countries—particularly the smaller ones—position themselves better to negotiate toward and participate in those agreements. Similarly, the ADB has been deeply engaged in the early stages of financial cooperation among the East Asian countries. For example, one essential part of the CMI is, of course, surveillance and peer pressure. The member countries have looked to the ADB to help develop the necessary mechanisms, first within ASEAN and then more broadly.

Countries in a given neighborhood are likely to know the neighborhood better than countries outside. Precisely for that reason, unlike many monetary economists, I believe that an Asian Monetary Fund would be a good idea, because if structured properly, it could help avoid future crises like that of 1997–98, as countries in the neighborhood are more likely to know if a neighbor is headed toward a crisis.

In addition, and this is critically important, countries in the neighborhood have more political legitimacy, more standing, in going to one of their neighbors and asking them to change their practices. It is true that Asians have traditionally been very reluctant to be quite so frank with each other, but the 1997–98 crisis may have changed that at the margin, because many now realize that if Malaysia or Singapore, or even Indonesia or the Philippines, had gone to Thailand in late 1996 and early 1997 and said, "Please change your ways, because if you don't you're going to ruin us as well as yourself," it might have had some effect. Peer pressure at the regional level could be very important and very positive. If regionalism moves in that direction, it could be extremely helpful.

I think the bottom line for the regional banks, as Devlin and Castro summarize it at the end of their chapter, is to provide intellectual leadership for the process, making sure that the interests of the individual countries do add up to a positive-sum game and that any new regional institutions coordinate effectively with the global institutions. Perhaps the regional banks could also, as the ADB has done, provide at least on a transitional basis an institutional home for some of the new arrangements that may be needed to get that process moving constructively, and therefore play a role in the global financial architecture and the global trade architecture.

I think this may, in fact, turn out to be a central role for the regional banks over the next five to 10 years. As Enrique Iglesias pointed out, the role of the banks may not now be primarily on the financial side but, indeed, more on the nonfinancial side.

Comment

WILLEM BUITER

A rather low-brow and narrow economic perspective on the regionalism issue is presented here. It is important, when considering the case for a regional approach in a given situation, to ask oneself which of the following two broad reasons for justifying regionalism one has in mind. The first is that regionalism is the second-best practical alternative to an unachievable global solution. The second is that regionalism is actually the first-best solution, because of externalities in public goods that have a strictly regional scope. To my mind, initiatives such as regional trade liberalization and regional monetary union fall into the second-best category. One would like to see them done on a global scale instead, but regionalism is the best one can do. With other issues, such as infrastructure, water use, public health issues, and certain cultural issues, the problem may be intrinsically regional, and therefore a regional approach is the first-best solution.

The dimensions of regionalism outlined in the chapter by Devlin and Castro include financial integration, monetary integration, and trade. The chapter has little to say about factor mobility, and about labor mobility at the regional level in particular, but I want to emphasize those issues as well.

To start with the easy issues, I do not see much of a role for regional financial integration. The key financial issues for any region, and indeed almost any country, are, first, strengthening the domestic financial system —banks, nonbank financial institutions, and capital markets—and, second, selectively tapping the resources of the global financial system. Ideally, one starts with foreign direct investment, which of course comes mainly

Willem Buiter is chief economist at the European Bank for Reconstruction and Development.

from the industrial countries, and then one graduates to trade finance and then to the long-term global bond markets and equity markets, so that the pension funds of both developing and industrial economies can diversify in a sensible way. Ultimately, when all is ready, countries allow short-term borrowing. In reality, the countries that I know about—developing and transitional countries alike—tend to seek financial integration with London, New York, Tokyo, Frankfurt, and Zurich, not with each other.

There may be one exception to that; namely, regional equity and bond markets. As regards the trading of equity and bonds, the location of the trading platform is not of primary importance. Equity claims on assets located anywhere could in principle be traded on a global platform somewhere in hyperspace. This is indeed increasingly the case. The challenge faced by developing and transition economies without a well-developed domestic equity market and bond market is, first, to gain access to these global trading platforms and, second, to bring to bear local and regional information on these global organized transactions, so that local risk and return can be properly priced. If global trading platforms are not efficient vehicles for dealing with small share or bond issues, a limited role may persist for decentralized, local (i.e., national) trading platforms.

As regards regional monetary integration, except for the common currency recently introduced in Europe, I do not think there is currently a case for regional monetary unions. I would change that view if monetary integration were matched by, and supported by, political integration. That means that it is an issue only for the countries looking forward to acceding to the European Union. In the rest of the world, whether it be monetary union between the United States and Canada in North America or dollarization in South America, unless the political institutions are created to support such unions, they will be short-lived affairs. Hence, I think efforts to create such unions would be destructive and dangerous.

Regional monetary funds, such as the proposed Asian Monetary Fund, would only be acceptable at all as a fourth- or fifth-best approach, and the same goes for regional bilateral swap arrangements. Such arrangements would be better than no financial swap arrangements, but clearly one wants to swap with countries with whom one's shocks are negatively correlated, and that is not likely to be the case at the regional level. The obvious case for having a single financial stabilization agent in the world is that it provides optimal diversification. If there are practical obstacles to such a regime, that is regrettable. In contrast, regional development assistance or transition assistance makes sense because such assistance supports a long-term process of structural change and institutional development, which requires intimate knowledge and ownership by the local and regional society.

I want to focus on the key role of interregional trade liberalization and also on the liberalization of transit, as distinct from trade, for goods, services, and people. Incidentally, the survey by Devlin and Castro cites not a single example from Central Asia, although it considers the Asian region, which is an interesting omission in the post–September 11 world.

Regional trade and transit for many countries, especially in Eastern Europe and Central Asia, is a necessary condition for global liberalization and global free trade. That is because of the simple fact that, of the 27 countries in which the European Bank for Reconstruction and Development (EBRD) operates, no fewer than 13 are landlocked. One, Uzbekistan, shares the unique distinction with Liechtenstein of being double-landlocked: goods from that country must pass through at least two countries to reach the sea. Incidentally, these 13 countries include 4 of the poorest countries in the region. Only Georgia, the fifth poorest country in the area, is not in this group of landlocked nations.

Of course, having access to the sea is neither necessary nor sufficient for economic prosperity. Switzerland and Austria are both landlocked countries, for example. However, being landlocked highlights the importance of regional liberalization of trade and transit of goods, services, and people as a precondition for global liberalization of trade and transit.

It also shows how, in this supposedly increasingly globalized world economy, geography continues to matter: It matters who your neighbors are. Landlocked countries are inherently more vulnerable to all the hold-up problems associated with a neighbor's ability to impose economic isolation through denial of transit and overflight rights. The only thing a landlocked country can do on its own is to beam digital information via satellite to customers abroad. For everything else, a country in such a situation depends on the goodwill of its neighbors.

For example, the fact that the Kyrgyz Republic is a member of the World Trade Organization does it little good unless it has free transit through its neighbors—China, Tajikistan, Uzbekistan, and Kazakhstan—to the rest of the world. If, hypothetically, I want to take my onions from the Kyrgyz Republic to Siberia, where there is a natural market for them, I have to go through Kazakhstan. By the time I get there, my onions will have rotted and I will have had to pay a thousand dollars in transit fees randomly imposed by rogue policemen along the way. This type of scenario is a huge issue for these countries. Similarly, hundreds of thousands of Tajiks traditionally work in Siberia, but they cannot pass freely through Kazakhstan. The official story of the Kazakh authorities is that they fear these transiting workers will bring in terrorism and drugs. Regional trade and transit are also key issues in the Caucasus and in southeastern Europe. These are extreme examples of the importance of regional barriers for establishing the preconditions for global integration, but they are worth mentioning.

Economists have long debated whether regional trade integration is a handmaiden or an obstacle to global trade integration. In theory, and in practice, it all depends. Consider perhaps the best-known example of a customs union: the European Union. Such a union is more likely to be trade-creating if the common external tariff is the minimum rather than the maximum of the former national tariffs. On that score, the European Union is doing fine. As measured by the common external tariff on those commodities to which it applies, the European Union is probably trade liberalizing.

The Common Agricultural Policy, of course, is a different matter, as are the nontariff barriers that are in place. These features may make regional integration and regionalism trade-diverting rather than globally trade-creating or enhancing. We know that the subsidies paid to agriculture in the United States and the European Union, when combined, amount to several times what these countries provide in overseas development assistance. The $52 billion of global development aid that The UK chancellor of the exchequer wants to double to about $100 billion is less than a third of the total explicit subsidies paid in the United States and the European Union to agriculture. This of course does not include the other barriers that these continent-size economies maintain to developing countries' exports of steel, textiles, and other sensitive goods, or the various nontariff barriers that they use to the great detriment of the world economy. Increasingly, these nontariff barriers are in the form of standards—health and safety standards, sanitary standards, labor standards, and environmental standards—as well as antidumping measures: the last popular refuge of protectionist scoundrels, both in the United States and in Europe.

The extension of the boundaries of the European Union all the way to Poland and beyond is particularly important and interesting from the EBRD's institutional point of view. Ten of the countries in which the EBRD operates are potential candidates for EU accession, but 17 are not.[1] This means that the EBRD will find looking at enlargement through from two different perspectives: that of the likely successful accession candidates and that of those countries that will remain outside the EU for the foreseeable future. The issue of who gains and who loses is a key one. With respect to the trade issue, strictly defined, there will probably be no great cost imposed on those who remain outside. However, with respect to the transit issue and labor mobility, the imposition of a common border with Ukraine, Belarus, and Moldova—countries that at the moment have free access for seasonal and short-term migrant labor—could become a very serious issue. The European Union has to make sure that its eventually expanded boundary does not become a Brussels Lace Curtain to replace the Iron Curtain of past decades. The Doha principles can be made compatible with regional integration and liberalization, but this change is not automatic.

---

1. At the time of publication, a number of candidates for EU accession had already effectively become EU members.

Harry Johnson used to say that the whole trade versus aid debate was something of a sideshow. If countries were serious about economic development and overcoming poverty, they would simply open their borders to all comers. At the regional level, the integration of labor markets, provided such integration is combined with sensible rules determining both entitlements to local public services and obligations to contribute to their cost, is an important issue that should be addressed alongside all the others.

Comment

GARY CLYDE HUFBAUER

Robert Devlin and Lucio Castro provide an excellent survey of regionalism, and they preview the potential role of the regional development banks in amplifying the economic gains from regional economic integration. The regional story since the late 1980s has been dominated by agreements centered on trade and investment issues. Devlin and Castro call these agreements the New Regionalism: Their inspiration and content differ greatly from agreements negotiated in the old, that is, postwar, period.

Agreements in the era of New Regionalism come in many flavors: bilateral, plurilateral, and subregional, as well as regional. Many are South–South, but a few are North–South. Chapter 2 provides a very useful overview of the numerous agreements involving at least one developing-country partner. The survey is organized by region: Africa, Asia, and Latin America. Even though trade and investment were the centerpiece of these agreements, the vast majority of the pacts achieved little in the way of trade or investment liberalization. Africa was especially prolific in creating paper agreements with limited economic substance. A common problem, which Devlin and Castro emphasize, is that many agreements were South–South, covering a small amount of trade, and hence provided little incentive for the partners to engage in precedent-setting liberalization. Fortunately, the emphasis is now turning to North–South agreements.

A few agreements that have emerged in the era of New Regionalism dramatically liberalized trade and investment, and these few successful

Gary Clyde Hufbauer is Reginald Jones Senior Fellow at the Institute for International Economics.

pacts furnish models for others. The Southern Cone Common Market and the North American Free Trade Agreement, in the Western Hemisphere, have been especially noteworthy. Other agreements, although not affecting significant volumes of trade or investment, are noteworthy as templates. Among these pacts, the Mexico–Chile agreement can be singled out.[1] Devlin and Castro usefully highlight the key objectives and ingredients of successful New Regionalism, as well as the potential costs. Outside the trade and investment area, the accomplishments of the New Regionalism have been modest. Financial and monetary cooperation has gone nowhere in Africa or Latin America, but in May 2000 Asia began a serious conversation under the auspices of the Chiang Mai Initiative.

As Devlin and Castro emphasize, the trade and investment accords of the New Regionalism operated against a background of multilateral trade liberalization resulting from the Tokyo and Uruguay Rounds. In addition, many countries embarked on unilateral liberalization, especially when their tariff peaks soared above 50 percent ad valorem. In this respect, the experience of Brazil and Argentina was striking, as discussed in Devlin and Castro's chapter. In other dimensions of economic policy there was a drift toward liberal reform: monetary and fiscal discipline, privatization of state-owned companies, and establishment of independent regulatory authorities. All in all, it is fair to characterize the 15 years from 1985 to 2000 as a period of global policy liberalization that was pursued more energetically in some countries and regions than others.

Except in Africa and the Muslim "-stans," liberal reform was a dominant theme on the economic policy agenda in this era. Latin America was at the forefront among developing countries in adopting the policy reforms that came to be labeled the Washington consensus and Anglo-Saxon capitalism.

Yet the last two decades of the 20th century did not, on average, yield better economic results for developing countries than the preceding two decades. Particularly disappointing was economic performance in Latin America and the Caribbean, where, according to one set of critics (Weisbrot et al. 2000, drawing on the *Human Development Reports* published by the United Nations Development Programme), income per capita grew 75 percent in the first period and only 6 percent in the second.[2] At the other end of the economic spectrum, income per capita in China grew by 300 percent in the second period, compared with 85 percent in the first. Apart from China and its East Asian neighbors, growth in income per capita in developing countries generally lagged in the second period.

---

1. In the near future, an agreement between the United States and the Central American Common Market may be added to the list of successful North–South agreements.

2. The data for the second period in the Weisbrot et al. (2000) paper cover 1980–98. Performance in 1999 and 2000 will add only a few percentage points to Latin America's cumulative two-decade growth record.

Critics who follow the banner of Dani Rodrik (1999) put the blame for poor performance variously at the feet of the IMF, the World Bank, or the liberal economic agenda.[3] By association, the regional development banks also number among the guilty. These critics claim that the international financial institutions and official Washington go overboard in promoting a one-size-fits-all agenda.[4] Another set of critics, to which I belong, views lagging growth as a consequence of insufficient reform, gaps in the reform agenda, and the time required for a new economic model to bear fruit. Devlin and Castro, one suspects, also belong to this second group, but we cannot be sure, as their chapter does not explicitly address the debate over the growth dividend (or is it the growth deduction?) emanating from regional economic integration and parallel reforms. The dividend or deduction debate provides exactly the context needed for discussing the role of the regional banks, particularly in Latin America. This context is what I miss in the chapter by Devlin and Castro.

Let me elaborate. In my view there are two major gaps in the reform agenda. The first is the regrettable correlation between the transition from autocratic state capitalism to market economics and the rise of corruption. Why the correlation? Because privatization provides a hunting ground for insider deals, liberalization of foreign direct investment invites joint ventures with politically connected partners, and a market economy empowers numerous government officials to demand—and private firms to supply—bribes to facilitate all sorts of transactions.[5] Once corruption has been institutionalized, it matures into a heavy and variable tax on capital, which is very discouraging to economic progress. A major gap

---

3. Weisbrot and his colleagues (2000) are prominent in this group of critics. More prominent from the media standpoint are various antiglobalization organizations such as Public Citizen, but their self-assigned role is exaggeration and misstatement, not analysis. Joseph Stiglitz (2000) is on the periphery of this group, as his criticism is directed at the short-term crisis policies of the IMF rather than the long-term success or failure of policy liberalization.

4. The one-size-fits-all criticism is, in my view, preposterous. The international financial institutions do not attempt, and could not succeed, in molding all countries into a single economic model. The size and structure of the public sector, the degree of independence of monetary and other regulatory authorities, the extent of state ownership—all these features and others differ enormously from country to country. The international financial institutions have never conceived of their mission as designing an approved template of development. A fairer criticism would be that the international financial institutions have been too tolerant of local idiosyncratic features, such as the nepotistic syndicalism of the Suharto regime or the chaebol industrial groups in Korea.

5. To be sure, primitive economies that are endowed with minerals and other natural resources frequently descend into systems of economic plunder. This happened in much of Latin America under Spanish and Portuguese rule, in parts of Africa under colonial rule (such as the Belgian Congo under King Leopold I), and in much of Africa under postcolonial military regimes. This unhappy phase is largely past in modern Latin America.

in the reform agenda, therefore, is its failure to establish institutions that curtail the choking grasp of corruption.

A second and related gap is the general weakness of financial institutions in developing countries, which includes a tendency toward connected lending for doubtful projects, slow recognition of nonperforming loans, mismatches in the term and currency structure of bank assets and liabilities, poor accounting standards throughout the corporate sector (as if Enron were the norm), and limited shareholder rights when it comes to voting out management. In the more spectacular episodes, these weaknesses combine with unsustainable exchange rate regimes and public debt dynamics to explode in financial crises. Equally damaging is the persistently high cost of dollar credit in developing countries—well above levels prevailing in the United States or Europe—partly as a consequence of lurking future crises.

In addition to their obvious importance in building hard infrastructure to support regional economic integration (e.g., the Puebla-Panama Plan), the regional banks can do a great deal more. This is particularly true in Latin America, where the scope of the Inter-American Development Bank's (IDB) operations coincides with the planned Free Trade Area of the Americas. It is less true in Asia (where the Asian Free Trade Area is stalled, and Association of South East Nations+3 is a distant prospect) and Africa (where trade and investment agreements are largely paper pacts, and basic development needs far exceed the modest resources of the African Development Bank).

Here is where I urge Devlin and Castro to strike bold notes. The regional banks, and in particular the Inter-American Development Bank, can do much to promote regional economic integration and faster growth by addressing the two gaps in the reform agenda. The regional banks can help curtail corruption by a variety of means:

- first and foremost, by insisting on high procurement standards, a policy already in place;

- by insisting on greater transparency in all public procurement, whether or not financed by the multilateral development banks;

- by providing resources to strengthen the capabilities of local prosecutors and judges; and

- by offering temporary teams of inspectors to countries that ask for outside assistance in exposing corrupt practices.

The regional banks—again with emphasis on the IDB—can also help strengthen financial institutions and practices. As Rojas-Suarez (2001) argues, this does not mean slavish adherence to the capital standards formulated at Basel. Instead, the regional banks should advocate institutions and practices adapted to regional needs. The acid test will be whether we see a diminished frequency of financial crises, lower interest rates across the credit risk spectrum, and deeper financial markets as measured by ratios of bank assets to GDP and capital market values to GDP. Here are a few suggestions for regional bank action:

- give guidance when regional members seem to be relying inappropriately on foreign capital, especially short-term bank loans denominated in dollars;[6]

- provide technical assistance for bank examiners, accounting boards, and capital market supervisors;

- suggest modalities for financial services liberalization, a topic on which Devlin and Castro are experts; and

- quietly campaign for proper pension fund management, and nudge countries in the direction of fully funded, as opposed to pay-as-you-go, pension systems.

References

Dobson, Wendy, and Gary Hufbauer. 2000. *World Capital Markets: Challenge to the G-10.* Washington: Institute for International Economics.
Rodrik, Dani. 1999. *The New Global Economy and Developing Countries: Making Openness Work.* Washington: Overseas Development Council.
Rojas-Suarez, Liliana. 2001. *Can International Capital Standards Strengthen Banks in Emerging Markets?* Working Paper WP01-10. Washington: Institute for International Economics.
Stiglitz, Joseph. 2000. The Insider: What I Learned at the World Economic Crisis. *The New Republic* (April 17).
Weisbrot, Mark, Dean Baker, Robert Naiman, and Gila Neta. 2000. *Growth May Be Good for the Poor—But Are IMF and World Bank Policies Good for Growth?* Unpublished paper. London: Center for Economic and Policy Research.

---

6. This theme is developed in Dobson and Hufbauer (2000), who advocate a more forceful supply side role by financial supervisors in the Group of 10 countries, but this is an area in which regional banks can make a useful demand side contribution.

3

Regional Public Goods: The Comparative Edge of Regional Development Banks

MARCO FERRONI

Although some development challenges undoubtedly need to be tackled globally, many issues of financing for development are more effectively dealt with at the regional level. An example is the provision of public goods and services needed for development that neither the market nor national governments will provide in the absence of external assistance. These include regional health programs to contain endemic diseases, coordination of transport infrastructure among neighboring countries, regional energy cooperation, and financial regulation to limit cross-border contagion, to name but a few. The regional development banks (RDBs) have a central role to play in the provision of these regional public goods (RPGs). However, this role, the mechanisms and constraints under which it operates, its relationship to country-focused assistance, and the challenge of financing RPGs have received little attention in the past.[1] This chapter attempts to fill the gap by examining these issues in the context of the broader, ongoing debate about cross-border public goods in international assistance.

Marco Ferroni is the principal evaluation officer at the Inter-American Development Banks's Office of Evaluation and Oversight. The views expressed in this chapter are those of the author and do not necessarily reflect institutional positions. This chapter draws on Ferroni and Mody (2002). Thoughtful contributions by Stephen Meardon and Ashoka Mody are gratefully acknowledged. Any errors are the author's responsibility.

1. For example, the Report of the High-Level Panel on Financing for Development (known as the Zedillo Report) has a section on global public goods but does not refer to RPGs or their potential role in supporting national development and the creation of global public goods (Zedillo 2001).

Background and Definitions

Notion of Public Goods

The concept of public goods can be traced at least as far back as David Hume's 1739 discussion of the common good. In 1954 Paul Samuelson developed a general theory of public goods, which stimulated a sizable literature, from which three interrelated characteristics of public goods have emerged: public goods generate significant externalities, or spillover effects; they are to a considerable degree nonrivalrous and nonexcludable (box 3.1); and they create opportunities for the enhancement of welfare through collective action (Institute of Development Studies 2001).[2]

In the 1990s, because of the intensification of economic integration and interdependence that has come to be referred to as globalization, the discussion of public goods went global.[3] Research and policy statements on international public goods began to emerge (including Development Committee 2001; IFIAC 2000; Kanbur and Sandler, with Morrison 1999; Kaul, Grunberg, and Stern 1999; and Soros 2001). It was noted that international public goods fall into two categories: global and regional. RPGs are a class of public goods that falls in between national and global public goods. The goods benefit what some have called spillover communities: communities that are close enough to each other geographically or in other ways such that the actions of one member can have effects on others. Depending on the problem being addressed, a spillover community can range from a couple of neighboring countries to a continent or a hemisphere. The production of RPGs typically requires cross-border collective action that engages all or most of the members of the spillover group. In exceptional cases, RPGs may be provided by one or a few leading nations motivated by a combination of self-interest and broader objectives.

Global public goods and RPGs include the knowledge, the regimes, and the standards and rules required to address cross-border problems or to engender desirable cross-border externalities; the institutions that monitor and enforce these rules and regimes; and the benefits that arise and are shared indiscriminately among countries. This definition implies that both types of public goods come in two forms: intermediate and final. Final public goods are broad outcomes or manifestations of well-being such as peace, the absence of extreme poverty, a well-managed physical environment, and convergent international economic conditions capable of lifting all boats. Intermediate public goods include shared policy

---

2. If collective action is difficult to achieve, it is in large measure because of the property of nonexcludability, which creates coordination and financing problems in the creation of public goods because of the incentive to have a free ride.

3. See Kindleberger (1986) for an early influential contribution.

Box 3.1 Regional public goods

A regional public good (RPG) is a service or resource whose benefits are shared by countries within a region.[1] The benefits of pure RPGs are nonrival (one country's consumption does not subtract from the amount available to other countries) and nonexcludable (no country in the region can be excluded from benefiting, except at prohibitive cost). In reality, most RPGs are significantly, but not wholly, nonrival and nonexcludable. They are thus mixed rather than pure public goods, meaning that they bestow a combination of national and transnational benefits. (The usual definitions of the characteristics of public goods take individuals as the relevant units. However, in the discussion of international public goods, countries, not individuals, are the relevant units.)

Three kinds of activities to pursue RPGs can be distinguished:

- non-country-specific investments in knowledge, dialogue, basic research into technologies meant to be in the public domain (e.g., vaccines), and negotiation of shared standards and policy regimes;

- intercountry mechanisms for managing adverse cross-border externalities or creating beneficial ones (such as coordinated public health measures to contain the spread of disease), investments in cross-border infrastructure to enhance the preconditions for growth through trade and integration among participating countries, and creation of regional institutions to facilitate solutions in areas ranging from financial and banking stability to the sustainable management of shared environmental resources; and

- country-specific action to take advantage (or enable absorption) of the benefits created by the first two activities, which will create national public goods, such as improved policy environments and institutional indicators, that in turn can engender transnational externalities.

---

1. This discussion is adapted from Kanbur (2001).

---

frameworks, regimes (such as regional integration schemes), institutions, and certain kinds of joint investments.

RPGs also arise when individual countries induce beneficial cross-border spillovers. Regional public bads arise, analogously, when the spillovers in question are undesirable. An epidemiological policy that improves health in the country practicing the policy while reducing the transmission of pathogens and disease across the country's borders is an example of an action generating a beneficial spillover.

Spillovers induce neighborhood effects, which may be positive or negative, and that in either case can play an important role in determining countries' development prospects.[4] Neighborhood effects provide a rationale for involvement by the RDBs at the regional and the subregional

---

4. William Easterly and Ross Levine (1997) estimate that neighborhood effects may reduce annual economic growth in sub-Saharan Africa by up to 1 percentage point.

level, in addition to these institutions' traditional, country-focused work. The task is to help prevent or contain negative neighborhood effects and to promote forces capable of engendering beneficial ones.

However, because neighborhood effects are the consequence of policies and measures taken individually by the countries that make up the neighborhood, they can also be seen as confirmation of the appropriateness of the RDBs' longstanding country focus. Wherever they generate cross-border externalities, national policies have some of the characteristics of international public goods (or public bads), which make it possible to say that, at bottom, good national policies are the premier RPG. Therefore, the merits of staking out a supranational (regional and subregional) role for the RDBs should be stated, not presumed, and should be spelled out precisely.

Merits of Regional Cooperation

The rationale for going regional is linked to the belief that the right combination of country-based and transnational measures leads to outcomes superior to those achievable by national measures alone. Countries engage in regional cooperation to realize benefits that cannot be obtained autonomously. Recent efforts at regional and subregional integration substantiate the point: regional integration agreements have proliferated in the past decade (most countries in the world are now members of at least one such agreement), and this is considered evidence that the demand for regional cooperation and for RPGs is growing (CEIP 2001).

The benefits pursued through regional integration are varied and include the following: locking countries into reform commitments, creating venues and peer pressure to address negative neighborhood effects, taking advantage of opportunities for liberalization and reform in a more controlled and predictable setting than that encountered in a multilateral context, and creating value by following up on a derived demand for cooperation in areas beyond trade, including infrastructure, finance, labor codes, product safety, law enforcement, and the environment. For example,

- The economic case for the coordination of transport infrastructure among neighboring countries is compelling when remote regions and landlocked countries can thereby be connected to urban centers and ports.[5]

---

5. The South American Regional Infrastructure Plan, unveiled at the Summit of South American Presidents in September 2000, identifies 12 key corridors linking the continent. The plan addresses transportation, energy, and telecommunications needs along these corridors and provides for an integral and multisectoral approach to infrastructure development in coming years, with financing from the private sector, the Inter-American Development Bank (IDB), the Andean Development Corporation, and other institutions (IDB 2000).

Similarly, there is often considerable scope for efficiency gains from integrating the supply and distribution of energy across borders. Making the supply of electricity more reliable and lowering unit costs requires competition and the attainment of economies of scale. This typically calls for integrating the power grids of small countries.[6]

- The possibility of cross-border financial contagion and, again, the desirability of bringing about economies of scale are among the considerations in favor of regional approaches to regulating and stabilizing financial markets. Indeed, some observers believe that the absence of a regional focus is the reason why financial sector reforms in sub-Saharan Africa during the 1990s were disappointing (World Bank 2000). The integration of the financial sectors of small, poorly diversified economies can help lower both the costs and the risks incurred by banks and financial services firms. Such integration is often achieved through cross-border consolidation of the industry. Policy measures to promote financial integration include harmonizing payment procedures, commercial and financial law, accounting standards, and prudential supervision. They also include appropriately endowed regional institutions to promote integration, help prevent crises through appropriate surveillance, and contribute to the stabilization of markets as a first line of defense, leaving the function of lender of last resort to global institutions such as the International Monetary Fund (Ocampo 2001).

- Infectious diseases severely disrupt economic life in many developing countries. Similar to financial contagion, they do not stop at national borders. One country's negligence can easily nullify a neighboring country's epidemiological efforts. Coordinated international action can help (box 3.2).

- Environmental policy and the management of shared natural resources are other fields in which cross-border cooperation has merit. Watershed management is particularly relevant in this context. When countries share a river system, the use of water resources in one country can profoundly affect the quantity and quality of water available to countries downstream. Diminishing water availability and water quality constrain economic development and can generate tensions, if not outright conflict. International law in the area of shared waters provides some guidance, but no universally accepted standards are available for the utilization and management of these waters.[7] Riparian

---

6. F. T. Sparrow and W. A. Masters (1999) provide estimates of cost savings from the electricity trade in southern Africa.

7. See World Bank, Berlin Recommendations for the International Roundtable at lnweb18.worldbank.org/ESSD/ardext.nsf/18bydocname/strategy_ preparation ofthestrategy _BerlinRoundtable.

Box 3.2 The River Blindness Control Program

Perhaps the best example of what a judicious combination of national and regional approaches can achieve in the domain of public health is the River Blindness Control Program in West Africa. The program, now extended to all countries in sub-Saharan Africa in which river blindness (onchocerciasis) is endemic, has operated since 1974 through a coalition of African governments, local communities, international organizations, bilateral donors, the business sector, foundations, and nongovernmental organizations. It combines a regional focus with capacity building at the national and the local levels, including the training of hundreds of epidemiologists, entomologists, and other specialists in national ministries of health, as well as the involvement of tens of thousands of community health workers. This debilitating, insect-borne disease has now been all but eradicated from the original program area, leading to enormous economic gains and improvements in the quality of life of affected communities and individuals. The coalition has been held together by a strong, shared sense of purpose, a judicious combination of leadership and deference on the part of individual contributors in accordance with their comparative advantages, a step-by-step approach following precisely defined and phased objectives, and what appears to have been the right amount of flexibility and compromise in execution (for more on the program, see www.worldbank.org/afr/gper/ocp.htm).

countries must search for cooperative solutions unique to their circumstances.[8]

The list of policy concerns in which regional cooperation can profitably complement national measures can easily be extended. Research cooperation and knowledge sharing are key among these concerns, as is cooperation in preserving or restoring peace and security. International initiatives in these and other areas, including regional integration, have been on the rise. The recognition that regional policies and programs can generate dividends, in terms of improved development outcomes at the national level, is spreading (box 3.3). This is a welcome trend from the perspective of development effectiveness. It does not, however, mean that the challenges of collective action have become less formidable. Longstanding challenges such as political tensions, lack of trust, and high coordination costs persist, as do the difficulties of engineering equitable solutions acceptable to all parties.

---

8. The International Consortium for Cooperation on the Nile is attempting such a solution. Like the River Blindness Control Program, the consortium, established in 1999, is a partnership of governments, donors, advocacy groups, the private sector, and international organizations. Its objective is to improve the management of the Nile River Basin, a resource shared by 10 countries from Egypt to Uganda, all of which suffer from water shortages and are affected by, from the collective viewpoint, suboptimal patterns of use of the Nile; see www.worldbank.org/afr/nilebasin.

Box 3.3. Regional public goods in the New Partnership for Africa's Development

The New Partnership for Africa's Development (NEPAD) exists today essentially as a manifesto of the development priorities on the African continent and the collective will and responsibility of its heads of state to address those priorities both singly and jointly.[1] The partnership's initiatives—political and economic governance, infrastructure, human resources, capital flows, market access, and environment—are intended, in the words of its primary document, "to eradicate poverty and to place [the] countries . . . on a path of sustainable growth and development." The initiatives are still unfunded, but financing through the African Development Bank as well as the World Bank and other donors is envisioned.

The partnership names several immediate priorities to be put on a fast track toward allocation of resources: communicable diseases (HIV/AIDS, malaria, and tuberculosis), information and communications technology, debt reduction, and market access. Although the plans to address these priorities are not yet sufficiently defined for detailed comment, one can expect projects addressing at least the first two priorities to constitute international and regional public goods. A peace and security effort subsumed by the political governance initiative, and a macroeconomic stability effort subsumed by the economic governance initiative, are also (if successful) likely to produce international public goods.

A conference on financing NEPAD was held in January 2002 in Dakar, Senegal. The conference document foresees an active role for the African Development Bank; it also implies considerable emphasis by NEPAD on the creation of international and regional public goods. The language of such goods is already written into the document with respect to the environment: "the ecological lung provided by the continent's rainforests . . . is a global public good that benefits all mankind." Because the language of the document is intended to be helpful in obtaining official funding for the partnership's initiatives, it may shift the priorities of the initiatives themselves still farther in the direction of international public goods.

---

1. Sources for this discussion include the Human Sciences Research Council, www.sarpn.org.za/nepad_1.php, and the NEPAD Web site, www.nepad.org.

It is possible to formulate some requirements that should be fulfilled if regional cooperation is to yield its full measure of benefits. First, the duration and depth of regional cooperation must be sufficient to make meaningful improvements possible. Nearly eradicating the scourge of river blindness in west Africa took a generation, and appropriate national measures to keep the disease at bay will need to continue indefinitely. Near eradication would not have been possible without persistence. Similarly, concluding a trade agreement is one thing, but persisting in the difficult effort of deepening integration is quite another. Such deepening is likely to be needed to consolidate the benefits of integration over time, but it is also expected to call for contentious structural change. Meaningful regional cooperation in policy domains such as those discussed earlier requires long-term commitments and a willingness to go into adequate depth. Deepening has to do with the complementary national measures needed to enable countries to contribute to, and absorb, the benefits of transnational cooperation (see below). This is the difficult part—much harder than signing an international agreement and rhetorically committing oneself to the course of action that it implies. Regional cooperation consists of national measures taken in accordance with some agreed international plan. The absence of, or lags in, complementary national measures can bring the best collective action framework to naught.

Second, in the interest of sustainability, those who lose (or those that gain less than others) from cooperation in a given field must be compensated to keep the coalition of actors and the pursuit of cooperative solutions alive. Again, this can be very difficult because of disagreements over the nature and extent of asymmetries and because of resource constraints.

Third, where feasible, contracting parties should bind themselves with treaties or agreements that are self-enforcing, because supranational authorities capable of exacting compliance are typically lacking. S. Barrett (2002) shows that the requirement of self-enforcement reduces the number of feasible cooperative solutions.

These are demanding conditions, and they are seldom completely satisfied. Nevertheless, protagonists of regional initiatives ignore them at their risk.

Core and Complementary Activities

The recognition that the production of RPGs requires the integration of regional programs and country-based activities has led to a distinction in the recent literature between core and complementary activities (World Bank 2001). As will be discussed later, this distinction is key to understanding the options for allocating official finance to RPGs. Core activities are those whose aim is to produce RPGs. They include regional programs and policy frameworks, as well as activities that are focused in one country but whose benefits spill over to others (these are called mixed goods). Complementary activities, however, prepare countries for consuming the RPGs that the core activities make available, while at the same time creating valuable national public goods. For example, a country cannot use international agricultural research goods effectively in the absence of adequate domestic agricultural services and incentives. Thus, core and complementary activities and investments go hand in hand. This indicates that the RPG agenda opens up new and heretofore little-explored dimensions of coordination in international assistance relating to matters of timing, balance, and synergy between core and complementary activities.

Role of the RDBs

Fostering cooperation among countries is difficult because, among other reasons, of a problem of valuation: Different countries and their citizens value the benefits of cooperation and public goods differently (World Bank 2001).[9] Regional policies to pursue transnational benefits tend to be in short supply because countries' first interest is their own national advantage. Countries acting on their own typically do not take into account the costs that their actions impose on others. They may recognize that they could further their national advantage by the right combination of national and regional policies, but this recognition by itself is usually not sufficient to overcome barriers to collective action.

This is where the RDBs come in. Regional organizations can act as catalysts of collective action. They are playing an increasingly important role in the provision of RPGs through their ability to convene potential participants, generate and transfer knowledge, assist negotiations, and transfer funding. As argued below, they have begun to step up their engagement at the regional and subregional levels. The principle of subsidiarity indicates a division of labor, with the global multilateral institutions supporting global public goods and the RDBs fostering RPGs. This appears to be largely borne out in practice.

However, the RDBs are not unconstrained in their endeavors to support regional policies and programs aimed at providing RPGs. Two factors affect the pace of progress: countries' limited ability (for political reasons or because of limited institutional capacity) to take the national measures needed to pursue joint projects, and a lack of adequate multilateral instruments to catalyze action. As a consequence, multilateral institutions face disincentives to lend—and governments to borrow—for the provision of RPGs. In addition, as explained later, grant-based funding faces constraints.

RDBs and Regional Public Goods

Participants in the Financial Architecture of RPGs

The RDBs have an important role in the architecture of official development finance. Figure 3.1 shows the distribution of net official flows by donor and recipient region. The Inter-American Development Bank (IDB), the Asian Development Bank (ADB), and the African Development Bank (AfDB) account for about 61 percent, 40 percent, and 13 percent of net

---

9. There are reasons to think that the challenges of coordination rise with the number of players involved. The presumption, therefore, is that coordination problems are less severe for RPGs than for global public goods.

Figure 3.1 Total net flows by donor and recipient region, 1990–2000

billions of 1999 dollars

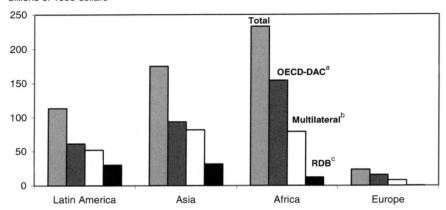

a. Flows from members of the Development Assistance Committee (DAC) of the Organization for Economic Cooperation and Development (OECD).
b. Includes flows from the corresponding regional development bank (RDB).
c. Flows from the RDB for the indicated region (Inter-American Development Bank, Asian Development Bank, African Development Bank, and European Bank for Reconstruction and Development, respectively).

Source: Data from Organization for Economic Cooperation and Development, Development Assistance Committee (OECD-DAC).

multilateral flows to their regions, respectively. Most of these flows finance domestic investments and policy reform (complementary activities and mixed goods). If, as noted above, good national policies are the premier RPG, the RDBs are an important transmission mechanism in their production.

However, the RDBs are also important direct sources of finance for international public goods. On the basis of a recently developed taxonomy of national and international public goods (partially congruent with the earlier definition of complementary and core activities), table 3.1 confirms the prominence of the RDBs in the first area, but it also indicates significant spending in the second are. In the case of the ADB and the AfDB, this spending actually accounts for a larger share of total multilateral commitments than does the banks' spending on national public goods. From their analysis of the sectoral breakdown of aid spending on international public goods, te Velde, Morrissey, and Hewitt (2002) conclude that in 1996–98, most of the spending of funds obtained through the concessional windows of the IDB, the ADB, and the AfDB was devoted to environmental programs aimed at generating a mixture of national and cross-border benefits.

Recent literature on the allocation of official flows to international public goods points to a growing involvement on the part of official (multilateral

Table 3.1 Commitments to national (NPGs) and international (IPGs) public goods by region and by institution, 1990–2000 (billions of dollars unless otherwise stated)

Region	Regional banks		Other multilaterals		Regional banks' share of all multilateral (percent)	
	NPGs	IPGs	NPGs	IPGs	NPGs	IPGs
Latin America and Caribbean	35.2	2.2	30.3	4.5	54	33
Asia	18.4	3.8	43.7	8.1	30	32
Africa	5.7	1.6	21.3	3.3	21	33
Total	59.3	7.6	95.3	15.9	38	32

Source: OECD Development Assistance Committee, based on classification methodology in te Velde, Morrissey, and Hewitt (2002).

and bilateral) agencies in endeavors of transnational scope (World Bank 2001; te Velde, Morrissey, and Hewitt 2002). However, the allocation of resources to core and complementary activities by RDBs in their respective regions is underresearched. The numbers in table 3.1 are quite disparate, which variety is assumed to be the result of different roles and emphases on the part of different RDBs. More detailed analysis is needed, as do such questions as how the RDBs prioritize the RPGs to be supplied (setting priorities for RPGs is less well established than country programming), and whether spending on RPGs is additional to spending on country programs. Although financial additionality is doubtful, judicious combinations of support to core and complementary activities are expected to yield additionality in terms of development effect. The nature and size of this additionality deserve to be investigated more systematically. Pending such an investigation, the remainder of this section presents an overview of activities at the regional and subregional levels by the IDB and the ADB.

IDB and Regional Cooperation

The IDB has fostered regional cooperation since its inception, and during the 1990s, it expanded its involvement in the context of new and unprecedented interest in Latin America and the Caribbean for regional integration (Iglesias 2000). In addition to country-level programming, the bank programs operations at the regional and the subregional levels and carries out research on regional integration. The Integration and Regional Programs Department, an institutional innovation with no counterpart in the other multilateral development banks, serves as a focal point for regional issues.

The IDB supports policy analysis and negotiations related to trade integration efforts at three levels: the subregional (the Caribbean Community and Common Market, the Andean Community, the Central American Common Market, Mercosur, and bilateral agreements), the hemispheric (the proposed Free Trade Area of the Americas), and the global (in the context of negotiations at the World Trade Organization). In the financial arena, the IDB promotes the application of international standards needed both to preserve stability and to promote financial integration. In the area of regional infrastructure, the IDB manages a portfolio of cross-border investments in transport infrastructure, border crossings, and energy, including gas pipelines. As an example, a privately owned and operated gas pipeline project received financing from the IDB's private sector window in 2000, together with support from a consortium of commercial banks, for a pipeline connecting northern Argentina and southern Brazil. New initiatives that the IDB will support include the South American Regional Infrastructure Plan and the Plan Puebla-Panama, a recently unveiled regional development initiative covering southern Mexico and parts of Central America.

The IDB has long provided technical assistance on a regional basis. Regional technical cooperation supports research and knowledge management, training, and the creation and strengthening of institutions that foster regional integration. In 1999, the IDB created the Regional Policy Dialogue, a forum for policy discussion and strategic thinking in key areas pertaining to national development and Latin America's insertion into the global economy.[10] The dialogue covers a variety of policy areas, including trade and integration, macroeconomic and financial policy, public management and transparency, poverty and social safety nets, education and human resources, and the environment and natural disaster management. It establishes networks of government officials proposed by the IDB's borrowing members, sponsors comparative studies that analyze experiences within and outside the region, maintains World Wide Web–based resources, and organizes meetings and the dissemination of good practice. The IDB's regional policies and programs are financed by the bank's administrative budget, income from the Fund for Special Operations (the IDB's concessional window), donor trust funds, and limited lending.

ADB and Regional Cooperation

The ADB supported regional policies and programs throughout the 1990s and has had a board-approved policy on regional cooperation since 1994.

---

10. For more on the Regional Policy Dialogue, see Inter-American Development Bank, Dialogo Regional de Política, www.iadb.org/int/DRP/.

The bank's mission statement on regional cooperation states that the bank (like the IDB) shall foster economic growth and cooperation in its region, collectively and individually, and use its resources for financing development in the region, giving priority to regional, subregional, and national projects.[11] Regional endeavors that the bank has supported include the promotion and institutionalization of economic cooperation in the Greater Mekong Subregion (GMS; discussed later), support for the Indonesia–Malaysia–Thailand growth triangle, promotion of subregional cooperation in South Asia, and fostering of trade cooperation among China, Kazakhstan, the Kyrgyz Republic, and Uzbekistan. The bank supports regional technical cooperation and policy forums in areas ranging from the social sectors to competition policy, and from regional energy cooperation to telecommunications and health, and its spending on regional technical cooperation is on the rise. The bank also supports a growing number of regional road construction and rehabilitation projects, financed by coordinated loans extended individually to the participating countries. More recently, a new unit at the bank initiated regional economic monitoring to complement economic and financial surveillance at the national and the global level.

The GMS comprises Cambodia, Laos, Myanmar, Thailand, Vietnam, and the Yunnan Province of China. A GMS program was instituted in 1992 to promote the subregion's economic development through projects in seven sectors: transport, telecommunications, energy, tourism, environment, human resources, and trade and investment. The ADB has supported intergovernmental coordination of the program and provided much of its financing. Of the approximately $2 billion allocated to the program from all sources through 1999, $39 million was allocated to technical assistance projects in all sectors. Meanwhile $1.96 billion—almost 50 times as much—was allocated to infrastructure projects consisting of seven roads, an airport, and two dams. The expected benefits of these infrastructure projects include the facilitation of commerce (including tourism) within and between countries, which is intended in turn to contribute to the reduction of poverty. Can it be said, though, that the GMS program is concerned principally with the provision of public goods—particularly international public goods and RPGs?

The road projects are certainly international in scope, but their status as public goods varies. Road access is excludable wherever tolls are charged, and rival wherever congestion is significant at the margin.[12] The Yunnan Expressway and Southern Yunnan Road projects, which at a cost of $1.25 billion dwarf the others, are intended to be toll roads; they are thus

---

11. The text of this mission statement may be found at Asian Development Bank's Web site, www.adb.org/countries/cooperation.asp.

12. For the concepts of "excludable" and "rival," see box 3.1.

excludable and, even if the congestion caused by an additional vehicle is negligible, are not international public goods. The Siam Reap airport will presumably exclude aircraft that do not pay a landing fee, and the airport will be subject to greater marginal congestion from each additional landing than that incurred by the roads because of an additional vehicle. The airport is thus excludable and somewhat rival, and therefore not an international public good. Although the two dams are international in that their electricity is intended for export, the electricity is intended presumably for paying customers, whose consumption lessens its availability to others; hence, the dams are surely not international public goods. The costs of these projects sum to just over $1.5 billion—three quarters of the cost of all the infrastructure projects and approximately the same fraction of the entire GMS program, including the relatively small technical assistance projects.

The aspects of the GMS program that come closest to being international public goods are the technical assistance projects. These include such projects as the building of a subregional environmental monitoring and information system, the mitigation of nonphysical barriers to cross-border movement of goods and people, and prevention and control of HIV/AIDS. All are international public goods as well as RPGs: Aside from protecting the environment, facilitating transportation, and controlling HIV, their components include the compilation and international dissemination of data through symposia and written reports. They are concerned, that is to say, with the production of knowledge that is published and shared internationally. Published knowledge is the classic example of a nonexcludable and nonrival good.

The GMS program thus consists of roughly $1.5 billion worth of dam, airport, and road projects that are international in scope but are not international public goods, half a billion dollars in road projects that arguably are international public goods, and $0.04 billion worth of knowledge production projects that are undoubtedly international public goods. These disparities do not constitute an indictment of the program: It may be that roads, airports, and dams are what are needed most for the subregion's development, and their excludability makes possible an efficient allocation of the benefits they confer. Nevertheless, it is a fact that knowledge production, the part of the program given the least emphasis in terms of funding, has the most characteristics of an international public good.

Financing of Regional Public Goods

Four Mechanisms

The provision of international public goods and RPGs can be financed through any of four mechanisms: public sources, private sources, payments

Table 3.2 Financing mechanisms for international public goods

Category	Sources
Public sources	Developed-country sources Developing-country sources International financial institutions International organizations and agencies
Private sources	Corporations (for profit) Corporations (not for profit) Individuals
Internalizing externalities	Market creation or strengthening Taxes, fees, and levies
Partnerships	Combination of various sources

Source: Institute of Development Studies (2001).

by users and beneficiaries (thus internalizing the externalities), and partnerships (table 3.2). Public sources include national contributions from developing and industrial countries and payments made by (or channeled through) international organizations and financial institutions. Private sources include contributions by foundations, nongovernmental organizations, individual philanthropists, and for-profit corporations. Payments by users and beneficiaries, to the extent that they are feasible today, take the form of market mechanisms and international taxes and fees (Institute of Development Studies 2001). Partnerships, finally, are combinations of these sources.

The economics of these mechanisms is set out in detail in Sandler (2002) and in World Bank (2001). R. Cooper (2001) provides a history of how international public goods have been financed over the decades. The remainder of this section focuses on public mechanisms alone; in particular, on the role of developing-country and donor-country governments, and in greater detail, on the role and modus operandi of contributions by the RDBs. The subsection devoted to the latter topic explores lending practices and the need for grants and suggests some scope for innovation in the financing of RPGs.

Developing-Country Governments

In poor and rich countries alike, domestically focused spending through government budgets in support of good policy is the key mechanism for financing international public goods and RPGs. In addition, three mechanisms, which overlap with the first, are at work for developing countries. These are their own spending on complementary activities to enhance their capacity to absorb international public goods; their financing of collaborative programs with other, mostly developing countries; and their contributions to core activities that directly help create international public goods.

An example of the first of these pathways is action to strengthen the institutional capacity of sector ministries, such as agriculture and health ministries, to enable them to access and intermediate new technologies relevant to their mission. An example of the second is technical cooperation and knowledge transfer among developing countries (of which there is a long tradition in Latin America; e.g., in health, agriculture, trade, finance, and more recently, information technology). An example of the third is resource allocation to transnational programs and to national activities that contribute to the creation of RPGs. Examples of this kind of research allocation include medical research, such as the efforts of China, India, and Brazil to provide inexpensive treatments for AIDS, and Vietnam's government-sponsored breakthroughs in locally produced malaria drugs and a vaccine against meningitis B (Institute of Development Studies 2001); agro-biotechnology research, such as the mapping of the genome of the bacterium *Xylella fastidiosa* by Brazilian scientists (*Washington Post*, December 29, 2001); and the costs of complying with international financial standards such as the bank solvency proposals advanced in early 2001 by the Basel Committee of Financial Regulators.

Donor Countries

Donor countries finance the provision of international public goods and RPGs through contributions from their official development assistance (ODA) budgets, through contributions from the budgets of non-ODA sector ministries and entities, and by means of tax incentives that aim to encourage private for-profit firms to contribute to the creation of international public goods through research and development and through donations of such resources as drugs and vaccines.

Multilateral Development Banks

The RDBs contribute to the financing of RPGs through allocations from their administrative budgets, limited transfers of net income, the expenditure of donor-funded trust funds administered by the RDBs, and lending. The first three of these modalities involve grant-based funding. The differing roles of grants and loans in financing RPGs are of considerable interest. Loans are the more abundant resource and should therefore be used before grants whenever possible. They are also preferable because they tend to strengthen borrowers' ownership of the activity in question, and because of their educational role in promoting a credit culture in recipient countries where this may be needed. However, loans may not work for all aspects of international public goods. The choice between loans and grants is informed by the distinction between core and complementary activities pertaining to the production and absorption of international public goods and RPGs.

Core activities have been defined above as those to create international public goods or mixed goods. The selection of the right funding instrument is relatively straightforward in the case of core activities for international public goods and in the case of complementary activities. It is more complicated in the case of mixed goods.

Core activities of the first kind tend to call for grant-based funding, whereas complementary activities can be financed through loans. Borrowers have an incentive to take out loans for complementary activities that support the absorption of public goods, because the associated benefits accrue primarily to the borrowers themselves, spilling over to others only in terms of higher-order effects. Such loans may be concessional or nonconcessional, depending on whether the borrower qualifies for loans from the soft window or the ordinary capital account.

Grants

The case for grants for core activities arises because these activities generate benefits that invite free riding. Nonpaying parties cannot be excluded from the benefits being created. Hence, partnerships such as the Consultative Group on International Agricultural Research, a global program, or the more recently established Regional Fund for Agricultural Technology in Latin America and the Caribbean are funded on a grant basis (the latter by an endowment provided by its regional member countries and institutions). Grant-based global and regional programs coordinated by the different multilateral development banks are similar in terms of their basic orientation and objectives. They promote research, knowledge management, emergency preparedness, training and institution building, and policy discussions among bank member countries to create awareness and possibly consensus regarding ways to address certain problems. The IDB's Regional Policy Dialogue is funded on a grant basis, and it is difficult to see how this could be otherwise.[13] Another example of a grant program sponsored by the IDB is the Inter-American Institute for Social Development, set up to provide strategic capabilities to the social area management teams of the governments of Latin America and the Caribbean.[14]

---

13. To be precise, grant funding is allocated to regional activities such as the production of background papers and knowledge management activities. The cost of participation in dialogue events is borne by the participating countries, which thereby signal a willingness to pay for the benefits that accrue to them.

14. For a description of this program, see Inter-American Development Bank's Web site, www.iadb.org/indes.

However, although grants are necessary for some kinds of programs, their allocation, governance, and management can be challenging. Because grants are free, an element of moral hazard may be associated with them: The demand for grants is, almost by definition, unlimited. Donors, international organizations, and issue-focused civil society groups formulate numerous calls for activities intended to produce international public goods and RPGs. Transparent and participatory methods for setting priorities are therefore extremely important, as is the provenance of grant funding in this context. The multilateral banks must strike the right balance between grants funded from the administrative budget (controlled by all members in accordance with their voting rights) and funds made available by individual donors.

The activities of the multilateral banks and their shareholders must also be transparent with respect to the issue of burden sharing. The allocation of income derived from lending operations to finance international public goods represents a cost to the banks' larger borrowers (which do not have access to concessional resources), because it leads to increased loan charges to meet income targets. In the eyes of the nonborrowers, "Because the loans are subsidized by their guarantee of the [banks'] liabilities, the effect on the cost of borrowing is not a measure of the cost of financing regional or global public goods" (CEIP 2001, 31).

Other issues include the leverage that grant funds should induce, for example, through cost sharing among the beneficiaries; the relationship between the grantor and the grantees, which should be arm's length; and the assurance that innovation is being fostered under grant programs. Further aspects include the existence of an exit strategy, clarity with respect to subsidiarity or the subordination of grants to lending, and awareness on the part of grantors that an entitlement mentality could spread among grantees, which could tie up funds in the long term that might more appropriately go to new endeavors. Therefore, although the call for grant funding for the production of international public goods is justified, the free (from the recipients' point of view) nature of this financial resource should not detract from the need for ambitious, goal-oriented standards of deployment and rigorous monitoring and evaluation.

However, grant programs are often not evaluated, except in the case of large and longstanding programs—such as the River Blindness Control Program—that are known to have produced important international and regional public goods. Unpublished evaluation reports produced by some of the multilateral banks indicate that many small grant programs and regional technical cooperation activities lack well-defined monitoring systems and are not systematically evaluated. The developmental effect of some longstanding grant programs administered by international agencies is likewise not well documented. Thus, calls for grant funding to support the provision of international public goods and RPGs should go hand in hand with calls for adequate monitoring and evaluation.

Loans

When it comes to financing mixed goods, borrowers hold loans in low esteem. They are reluctant to take on loan charges when they cannot capture most of the benefits expected from the investment being financed. Countries' reluctance to borrow is likely to grow with the magnitude of the expected cross-border externality relative to the country's own gain. Eradicating (or greatly lowering the prevalence of) tuberculosis in a country in which the disease is endemic yields a larger gain to that country than to others as long as much of the world is still prone to this disease, but eradicating the remaining pockets of poliomyelitis yields a larger gain to the rest of the world than to the few developing countries where the disease occurs sporadically. Similarly, preserving forests and biodiversity may produce a larger gain for the rest of the world than for individual forest-rich lands. Should these countries be the only ones to pay for vestigial disease eradication campaigns or the preservation of natural resources? Or should those benefiting from the externalities compensate them?

Compensation brings up the issue of differential pricing for services that generate cross-border benefits. Differential pricing has in recent times been on the table in discussions spearheaded by the Group of Seven on the products and governance of the multilateral banks. These discussions have not focused explicitly on financing global public goods and RPGs, but they could be extended to this topic. In between grants and regularly priced nonconcessional loans at near-market rates, there is room for a gradient of incentives in the form of differentially priced concessional loans that would compensate borrowers for precious externalities originating in their territory.

The World Bank (2001) argues that differential pricing, that is, lower interest charges for some investment loans, needs to be judged on efficiency grounds, because it does not expand the envelope of resources. Differential pricing would, in theory, permit fine tuning of subsidies for different kinds of international public goods, but it could also be difficult to administer, and its administration would likely become a politically charged exercise. Multilateral financial institutions have basically offered two kinds of loans—concessional and nonconcessional—for many years, with borrowers' eligibility for each type a function of their income and (implicitly) their creditworthiness. The addition of an international public goods criterion, although worthwhile, could complicate matters considerably. Borrowing and nonborrowing shareholders would have to engage in negotiations to agree about which international public goods to pursue, and nonborrowing shareholders would have to admit in principle the appropriateness of loan subsidies for the better-off developing countries that do not qualify for concessional loans.

In the absence of differential pricing, loans will need to be combined with grant funding in appropriate combinations to foster the production of mixed goods. This is already being done in the form of hybrid financial products combining concessional or nonconcessional lending and grant-based cofinancing from bilateral donors. The Global Environment Facility is a source of grant-based cofinancing for operations that address global environmental issues, but this facility is small in relation to the need, as are the resources that bilateral donors have been able to make available. No dedicated international funds for priorities other than the global environment are available (although the international community has recently agreed to establish a global AIDS fund). Funds for regional priorities are even scarcer. In addition, grant funding tends to go largely to the poorest countries, which is appropriate from the point of view of fostering development within national confines, but may be inappropriate if one seeks to maximize cross-border externalities in key areas of transnational public policy.

In principle, a solution exists to the problem of financing such endeavors as cross-border infrastructure and campaigns to combat contagious disease: multicountry loans taken out jointly by the members of a spillover community or by countries that otherwise stand to benefit from coordinated action. In practice, however, such loans are difficult to manage. The difficulty lies in figuring out and obtaining agreement on who should pay what share of the cost of borrowing. This makes it difficult for official financial institutions to employ their basic financial instrument, namely, a government-guaranteed loan, to support the creation of international public goods and RPGs.

The wider deployment of the described approach to coordinated lending would require that institutions overcome internal organizational setups that militate against communication across divisions and departments responsible for different countries belonging to the same spillover group. More generally, the culture of approaching problems from a regional point of view would have to be further strengthened, and the institutions' administrative budgets would have to accommodate what must be assumed to be heavy transaction costs of building partnerships and coalitions for joint action financed on the basis of loans. Coordinated loans extended under a common policy framework, but permitting as much national autonomy in program execution as possible without jeopardizing the common framework, would appear to offer the greatest scope for purposeful, loan-financed, regional cooperation.

Conclusion

This chapter has sought to introduce the case for RPGs as a recommended area of engagement for the RDBs in the interest of development effectiveness. The analysis is premised on the notion of complementarity between national and regional policies. A number of issues that are as yet unresolved and deserve further analysis and discussion have been explored, including more detailed description and measurement of the RPGs and beneficial cross-border externalities that could be realized by going regional in given policy domains; a more in-depth investigation of the implied additionality in terms of development impact; discussion of the mechanisms and processes whereby the pursuit of different RPGs is prioritized; clarification of the issues of timing, balance, and coordination between core and complementary activities in given policy domains; assessment of potential synergies and needed cooperation among subregional, regional, and global institutions in the production of international public goods and RPGs (an issue not addressed in this chapter); and analysis of financing constraints.

The chapter has also analyzed how RPGs are being financed through lending and nonlending operations and has sought to clarify the circumstances in which lending is possible and when grant funding is in order. Some scope for innovation in regional lending has been identified, with the instrument of choice being a program of coordinated loans offered to and taken out by countries that belong to a given spillover community. Brokering arrangements of this kind is challenging, yet the rewards could be substantial in an era in which growing international interdependence calls for an increased supply of RPGs.

References

Barrett, S. 2002. Supplying International Public Goods: How Nations Can Cooperate. In *International Public Goods: Incentives, Measurement, and Financing*, ed. M. Ferroni and A. Mody. Boston: Kluwer Academic Publishers and World Bank.

CEIP (Carnegie Endowment for International Peace). 2001. *The Role of the Multilateral Development Banks in Emerging Market Economies: New Policies for a Changing Global Environment*. Report of the Commission on the Role of the Multilateral Development Banks in Emerging Markets. Washington: Carnegie Endowment for International Peace.

Cooper, R. 2001. Global Public Goods: A Historical Overview and New Challenges. In *Global Public Policies and Programs: Implications for Financing and Evaluation: Proceedings from a World Bank Workshop*, ed. C. Gerrard, M. Ferroni, and A. Mody. Washington: Operations Evaluation Department, World Bank.

Development Committee. 2001. *Poverty Reduction and Global Public Goods: A Progress Report*. World Bank Document SecM2001-0527. Washington: World Bank.

Easterly, William, and Ross Levine. 1997. Africa's Growth Tragedy: Policies and Ethnic Divisions. *Quarterly Journal of Economics* 112 (November): 1203–50.

Ferroni, M., and A. Mody, eds. 2002. *International Public Goods: Incentives, Measurement, and Financing*. Boston: Kluwer Academic Publishers and World Bank.

Iglesias, Enrique. 2000. *Twelve Lessons from Five Decades of Regional Integration in Latin America and the Caribbean*. Presentation given at the Policy Forum, INTAL: 35 Years of Commitment to Regional Integration, Buenos Aires, November 27–28.

Institute of Development Studies. 2001. *International Public Goods: Challenges, Problems and the Way Forward*. Draft Report submitted to Ministry of Foreign Affairs, Government of Sweden.

IDB (Inter-American Development Bank). 2000. *Integration and Trade in the Americas.* Periodic Note. Washington: Inter-American Development Bank.

IFIAC (International Financial Institutions Advisory Commission). 2000. IFIAC (Meltzer) Commission Report. www.house.gov/jec/imf/meltzer.htm (accessed January 2002).

Kanbur, R. 2001. *Crossborder Externalities, International Public Goods and their Implications for Aid Agencies.* www.people.cornell.edu/pages/sk145/papers/IPGWB.pdf (accessed April 2003).

Kanbur, R., and T. Sandler, with K. Morrison. 1999. *The Future of Development Assistance: Common Pools and International Public Goods.* Policy Essay 25. Washington: Overseas Development Council.

Kaul, I., E. Grunberg, and M. Stern. 1999. *Global Public Goods: International Cooperation in the 21st Century.* New York: Oxford University Press.

Kindleberger, C. P. 1986. International Public Goods without International Government. *American Economic Review* 76, no. 1: 1–13.

Ocampo, J. A. 2001. Recasting the International Financial Agenda. In *External Liberalization, Economic Performance, and Social Policy,* ed. J. Eatwell and L. Taylor. New York: Oxford University Press.

Sandler, T. 2002. Financing International Public Goods. In *International Public Goods: Incentives, Measurements, and Financing,* ed. M. Ferroni and A. Mody. Boston: Kluwer Academic Publishers and World Bank.

Soros, G. 2001. *The Soros Report on Globalization* (draft). New York: Soros Fund Management.

Sparrow, F. T., and W. A. Masters. 1999. *Modeling Electricity Trade in Southern Africa 1999–2000.* West Lafayette, IN: Purdue University.

te Velde, D. W., O. Morrissey, and A. Hewitt. 2002. Allocating Aid to International Public Goods. In *International Public Goods: Incentives, Measurement, and Financing,* ed. M. Ferroni and A. Mody. Boston: Kluwer Academic Publishers and World Bank.

World Bank. 2000. *Can Africa Claim the 21st Century?* Washington: World Bank.

World Bank. 2001. *Global Development Finance: Building Coalitions for Effective Development Finance.* Washington: World Bank.

Zedillo, E. 2001. *Report of the High-Level Panel on Financing for Development.* New York: United Nations.

Comment

TODD SANDLER

Marco Ferroni's chapter raises some essential issues with respect to the role of the regional development banks in the financing of regional public goods (RPGs). The current focus of the donor community on global public goods for development, spurred by globalization, appears to ignore RPGs. At this juncture, an empirical breakdown of official development assistance into support for national public goods, global public goods, and RPGs is not available (see, e.g., Hewitt, Morrissey, and te Velde 2001). However, regional aid unallocated by country is a tiny fraction (less than 8 percent) of regional assistance, indicating that most support goes to national public goods and other forms of country-specific aid (Cook and Sachs 1999, 444). This apparent lack of attention to RPGs is particularly ironic, because there are far more examples of RPGs (energy grids, waterways, peacekeeping operations, pest control, forest fire suppression, health care infrastructure, curbing acid rain, geoclimatic-specific agricultural research) than of truly global public goods (such as eliminating polio and curbing global warming; see Sandler 1997, 1998, 2002; Kanbur and Sandler, with Morrison 1999; Arce and Sandler 2002). RPGs are also more prevalent than interregional public goods—those whose benefits affect two or more regions (such as transtropical public goods) but not the entire world.

Ferroni's message is that a division of labor among the global multilateral institutions and the regional development banks is necessary for

Todd Sandler is the Robert R. and Kathryn A. Dockson Professor of International Relations and Economics at the University of Southern California.

effective support of public goods. This message must be taken seriously if foreign assistance is to have its greatest possible effect, as some portion of this assistance is directed to supporting public goods. In making his case, Ferroni follows the lead of the *Global Development Finance* report (World Bank 2001) and appropriately distinguishes between core activities, which provide global public goods and RPGs directly, and complementary activities, which allow developing countries to absorb these RPGs. Parts of those complementary activities include national public goods in the form of education, health care infrastructure, Internet connectivity, and national institution building. Ferroni also makes a crucial distinction, with respect to the financial instruments for funding these activities, between loans for complementary activities with little regional benefit spillovers, and grants for core activities with significant regional benefit spillovers. For core activities, grants are required to motivate recipient countries to account for the benefits that the supported RPGs confer on other countries.

As I will show, regional development banks are uniquely positioned to assist in the financing of RPGs. Not only can these banks coordinate diverse donors—for-profit corporations, not-for-profit organizations, charitable foundations, donor countries, and nongovernmental organizations—but they can also foster partnerships and networks for the provision of RPGs and complementary activities. Like their global counterpart the World Bank, the regional development banks can also collect and disseminate information on RPGs.

To an untrained eye, RPGs appear to present an easier collective action problem than do global public goods, because fewer countries are involved (Barrett 2001). Group size is, however, just one consideration when assessing the difficulty of collective action (Sandler 1992, 1997). A number of factors inhibit the financing of RPGs relative to global public goods. First, donors have more experience in supporting national and global public goods, as recent statistics indicate. Second, a culture has developed in which donors are comfortable giving loans or grants to countries to support development-enhancing national public goods or donating to global multilaterals (such as the World Bank or the United Nations) to finance global and other transnational public goods with wide-ranging spillovers. For loans for national public goods, donors can hold the recipient country accountable; for support given to world bodies, donors can rely on these bodies for a subsequent accounting of the funds. RPGs, in contrast, fall between the chairs, because loan contracts written to a group of countries are difficult to draft and even more difficult to enforce. In addition, many regional bodies in the developing world, although maturing, are still weak compared with their counterparts in the industrial world, such as the European Union. Third, unlike global and other transnational public goods whose benefits have wide-ranging spillovers, RPGs may not provide any direct benefit spillovers to the donors, and this factor limits donors' altruism. For example, the curing of an infectious disease (a global public good) that poses a threat to industrial countries mobilizes action to limit the disease's foothold in developing countries. Consider the successful international efforts, coordinated by the World Health Organization, to eradicate smallpox. RPGs do not provide similar spillovers, and so donors may be less motivated. Fourth, many regions in the developing world lack a wealthy dominant nation that can spearhead the requisite collective action for RPGs. Fifth, rivalries among developing countries at the regional level can block localized actions to fund RPGs (Cook and Sachs 1999; Stålgren 2000; Arce and Sandler 2002).

If efforts to support these RPGs are to be fostered, these collective action difficulties must be overcome. Intervention by institutions and coordination of potential supporters of RPGs are required to address such difficulties. Although RPGs have received relatively scant attention from the international community, the same is not true of the academic community, as the references herein indicate. Earlier pieces by Todd Sandler and Keith Sargent (1995) and Sandler (1998) focus on the subtleties of collective action problems associated with RPGs in contrast to global public goods. These papers also indicate those cases involving RPGs in which intervention may or may not be needed.

Clearly, a division of labor must emerge between the global multilateral institutions and the regional development banks in their support of development-enhancing public goods with differing spillover ranges (Kanbur and Sandler, with Morrison 1999). This key message cannot be emphasized enough. From an institutional perspective, the comparative advantage of alternative institutions needs to be exploited to limit transactions costs and to maximize allocative efficiency. As a first cut at this division of labor, the World Bank, the United Nations Development Programme, and other global institutions should support the provision of transnational public goods, including global public goods, whose benefit range extends beyond a single region. Transtropical public goods, such as population control and curing malaria, are examples. In contrast, regional development banks should support RPGs whose benefits are primarily confined to their region. If, for some transnational public goods, contiguous regions constitute the range of benefit spillovers, then networks involving regional development banks in these neighboring regions may be best relied on to finance the public good. For transnational public goods with noncontiguous regional spillovers, the global bodies should assist in the financing.

Greater reliance on these regional development banks for financing RPGs fosters efficient allocation of resources in a number of ways. First, the regional development banks are better equipped to acquire knowledge of the potential recipients' tastes for and capacity to absorb RPGs. The banks are positioned, through their support of complementary activities, to know how well prepared their client states are to take advantage of RPGs. Second, as Ferroni indicates, regional development banks have displayed a real willingness, as measured by their past contributions, to support RPGs—the track record is there. Third, with fewer participants at the regional than at the global institutional level, transactions costs are saved. Fourth, repeated interactions among regional development banks and their client countries also limit transactions costs by reducing information asymmetries and building trust. Fifth, regional development banks have a greater propinquity in space and culture with their recipient countries than is true of their global counterparts. Sixth, and of utmost importance, these regional development banks have a familiarity with emerging regional trade pacts, such as the Southern Cone Common Market, the Andean Community, and the Central American Common Market, whose organizations can form partnerships with the regional development banks to finance RPGs. Many of these trade pacts have greater economic integration as a goal and, as such, have a desire to supply RPGs. The regional development banks are positioned to work with such emerging common markets, which may eventually be able to organize members to collectively provide collateral for loans supporting RPGs.

To fulfill the vision of Ferroni and of Kanbur, Sandler, and Morrison (1999) regarding RPGs, the regional development banks must be strengthened in terms of their funding. This strength can come from support by the World Bank or by the diverse donors. Donors must come to understand that the regional development banks are uniquely suited to finance a wide range of RPGs, and they must recognize that funds channeled through these banks can support essential core and complementary activities that are related to RPGs and are needed to further development. I fully endorse the case made by Ferroni: His chapter does an excellent job in identifying the rich array of RPGs that can be best supported by the regional development banks.

In closing, I should emphasize that aid for both RPGs and global public goods will require additional amounts and sources of funds. The inflow of money from nongovernmental organizations, partnerships, and charitable foundations will be very helpful. If poverty is really to be alleviated through official development assistance, support for these public goods must be greater than the traditional forms of foreign assistance. More empirical work is also needed to distinguish the flows of funds to the various classes of public goods and to the traditional kind of poverty-alleviating activities, so that relative support can be properly judged.

References

Arce, Daniel, and Todd Sandler. 2002. *Regional Public Goods: Typologies, Provision, Financing, and Development Assistance.* Stockholm: Almkvist and Wiksell International for the Expert Group on Development Issues, Swedish Ministry for Foreign Affairs.

Barrett, Scott A. 2001. Financing Global Public Goods. In *Global Public Policies and Programs: Implications for Financing and Evaluation, Proceedings from World Bank Workshop,* ed. Christopher D. Gerrard, Marco Ferroni, and Ashoka Mody. Washington: World Bank.

Cook, Lisa D., and Jeffrey Sachs. 1999. Regional Public Goods in International Assistance. In *Global Public Goods: International Cooperation in the 21st Century,* ed. Inge Kaul, Isabelle Grunberg, and Marc A. Stern. New York: Oxford University Press.

Hewitt, Adrian, Oliver Morrissey, and Dirk Willem te Velde. 2001. *Financing International Public Goods: Options for Resource Mobilisation.* Preliminary draft. London: Overseas Development Institute.

Kanbur, Ravi, and Todd Sandler, with Kevin Morrison. 1999. *The Future of Development Assistance: Common Pools and International Public Goods.* Baltimore, MD: Johns Hopkins University Press for the Overseas Development Council.

Sandler, Todd. 1992. *Collective Action: Theory and Applications.* Ann Arbor: University of Michigan Press.

Sandler, Todd. 1997. *Global Challenges: An Approach to Environment, Political, and Economic Problems.* Cambridge: Cambridge University Press.

Sandler, Todd. 1998. Global and Regional Public Goods: A Prognosis for Collective Action. *Fiscal Studies* 19, no. 3: 221–47.

Sandler, Todd. 2002. Regional Public Goods: Demand and Institutions. Unpublished manuscript. Los Angeles: University of Southern California.

Sandler, Todd, and Keith Sargent. 1995. Management of Transnational Commons: Coordination, Publicness, and Treaty Formation. *Land Economics* 71, no. 2: 145–62.

Stålgren, Patrik. 2000. *Regional Public Goods and the Future of International Development Co-operation.* EGDI Working Paper 2000:2. Stockholm: Swedish Ministry for Foreign Affairs.

World Bank. 2001. *Global Development Finance: Building Coalitions for Effective Development Finance.* Washington: World Bank.

Comment

OMAR KABBAJ

In the last few years, the issue of global and regional public goods has caught the imagination of policymakers as well as that of civil society and nongovernmental organizations around the world. There is today a lively debate on the nature of these goods, their optimum level of supply, who should provide them, and how best to mobilize the resources to pay for them. There is also an increasing call for international development organizations to devote more of their energies and resources to the provision of these goods. My brief discussion of the role that the regional development banks (RDBs) should play in the supply of regional public goods has been made easier by the excellent chapter prepared by Marco Ferroni and by the comments made by Todd Sandler on that chapter. Together these authors have provided essential background on the current debate.

I will focus my remarks on two issues. First, where do the RDBs currently stand with respect to the provision of regional public goods? Second, what are the major challenges facing the RDBs as they attempt to mobilize the support of the international community and of governments in their regions to supply adequate amounts of these goods?

On the first question, all five multilateral development banks—the four RDBs and the World Bank—have in the recent past become active players in the provision of global and regional public goods. Although these institutions have yet to place their interventions in the context of the evolving policy debate on global and regional public goods, they are nonetheless all active and engaged.

Omar Kabbaj is the president of the African Development Bank.

It is important to stress at the outset that the RDBs cannot be expected to supply all regional public goods. Aside from the clear resource constraints they all face, the engagement of the RDBs must necessarily be focused on those goods that have clear links to their mandates. For the African Development Bank (AfDB), the Asian Development Bank (ADB), and the Inter-American Development Bank (IDB), priority must be given to fulfilling their core mandate of poverty reduction and sustainable economic development, whereas for the European Bank for Reconstruction and Development (EBRD), the focus is on those goods related to the transition to the market economy.

At the request of their shareholders, the multilateral development banks recently completed a progress report on their support for global and regional public goods. That report identified five areas—communicable diseases, global and regional environmental issues, market integration, investment climate and financial stability, and creation and dissemination of knowledge—in which the banks have been actively involved. As one would expect, the nature and intensity of their involvement varies considerably across these five areas, yet despite these variations, the report clearly highlights the considerable engagement of the RDBs.

In the fight against communicable diseases, each RDB, with the exception of the EBRD, provides considerable financial and technical support while focusing on those diseases that are of particular concern to its region. Just as important, each RDB has also established strong partnerships with the specialized agencies of the United Nations, thus favoring a clear division of labor. These specialized agencies support the core activities in this area, whereas the RDBs fund complementary activities to enable their borrowing countries to implement effective strategies and programs to fight these diseases.

With respect to global and regional environmental issues, each RDB has developed active programs, again in collaboration with the relevant international organizations, in this case including the Global Environment Facility and the United Nations Environment Programme. Here again we witness a natural regional differentiation, with the AfDB, for example, focusing on desertification and deforestation, the EBRD on nuclear safety and decommissioning, the ADB on biodiversity conservation, and the IDB on promoting environmental services.

All four RDBs have active programs to promote regional cooperation and integration. Indeed, for the AfDB and the IDB, such support is an integral component of their mandate. In recent years, regional infrastructure and its financing, including private finance, have become key components of such efforts. Increasingly, with the strengthening of regional bodies, greater attention is being given to efforts at harmonizing macroeconomic policy among member states. For the AfDB, the New Partnership for Africa's Development, which was adopted by African heads of state at the Lusaka Summit of the Organization for African Unity in 2001, has become an important instrument for energizing regional efforts at cooperation and integration, as well as for increasing the supply of other regional public goods. At the request of the initiating countries, we are today providing intellectual and technical support to help our countries draw up action plans and programs to realize the ambitious goals of this important initiative.

All four RDBs are also actively involved in improving the investment climate and financial stability in their regions. At the AfDB, promoting good governance, including reforming the financial sector and supporting banking and financial standards, has become a priority area for our interventions. This focus has the support of all our shareholders, both inside and outside the region. Similarly, our three sister institutions all provide support for strengthening financial institutions and provide technical assistance and support for the adoption of international norms and standards.

Finally, in the area of creation and dissemination of knowledge, all four RDBs have specific programs in place. These programs increasingly focus on strengthening the information and communications capacity of our borrowing member countries to enable them to bridge the digital divide. The RDBs are also active supporters of global and regional research institutions such as the Consultative Group on International Agricultural Research. In the case of the AfDB, the Joint Africa Institute, jointly established with the International Monetary Fund and the World Bank in 1999, is an important initiative for disseminating knowledge on current development issues and for capacity building.

Turning to the second question that I posed earlier, I believe that the RDBs will face four major challenges in the years ahead. First, as they define more sharply their policy stance, the RDBs will need to clearly delineate, in close consultation among themselves and with their partners, those core and complementary activities in which they themselves will take the lead, and those in which they will provide support to the specialized agencies. Second, the RDBs will need to strengthen their partnerships with other international institutions to ensure that regional public goods are provided both efficiently and effectively, and in line with the comparative advantage of each institution. Third, the RDBs will need to continue to strengthen the capacity of their borrowing member countries to provide an increasing supply of these goods at both the regional and the national level. Fourth, the RDBs will need to develop, in close collaboration with the international donor community, more effective mechanisms for financing regional public goods. In particular, a greater consensus will need to be established as to which public goods should be financed by grants, which by loans, and which public goods the private sector can be expected to take part in financing.

Comment

GUN-BRITT ANDERSSON

The objectives for development cooperation are clear: We should work toward the attainment of the Millennium Development Goals. There is and can be, however, no single blueprint for attaining those goals. The development challenges differ from country to country and from region to region. A variety of actions and measures is required. The actors include individuals, communities, authorities at different levels, corporations, nongovernmental organizations, and national as well as international institutions. Through the Millennium Development Goals and a series of UN conferences during the 1990s, the world community has reached a degree of consensus on what we want to achieve in terms of development. The urgency of the consensus on the need to eradicate poverty was underscored on September 11, 2001. The focus of this text is on the regional dimension of this undertaking, which I consider to be of great importance.

There have been many paradigms in development, among the latest of which are the Washington consensus and the Asian model. All have provided some useful insights. We now need to take those insights further and examine, from the perspective of the developing countries themselves, how development is conditioned and how it can best be promoted. We must understand that the reality of an African schoolgirl, an African entrepreneur, or an African finance minister is rooted in that

Gun-Britt Andersson is the ambassador and permanent representative of Sweden to the Organization for Economic and Development (OECD) and UNESCO.

region of the world. Change will have to start from there. Of course, it also can be facilitated through a conducive international environment.

Unfortunately, development cooperation, and before it, colonialism, has over the years had a bilateral bias. This has led partner governments in the developing world to look to donors and international institutions for help rather than to build relationships and explore the potential for gainful exchange within their own region. Thus, regional institutions in the developing world are far weaker than those in Europe. In an era of globalization, it is, of course, possible to learn directly both from the mistakes and from the achievements of others, but the routes toward development and poverty eradication will not be the same today as they were in the past. Therefore, I still believe that Africa, Asia, and Latin America will tend to gain from greater regional cooperation, as Europe has done and is still doing.

An account of the regional public goods produced and consumed in Europe since World War II would show great abundance and variety. One of the fruits of the Marshall Plan for the reconstruction of Europe after World War II was the Organization for Economic Cooperation and Development (OECD). Intense peer review and learning, organized from the OECD's headquarters in Paris, developed knowledge and standards that the member countries could adopt or adjust to their various circumstances and priorities. Later, through the European Union, Europeans extended direct cooperation to most sectors of society, from settlement of international payments, to acid rain, to peace building. This legislative and institutional framework for running our countries now constitutes a regional public good from which the transition countries of central and eastern Europe can benefit as candidates for membership.

The question is not whether we should continue to provide country-focused or so-called traditional aid, whatever that is; the choice is not between that kind of aid and more production of global and regional public goods. The issue, rather, should be how to determine where sustainable development and poverty reduction require collective action at the regional level and where they require such action at the global level.

For example, I believe it is efficient to do much more building of dams upstream. Two years ago, a large part of Mozambique was under water. Dams upstream in neighboring countries were overflowing and threatening to collapse. This problem dramatically demonstrated the need for cooperation to protect, regulate, and secure the benefits of a common watershed.

To reduce its poverty by half by 2015, Africa needs much faster economic growth. Only a few countries are reaching their required level of growth of 6 to 8 percent a year. In many other countries, human endeavors and economic activity are hampered by tension and violent conflict. Serious trouble in one country often becomes a regional public "bad." The hope that blossomed some years ago for mutually reinforcing positive developments in southern Africa has been frustrated by the sad sequence of events in Zimbabwe.

The New Partnership for Africa's Development (NEPAD) initiative defines as a first priority the need for cooperation to promote peace and stability. Support for the provision of this regional, and indeed global, public good needs to be a priority in development cooperation. NEPAD partners are also conducting a range of other very important undertakings aimed at creating conditions in Africa conducive to development. Good governance, both political and economic, is a priority, as are improved trade policies.

In this endeavor, African countries can learn from and encourage one another. Decisions have been made to introduce peer review processes, but there is no point in just holding meetings and discussing matters politely. Serious comparative analysis is required to underpin the efficiency of the peer review process. Regional institutions such as the African Development Bank and the UN Economic Commission for Africa now have a clear comparative advantage in playing a critical role in the service of their continent.

One obvious role for the regional banks is to help build regional infrastructure. Long a main preoccupation of these banks, building infrastructure remains an important task, and maybe the time has come for a renaissance, now that some of the poorest countries are, we hope, moving out of their paralyzing debt crisis. However, this is also an area in which careful balancing is required between the grandiose plans of the engineers and the actual needs and demands of member countries. It is easy to say yes to a regional grid connection, but policymakers need to consider whether its funding is in competition with other priority needs at the national level. In the same way, it is all too easy to refrain from any commitment to supply regional or global public goods, even where little can be done to influence this production at the national level. The southern African watershed again provides an example.

The regional development banks, together with other regional institutions, must use their convening power to help determine these priorities and forge efficient regional clubs among stakeholders and financiers. Not all regional cooperation is efficient. In their chapter, Robert Devlin and Lucio Castro referred to the "spaghetti bowl" phenomenon in the area of trade agreements. Promotion at the regional level of a well-researched debate on trade policy choices is especially crucial now that we have decided to negotiate a global trade regime with development at its forefront.

Europe is well aware of the need to reform its gigantically trade-distorting agricultural policy. Are there enough institutions in other regions to provide critical analysis and spearheading of reform? How much can the regional development banks take on without losing their focus? What are their true comparative advantages? The existing regional institutions are few and precious and should be strengthened.

The regional development banks are also needed in their role as banks. Some years ago there was general optimism about the flow of private capital to developing countries. We have since seen how a financial crisis in one developing region can influence for the worse the confidence of investors more generally. Development suffers from the excessive volatility of financial markets, as well as from the present general slowdown of the global economy.

Issues of financial stability are also on the agenda: One of the conclusions of the Monterrey consensus document is that a first priority is to find pragmatic and innovative ways to further enhance the effective participation of developing countries, both in the international dialogue and in the decision-making processes for financial matters.

The regional development banks should define their roles, together with their constituencies. It appears natural that they have a particular role to play in representing development concerns in the management of global financial issues, as well as in promoting the application of sound standards in their respective regions. I think much of the debate here has confirmed that.

Resources, both public and private, are limited. I sincerely hope that soul-searching discussions are going on in national capitals around the world on how we can do better together to mobilize the necessary and catalytic public resources for development. Of course, we have to work hard to secure efficiency in the use of aid funds, but concern for efficiency can no longer be used as an excuse for keeping aid at its present minuscule level of 0.22 percent of the OECD countries' GDP.

The number of developing countries with poverty-reduction strategies or other prudent and ambitious economic policies in place is increasing. Reforming countries need and deserve more resources to meet their—and donors'—objectives of poverty eradication. There is also an abundance of unmet needs for provision of regional and global public goods. If we believe that only a more-just world will be a decent and secure place in which to live, we need to mobilize resources for building that world.

Determined progress toward achieving the UN target for overseas development assistance is what governments in the OECD countries should contribute. We should also look for innovative sources of finance and invite contributions from the private sector. In the production of regional public goods in particular, the role of regional partners as emerging donors should also be discussed, particularly to provide the fora for further discussions on regional issues.

On this note, it was surprising that there was no reference in the Monterrey consensus document to the financing of our common concerns from other than OECD countries. This omission is all the more surprising given the large number of emerging market donors that have already come forward as contributors to urgent new common tasks. The latest, very encouraging, example was the donor meeting on Afghanistan in Tokyo, where countries in the region that have suffered from the turmoil and drug trafficking out of that country pledged impressive amounts.

In our activities at the think tanks in Sweden, we have recognized the importance and the relevance of deepening our understanding of global public goods. As part of these efforts, we recently carried out two major studies of the financing and provision of global and regional public goods, as well as a more specialized study on transboundary water management. In one of these studies we suggest pursuing these concepts further and perhaps establishing an international task force on how to strengthen the production of these goods and on how to approach the issue of financing.

There will be agreement on certain general principles, but we must also commit ourselves to act on them. One priority for such action will be to further pursue the discussion both on how to provide enough global and regional public goods and on how to share in financing them.

4

International Standards for Strengthening Financial Systems: Can Regional Development Banks Address Developing Countries' Concerns?

LILIANA ROJAS-SUAREZ

Following the eruption of the Asian crisis in mid-1997, the international community has increasingly focused on developing new mechanisms for preventing financial crises. These efforts respond to the realization that, although globalization can bring significant benefits to countries undertaking transparent and sustainable policies, it can also lead to severe disruptions in countries that liberalize their financial systems without having fully dealt with domestic economic and financial weaknesses and fragilities. It is therefore no coincidence that the frequency of financial crises worldwide has increased in recent years in the context of dramatic growth of international capital markets, which followed the liberalization of financial systems and the development of new financial technology without adequate regulatory and supervisory frameworks.

Weak domestic financial systems have not been the only source of severe financial problems, however. In the absence of complete information about a country's capability to deal with external shocks, concerns about one country's financial stability can lead markets to question the financial soundness of other countries broadly viewed as similar, in what has come to be called contagion.[1] Countries can be regarded as similar because of any of a number of factors, including geographical location

---

Liliana Rojas-Suarez is a senior fellow at the Center for Global Development. She acknowledges helpful comments from Eduardo Aninat, Charles Calomiris, and Helmut Reisen and the excellent research support and valuable suggestions of Trond Augdal, but absolves them of responsibility for any remaining errors.

1. Many recent papers attempt to explain this phenomenon; for example, Calvo (2000), Claessens, Dornbusch, and Park (2000), Pericolli and Sbracia (2002), Perry and Lederman (1999), and Reinhart and Kaminsky (2000).

(the neighborhood effect) and comparable economic and financial ratios (such as the debt-to-GDP ratio or the current account deficit-to-GDP ratio). The lesson learned from these episodes is that the intricate workings of global markets need new and better-coordinated global regulatory and supervisory frameworks. Effective domestic regulatory frameworks are essential but are not sufficient to ensure financial stability, because they do not take into account the new interrelationships across countries created by globalization in a world of imperfect information. Efforts to promote financial stabilization, therefore, must focus simultaneously on strengthening domestic financial markets and on improving the international regulatory framework.

It was precisely this discontent with the capacity of the existing international architecture to prevent financial sector crises that led to the creation of the Financial Stability Forum (FSF) in April 1999. The FSF was established for the specific purpose of promoting international financial stability by engaging the cooperation of governments, markets, and international organizations in improving financial supervision and surveillance. A major component of the activities of the FSF has been the coordination of a comprehensive set of international standards and codes to strengthen financial systems. In a nutshell, common standards attempt to tackle two main objectives. First, because they are common, the standards facilitate international comparisons and, hence, avoid the negative externalities created by confusing and incomplete information about a country's economic policies. Second, if these common standards are set at high levels, they can enhance the role of market discipline: countries that want to improve their access to international capital markets (i.e., to obtain more financing at lower cost) will have an incentive to enforce the standards, which can then act as benchmarks to guide policymakers' reform efforts.

Identifying appropriate codes and standards, however, is not an easy task. To the question of what guarantees the stability of financial systems there is a multitude of answers, ranging from the familiar prescription of macroeconomic consistency and sound domestic regulatory financial frameworks to reforms in a number of economic and institutional sectors to the full dissemination of a wide variety of information.

Setting priorities thus becomes a key issue when establishing and implementing standards and codes. The FSF has identified over 60 standards, but it has highlighted a smaller set of 12 principles, grouped in three areas, that the forum deems essential for sound financial systems. These standards have been set by a number of international institutions and are understood as being minimum requirements for good practice (table 4.1; FSF 2001). Each standard, in turn, contains a number of guidelines. Some are very specific, such as the standards on data dissemination, but others, including those governing certain aspects of the transparency of monetary policy, are quite general and allow for variation from country to country.

Table 4.1 Key standards for sound financial systems

Subject area	Key standard	Issuing body
Macroeconomic policy and data transparency		
Monetary and financial policy transparency	Code of good practices on transparency in monetary and financial policies	International Monetary Fund
Fiscal policy transparency	Code of good practices on fiscal transparency	International Monetary Fund
Data dissemination	Special Data Dissemination Standard (SDDS) and General Data Dissemination System (GDDS)	International Monetary Fund
Institutional market infrastructure		
Insolvency	Principles and guidelines on effective insolvency and creditor rights systems	World Bank
Corporate governance	Principles of corporate governance	Organization for Economic Cooperation and Development
Accounting	International accounting standards (IAS)	International Accounting Standard Board
Auditing	International standards on auditing (ISA)	International Federation of Accountants
Payment and settlement	Core principles for systemically important payment systems	Committee on Payment and Settlement Systems
Market integrity	The forty recommendations of the financial action task force on money laundering	Financial Action Task Force
Financial regulation and supervision		
Banking supervision	Core principles for effective banking supervision	Basel Committee on Banking Supervision
Securities regulation	Objectives and principles of securities regulation	International Organization Securities Commissions
Insurance supervision	Insurance core principle	International Association of Insurance Supervisors

Source: Financial Stability Forum.

Given the importance that the multilateral organizations attach to the observance of standards and codes, in 1999 the International Monetary Fund (IMF) initiated the preparation of Reports on the Observance of Standards and Codes (ROSCs). Assessments of the status and progress of countries on one or more standards are conducted on a voluntary basis. Sometimes these assessments take place in the context of the IMF surveillance process (Article IV consultations). It is the intention of the IMF to maintain a standardized format for all ROSCs and to publish them on the institution's Web site.[2]

Table 4.2 lists those ROSCs that had been published as of July 27, 2004. (Other ROSCs not listed might have been completed but not yet published.) For each individual international standard, the table indicates which countries either have conducted a self-assessment on that standard or have been assessed by a group of experts from the IMF or the World Bank or both. As the table shows, by far the majority of countries that have participated in this process are developing countries.[3] It also shows that the standards on which the greatest number of countries has sought assessments are those related to transparency and banking supervision; this is not at all surprising, given the recent emphasis on strengthening domestic banking systems. Finally, the table reveals a large disparity in the degree of countries' participation in standards assessment. For example, only three ROSCs have been prepared for Chile, but Argentina has been involved in eight (although four of these were self-assessments).

Policymakers' responses to the establishment, implementation, and assessment of international standards and codes have been mixed. Although the potential benefits of common standards are generally recognized, a number of policymakers and analysts have raised important concerns about the process. Their criticisms cover a wide range of issues: Some claim that the standards do not adequately take into account certain key features of developing countries, whereas other critics argue that an inappropriate sequencing in implementing the standards can create more problems than it solves.

This chapter examines the appropriateness and effectiveness of international standards for the purpose of financial crisis prevention in developing countries. It begins by reviewing a variety of concerns raised by analysts and policymakers. To fully illustrate the nature of these concerns, the chapter also discusses in greater detail recent criticisms of one of the key guidelines for effective banking supervision: the banking capital

---

2. A reading of the ROSCs that had been published as of July 16, 2002, however, indicates that important efforts are still needed to achieve the desired standardization.

3. Of course, one would expect this simply because there are more developing countries than industrial countries in the world. However, industrial countries have not participated in the process to the extent that they should. For example, no industrial country is listed as participating in the standard on corporate governance.

Table 4.2 ROSC modules published on the International Monetary Fund and World Bank Web sites as of July 27, 2004

Module	Countries publishing
Monetary and financial policy transparency	Algeria, Argentina, Australia, Barbados, Bulgaria, Cameroon, Canada, Costa Rica, Croatia, Czech Republic, Estonia, Euroland, Germany, Finland, France, Gabon, Georgia, Hong Kong SAR, Hungary, Iceland, Ireland, Israel, Japan, Korea, Kyrgyz Republic, Lativa, Lithuania, Luxembourg, Macedonia, Malta, Mauritius, Mexico, Morocco, New Zealand, Pakistan, Poland, Romania, Senegal, Singapore, Slovak Republic, Sweden, Switzerland, Tunisia, Uganda, Ukraine, United Arab Emirates, United Kingdom
Fiscal transparency	Albania, Argentina, Armenia, Australia, Azerbaijan, Bangladesh, Benin, Brazil, Bulgaria, Burkina Faso, Cameroon, Canada, Chile, Colombia, Czech Republic, Estonia, Fiji, France, Georgia, Germany, Chana, Greece, Honduras, Hong Kong SAR, Hungary, India, Iran, Israel, Italy, Japan, Kazakhstan, Korea, Kyrgyz Republic, Latvia, Lithuania, Malawi, Mali, Mauritania, Mexico, Mongolia, Mozambique, Nicaragua, Pakistan, Papua New Guinea, Peru, Philippines, Poland, Portugal, Romania, Rwanda, Slovak Republic, Solvenia, Sri Lanka, Sweden, Tanzania, Tunisia, Turkey, Uganda, Ukraine, United Kingdom, Uruguay
Data dissemination	Albania, Argentina, Armenia, Australia, Azerbaijan, Botswana, Burkina Faso, Bulgaria, Cameroon, Canada, Chile, Costa Rica, Czech Republic, Ecuador, Estonia, France, Georgia, Greece, Hong Kong SAR, Hungary, India, Italy, Jordan, Kazakhstan, Korea, Kyrgyz Republic, Latvia, Lithuania, Mauritius, Mexico, Mongolia, Mozambique, Namibia, Norway, Peru, Poland, Romania, Russian Federation, Senegal, South Africa, Sri Lanka, Sweden, Tanzania, Tunisia, Turkey, Uganda, United Kingdom, Uruguay
Insolvency and creditor rights systems	Argentina, Czech Republic, Lithuania, Mauritius, Slovakia
Corporate governance	Bulgaria, Chile, Colombia, Croatia, Czech Republic, Egypt, Georgia, Hong Kong SAR, Hungary, India, Korea, Latvia, Lithuania, Malaysia, Malta, Mauritius, Mexico, Morocco, Philippines, Poland, Slovak Republic, Slovenia, South Africa, Turkey, Uganda, Zimbabwe
International accounting standards	Argentina,[a] Bangladesh, Bulgaria, Colombia, Croatia, Czech Republic, Egypt, Hong Kong SAR,[a] Jamaica, Kenya, Philippines, Poland, Romania, Slovak Republic, Sri Lanka, South Africa, Ukraine, United Kingdom[a]

(table continues next page)

Table 4.2   ROSC modules published on the International Monetary Fund and World Bank Web sites as of July 27, 2004 *(continued)*

Module	Countries publishing
International auditing standards	Argentina,[a] Bangladesh, Bulgaria, Colombia, Croatia, Czech Republic, Egypt, Hong Kong SAR,[a] Jamaica, Kenya, Lebanon, Lithuania, Macedonia, Mauritius, Morocco, Philippines, Poland, Romania, Slovak Republic, Sri Lanka, South Africa, Ukraine, United Kingdom[a]
Systemically important payment systems	Barbados, Bulgaria, Cameroon, Canada, Costa Rica, Croatia, Czech Republic, Estonia, Euroland, Finland, Georgia, Germany, Hong Kong SAR, Hungary, Iceland, Ireland, Israel, Japan, Korea, Kyrgyz Republic, Latvia, Lithuania, Luxembourg, Macedonia, Malta, Mauritius, Mexico, Morocco, Mazambique, Poland, Singapore, Slovak Republic, Slovenia, Sweden, Switzerland, Tunisia, Uganda, Ukraine, United Arab Emirates, United Kingdom
Banking supervision[b]	Algeria, Argentina, Australia, Barbados, Bulgaria, Cameroon, Canada, Costa Rica, Croatia, Czech Republic, Estonia, Finland, Gabon, Georgia, Germany, Ghana, Hong Kong SAR, Hungary, Iceland, Ireland, Israel, Japan, Korea, Kuwait, Kyrgyz Republic, Latvia, Lithuania, Luxembourg, Macedonia, Malta, Mauritius, Mexico, Morocco, Mozambique, New Zealand, Pakistan, Philippines, Poland, Romania, Senegal, Slovak Republic, Slovenia, Sweden, Switzerland, Tanzania, Tunisia, Uganda, Ukraine, United Arab Emirates, United Kingdom
Securities regulation	Argentina,[a] Barbados, Bulgaria, Canada, Croatia, Czech Republic, Estonia, Finland, Germany, Ghana, Hong Kong SAR, Hungary, Iceland, Ireland, Israel, Japan, Korea, Kuwait, Latvia, Luxembourg, Malta, Mexico, Morocco, New Zealand, Pakistan, Philippines, Poland, Romania, Senegal, Singapore, Slovak Republic, Slovenia, Sweden, Switzerland, Tunisia, Uganda,[a] United Kingdom
Insurance core principles	Argentina,[a] Barbados, Bulgaria, Cameroon, Canada, Croatia, Czech Republic, Estonia, Finland, Gabon, Georgia, Germany, Ghana, Hong Kong SAR, Hungary, Iceland, Ireland, Israel, Japan, Korea, Latvia, Lithuania, Luxembourg, Malta, Mexico, Morocco, Poland, Senegal, Singapore, Slovak Republic, Slovenia, Sweden, Switzerland, Tunisia, Uganda,[a] United Kingdom[a]

a. Self-assessment.
b. Not all countries are considered against all core principles for effective banking supervision.

Sources: IMF and World Bank Web sites, www.imf.org/external/np/rosc/rosc.asp and www.worldbank.org/ifa/rosc.html.

adequacy standard as recommended by the Basel Committee on Banking Supervision. Focusing on this standard should prove useful given the importance attached by the international community to ensuring a sound regulatory and supervisory framework for the banking sector in developing countries. The chapter goes on to address these concerns and advance policy recommendations. Central to this discussion is the identification of a key role for the regional development banks (RDBs).

Concerns about Common International Standards as Applied to Developing Countries

There is general agreement about the long-term benefits of establishing international standards to guide individual countries' policies for the purpose of achieving financial stability. Most analysts agree with the principle that under ideal conditions, policy standards, and especially those for the financial sector, should converge across countries in the long run. However, many analysts argue that the pressing issue for developing countries is how to handle the transition period, when the preconditions needed for the effective implementation of international standards may not yet be in place. Concerns raised regarding the setting and implementation of international standards in general are summarized here. To exemplify these concerns, the capital adequacy requirement recommended by the Basel Committee on Banking Supervision—a standard that has been the center of much attention and criticism—then will be explored in greater detail.

General Concerns

The general concerns about standards that have been raised are all interrelated. However, for expositional purposes they can be classified into four categories: perceptions of and discontent with a one-size-fits-all approach, problems with the sequencing of and countries' capacity to implement the standards, the ownership problem arising from lack of sufficient participation by developing countries in setting the standards, and questions about the effectiveness of the standards methodology.

One-Size-Fits-All Approach

From the perspective of this chapter, the most important concern is the first one. Because developing countries face different constraints than do industrial countries, at least in the short run, standards designed for the latter may not be appropriate for the former. Perhaps one of the clearest formulations of this concern is that of Jin Liqun, deputy finance minister of China, at a conference organized by the IMF:

Developing countries are given to understand that they can preempt a financial crisis and achieve economic stability, provided they follow rigorously the international standards and codes. But there are two questions to answer: first, are the standards and codes suitable to the developing country at their stage of development; and second, do they have a minimum institutional capacity to apply these standards and codes at the same level as developed countries?[4]

Notice that the minister's concern is not with the establishment of common principles in the long run, but with the adequacy of common standards at this time, for countries at any level of development. High-level officials from some of the industrial countries have raised the same concern. For example, Gordon Brown, UK chancellor of the exchequer, has written that, "there exists a danger of pushing inappropriate measures for a given country's state of financial and institutional development, and any order of priority for implementation of the codes and standards must be carefully established on an individual basis to ensure positive net benefits" (Brown 1998, 8). Although the relevance of this concern depends on the standard in question, it will be argued next that it is fully relevant for the banks' capital adequacy standard.

Sequencing and Issues of Implementation Capacity

Concerns about sequencing and implementation capacity are closely related to those concerns about uniformity of standards. A main issue is that, without appropriate institutions such as adequate legal frameworks and appropriate judicial systems, compliance with the so-called key standards may not produce the desired results. For example, a government may fully comply with standards for disclosure yet actually disclose very little, because ineffective control within the government results in a lack of accurate data.[5] A natural, yet unresolved question is, therefore, should countries not first set up appropriate institutions to guarantee the quality (and quantity) of data to be disseminated before actually testing whether the country meets the standard for disclosure?

Policymakers' concern about inappropriate sequencing when applying to developing countries' policy recommendations largely designed in and for industrial countries is based on past disastrous experiences. For example, the liberalization of domestic financial markets, a prescription whose long-run benefits are widely accepted, became a popular policy in Latin America in the late 1970s and early 1980s. The banking crises that followed, which resulted in the worst economic episode in the region in recent history—the lost decade—are well known. Was financial liberalization the

---

4. Quoted in *IMF Survey*, April 2, 2001, 103.

5. This was the outcome in the 1998 Uganda case study on transparency practices as reported by Brown (1998).

culprit? Not really. Rather, it was a sequencing problem. Successful financial liberalization requires the adoption of sound regulatory and supervisory frameworks, and those preconditions were not in place in the region. This was a lesson well learned—but only after the fact.[6]

Further examples of the right sequencing of reforms abound in the literature. One of the best-known arguments is that liberalization of the capital account should only be undertaken when a sound banking system is in place and fiscal stability has been achieved.[7] Notwithstanding the proliferation of examples supporting the need for such sequencing, only very recently has the IMF published statements supporting the maintenance of controls on capital inflows in cases in which the domestic financial system may not be sound enough to intermediate those inflows (see, e.g., Fischer 2001).

Having suffered through many cases of wrong sequencing in policy reform, it is only natural that this issue appears high on the list of developing-country policymakers' concerns. Even if the timing of the implementation of standards is right, however, a number of countries are concerned about their capacity to pursue the task effectively. The requirements, in terms of resources and technical ability, may well surpass those available to some countries, especially in the poorest regions of the world, such as sub-Saharan Africa.

Ownership Problem

Another concern often voiced by representatives of developing countries is that their countries do not participate fully in the design and prioritization of the standards that they are then asked to adopt. The argument is that underrepresentation of developing countries in standards-setting institutions and forums contributes to the problems of adequacy, sequencing, and implementation already discussed. A complementary argument is that is their limited involvement leads to a lack of "ownership" by developing countries of the proposed reforms, and that this is an important deterrent for national legislatures in supporting the implementation of the standards.

Table 4.3 shows that the number of countries participating in the different standards-setting bodies varies considerably. For example, standards set by the IMF and the World Bank, such as those on transparency and dissemination, enjoy the participation of the entire membership of those institutions (184 countries). In contrast, the Basel Committee on Banking Supervision has a membership of only 13 countries, all from the

---

6. The seminal work by Carlos Diaz-Alejandro (1985) was one of the first studies establishing the importance of sequencing.

7. For a full discussion of the preconditions needed for an effective and sustained liberalization of the capital account, see Mathieson and Rojas-Suarez (1993).

Table 4.3 Countries participating in standards-setting bodies

Type of standards	Organization	Number of countries participating
Monetary and financial policies	International Monetary Fund	184
Fiscal transparency	International Monetary Fund	184
Data dissemination	International Monetary Fund	184
Insolvency and creditor rights	World Bank	184
Corporate governance	Organization for Economic Cooperation and Development	30[a]
International accounting standards	International Accounting Standards Board	106
International auditing standards	International Federation of Accountants	118
Systemically important payment systems	Committee on Payment and Settlement Systems	10[b]
Banking supervision	Basel Committee on Banking Supervision	13[c]
Securities regulation	International Organization of Securities Commissions	105
Insurance core principles	International Association of Insurance Supervisors	94

a. Australia, Austria, Belgium, Canada, Czech Republic, Denmark, Finland, France, Germany, Greece, Hungary, Iceland, Ireland, Italy, Japan, Korea, Luxembourg, Mexico, Netherlands, New Zealand, Norway, Poland, Portugal, Slovak Republic, Spain, Sweden, Switzerland, Turkey, United Kingdom, and United States.
b. Group of Ten countries: Belgium, Canada, France, Germany, Italy, Japan, Netherlands, Sweden, Switzerland, United Kingdom, and United States.
c. Belgium, Canada, France, Germany, Italy, Japan, Luxembourg, Netherlands, Spain, Sweden, Switzerland, United Kingdom, and United States.

Source: Web sites of the organizations listed: www.fsforum.org/compendium/who_ are_ the_standard_setting_bodies.html.

industrial world. It is true that the Basel Committee consults intensively with a large number of developing countries, especially through the Core Principles Liaison Group, but the strong perception in developing countries is that the last word remains within the membership.

Perhaps the most frequently voiced concern about developing-country involvement is the limited membership of the FSF, the main institution in charge of coordinating financial standards and codes. The FSF's membership consists of the Group of Seven major industrial countries plus four countries that represent important financial centers: Australia, Hong Kong, Singapore, and the Netherlands. The response of the FSF to this concern has been not to broaden its membership but, rather, to establish a number of working groups with significant participation by developing countries.

Table 4.4 lists the members of the FSF working groups. The degree of developing-country participation varies significantly, depending on the subject matter. For example, whereas the working group on highly leveraged institutions remains limited to industrial countries, half the members participating in the working group on deposit insurance are developing countries. However, in spite of these efforts by the FSF to diversify countries' participation, the perception of lack of ownership of the standards remains strong among developing countries.[8]

Are the Standards Producing the Expected Results?

The institutions engaged in setting and assessing international standards fully recognize that adoption of these standards is simply an additional instrument in the policymakers' toolbox for crisis prevention, not a magic wand that can ensure financial stability. Indeed, some analysts and members of the press have recently questioned the effectiveness of the policy recommendations, including international standards, made by multilateral institutions. The Argentinean crisis of early 2002, which combined severe banking disruptions with defaults on domestic and international obligations, has heightened this concern, summarized in the following two questions: first, why did Argentina, one of the developing countries most involved in the ROSC process (as already noted, it has four official ROSCs and four self-assessments published on the IMF Web site), suffer what appears to be one of the deepest and lengthiest financial crises in recent history? Second, why did a positive assessment by the IMF and the World Bank of Argentina's progress in the implementation of four standards not help shield the country against this crisis? An explanation of the Argentinean crisis is certainly beyond the scope of this chapter, but it is not difficult to predict that this episode will be cited over and over again by those who are skeptical about the usefulness of standards.

Concerns with a Key Standard: Banks' Capital Requirements

The capital adequacy standard recommended in the Basel Capital Accord is a key item in the Core Principles for Effective Banking Supervision,

---

8. Some representatives from industrial countries agree with this view; see, for example, Brown (1998).

Table 4.4 Membership in Financial Stability Forum working groups

Working group	Terms of reference	Final report	Countries participating
Task Force on Implementation of Standards (September 1999 to March 2000)	Explore issues related to and consider a strategy for fostering the implementation of international standards for strengthening financial systems	Issues of the Task Force on Implementation of Standards	Australia, Canada, China, France, Germany, Hong Kong SAR (chair), India, Italy, Japan, Mexico, Netherlands, South Africa, Sweden, United Kingdom, United States
Incentives to Foster Implementation of Standards (April 2000 to September 2001)	Monitor progress in implementing core standards and further raise market awareness of standards	Final Report of the Follow-up Group on Incentives to Foster implementation of Standards	Argentina, Australia, Canada, France, Germany (chair), Hong Kong SAR India, Italy, Japan, Sweden, United Kingdom, United States
Working Group on Capital Flows (April 1999 to April 2000)	Evaluate measures in borrower and creditor countries that could reduce the volatility of capital flows and the risks to financial systems of excessive short-term external indebtedness.	Report of the Working Group on Capital Flows	Brazil, Canada, Chile, France, Germany, Italy (chair), Japan, Malaysia, South Africa, United Kingdom, United States
Working Group on Offshore Centres (April 1999 to April 2000)	Consider the significance of offshore financial centers for global financial stability	Report of the Working Group on Offshore Centres	Canada (chair), France, Germany, Italy, Japan, Singapore, Switzerland, Thailand, United Kingdom, United States
Working Group on Enhanced Disclosure (June 1999 to April 2001)	Assess the feasibility and utility of enhanced public disclosure by financial intermediaries	Multidisciplinary Working Group on Enhanced Disclosure Final Report	Australia, Canada, France, Germany, Japan, Mexico, Sweden, United Kingdom, United States
Working Group on Highly Leveraged Institutions (April 1999 to April 2000)	Recommend actions to reduce the destabilizing potential of institutions employing a high degree of leverage in the financial markets of developed and developing countries	Report of the Working Group on Highly Leveraged Institutions	Australia, Canada, France, Germany, Hong Kong SAR, Italy, Japan, Netherlands, United Kingdom (chair), United States
Working Group on Deposit Insurance (April 2000 to September 2001)	Review recent experience with deposit insurance schemes and consider the desirability and feasibility of setting out international guidance for such arrangements	Guidance for Developing Effective Deposit Insurance Systems	Argentina, Canada (chair), Chile, France, Germany, Hungary, Italy, Jamaica, Japan, Mexico, Philippines, United States

Source: FSF (2001a).

which in turn form the basis for the FSF standards on banking supervision.[9] Although strictly speaking, minimum capital requirements as recommended by the Basel accord were established only for internationally active banks, in practice they have formed the basis for assessing capital adequacy in all banks, including those that operate only domestically. In fact, this practice is fully recognized in the core principles themselves, with no other comment than that the recommended capital requirement is intended as a minimum and that national supervisors may set more stringent requirements.

The international capital standard can be used to exemplify widespread concerns about financial standards in general, as discussed above. The fundamental reason for the concern is that there is evidence showing that capital standards have not been very useful as a supervisory tool in a number of crisis episodes in developing countries. In these episodes, capital requirements were unable to prevent the eruption of a severe banking crisis. The rest of this subsection explores how each of the concerns with the standards applies to the capital adequacy ratio.[10]

Basel Capital Standard Has Not Always Produced the Expected Results in Developing Countries

Encouraged by the perceived success of capital requirements as a supervisory tool in industrial countries, developing countries have been advised to adopt similar rules governing capital adequacy.[11] Indeed, during the 1990s many developing countries directed their financial reform efforts toward implementing the recommendations of the Basel accord. However, the recent experience of banking problems in developing countries (despite their diverse outcomes), especially in emerging markets, indicates that capital requirements often have not performed their expected role as an effective supervisory tool: The accumulation of capital on banks' balance sheets failed to act as a buffer against unexpected adverse shocks.

Recent evidence supports this view. Figure 4.1 shows, for a group of eight countries, the rate of growth of the banking system's net equity

---

9. As established in the FSF's *Compendium of Standards* (2001b), the standard on Banking Financial Regulation and Supervision were set by the Basel Committee on Banking Supervision in its 1997 document (Basel Committee on Banking Supervision 1997). This document contains 25 principles. Principle 6 states that capital requirements should be those established in the Basel Capital Accord (Basel Committee on Banking Supervision 1988).

10. For a full discussion of the issues raised here, see Rojas-Suarez (2001a).

11. Undoubtedly the preferred summary statistic for bank risk, one that includes a composite assessment of credit and market risk, is the capital-to-risk-weighted-assets ratio. This ratio can serve this function because, at least in theory, enforcement of each of the other supervisory ratios implies an adjustment in the value of assets and liabilities that ultimately affects the size of the bank's capital account.

Figure 4.1 Real net equity growth in selected banking systems on the eve of a crisis

percent

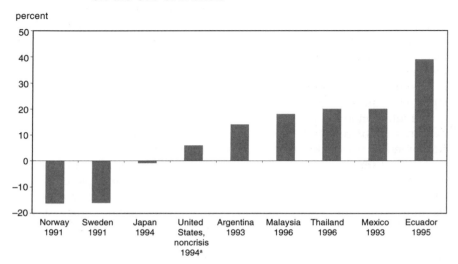

a. The United States did not experience a crisis in 1994 but instead is used here as a benchmark.

Source: Rojas-Suarez and Weisbrod (1997), Rojas-Suarez (2001b), various central bank statistics, and IMF *International Financial Statistics* (various issues).

during the year before the eruption of a major banking crisis. If equity capital were at all a good indicator of banking soundness (i.e., if insufficient or decreasing capital accurately signaled banking weaknesses), banks in countries about to fall into a major crisis should be facing difficulties in raising capital. This has indeed been the case in banking crises in industrial countries. As the figure shows, during the year before banking crises erupted in Sweden, Norway, and Japan, net real equity growth became negative. (The figure also illustrates a noncrisis episode in the United States to show that, in normal times, net real equity grows at moderate rates.) In contrast, however, on the eve of disastrous crisis episodes in several developing countries, real net equity growth was not only positive but indeed reached very high levels. Cases in point are Thailand, Mexico, and Ecuador, where this indicator did not serve as a warning signal of major banking turbulence. Large and growing stocks of net equity did not prevent the eruption of severe banking crises. Notice also that the behavior of net equity growth was related to the country's level of development, not to its size. For example, banks' real net equity growth was negative on the eve of the banking crises in the two small industrialized countries in the sample: Norway and Sweden. Thus, net equity behaved as expected for industrial countries in these two countries, despite their small size.

Rojas-Suarez (2001b) presents further evidence that capital ratios have been meaningless in signaling banking problems in many developing countries. The main result is that, among traditional indicators used by supervisors as early warning indicators of banking problems, the capital-to-assets ratio has performed the worst. For example, in Mexico, a country that claimed to have adopted the Basel capital standards recommendations just before the 1994 banking crisis, the behavior of the capital-to-risk-weighted-assets ratio was useful in predicting problems in only 7 percent of the banks that experienced severe crises. Indeed, according to the data provided by the Mexican bank supervisory authority, most banks in Mexico were in full compliance with the capital requirements, with ratios well above 8 percent.

The conclusion to be drawn from this evidence is not that capital requirements can never be of use for supervisors in developing countries. As the discussion below will demonstrate, the appropriate conclusion is instead that, for capital standards to work, some preconditions must be met that many developing countries may not be meeting today. Effective banking supervision may therefore need to take into account certain important differences between developing countries and industrial countries.

What Will It Take for Capital Standards to Work?

There are a number of reasons for the disappointing performance of capital requirements as an effective supervisory tool in developing countries. The main argument of this chapter is that, for this standard to work, two sets of conditions need to be met. The first relates to the quality of data and the overall supervisory framework, and the second to the depth and efficiency of markets. The first set of conditions is well known and is fully recognized by members of the standards-setting bodies: compliance with adequate accounting and regulatory frameworks is necessary to make the capital adequacy standard work. Inappropriate accounting standards and reporting systems, improper classification of nonperforming loans, and underprovision of reserves against credit losses stand out as the best examples of inadequacies that reduce the effectiveness of capital requirements. In addition, a deficient judicial framework, one that is unable to enforce supervisory actions when a bank's performance is deemed faulty, seriously undermines the effectiveness of bank ratios.

If these were the only preconditions, however, concerns about the appropriateness of the capital standard for developing countries would be exaggerated. All that would be needed is an adequate prioritization and ordering of the Basel Committee's core principles. This, indeed, is often done in practice. A more fundamental problem with the capital standards, however, goes beyond the establishment of rules and regulations to highlight a feature that is unique to developing countries; namely, the lack of deep and liquid capital markets. Even when accounting, reporting, and legal frameworks are adequate, capitalization ratios will be less effective if liquid markets for bank shares, subordinated debt, and other bank liabilities and assets are not available to validate the real value of bank capital as distinct from its accounting value. Therefore, changes in the market value of bank capital that provide supervisors in industrial countries with information regarding the quality of reported capital will not be effective in developing countries. A second set of conditions for the appropriate performance of capital standards is needed to address this problem.

In contrast to the situation in industrial countries, asset ownership, both financial and real, in many developing countries remains highly concentrated, making the potential market for equity capital small and uncompetitive. In such an environment, the intent of the capital standard—to increase the ratio of uninsured funding (equity and subordinated debt) to insured funding (deposits) in order to reduce bank stockholders' incentive to take risks at the expense of existing public safety nets—can easily be subverted.[12] Shareholders' wealth may not really be at risk when they supply equity capital to a bank, because shareholders can finance their stake with a loan from a related party, which may even be a nonfinancial corporation and hence outside the regulators' purview. Thus, concentration of wealth provides incentives for bank owners in developing countries to supply low-quality bank capital and, therefore, to take on greater risks than do their counterparts in industrial countries.

This indicates that it can be relatively easy for bank owners in some developing countries to raise large amounts of low-quality equity capital relative to the bank's capital base in a short time. Indeed, this may explain the results shown in figure 4.1: The rapid growth of net accounting equity on the eve of banking crises in several developing countries may reflect the low quality of capital in these economies. In countries that lack a market that can accurately assess the quality of bank capital, capitalization ratios cannot reveal the true riskiness of bank activities and therefore cannot serve as an effective supervisory tool.

Clearly, the severity of this problem varies widely across developing countries. In many of these countries, the constraints limiting the usefulness of capital requirements are extremely binding. This raises the question of whether there is an alternative to the use of capital standards for assessing the strengths of banks now, or in the immediate future, until the preconditions for the effectiveness of the capital standard are in place. I address this issue later in this chapter.

In some countries, however, a continuous increase in the participation of banks based in industrial countries is effectively reducing the prevalence of connected lending both among financial institutions and between financial institutions and the real sector. Furthermore, in this (still small)

---

12. This point has been advanced by Rojas-Suarez and Weisbrod (1997) and by Rojas-Suarez (2001b).

group of countries, the accounting, regulatory, and supervisory frameworks have improved dramatically. Although very few developing economies have sufficiently deep and liquid capital markets (Chile, Hong Kong, and Singapore may be the leaders on this score), the participation of foreign banks can provide an outside source of capital for the pursuit of new wealth. The competition induced by the entry of new providers of wealth can indeed contribute to improving the usefulness of capitalization ratios. For this group of countries, the relevant question is whether adopting the internationally accepted capital standards recommended by the Basel Committee (both the current and the newly proposed accords) is appropriate.

Sequencing and the Level of Development Matter

The foregoing discussion clearly demonstrates the importance of the level of financial development for the effectiveness of capital standards. For industrial countries, in which deep and liquid capital markets validate the value of accounting capital, the standard has proved useful. In contrast, in the least developed countries in the world, wealth concentration and the resulting absence of competitive capital markets severely hinders the usefulness of any bank capital standard. Between these two extremes there is a group of developing countries in which the participation of foreign banks has improved the functioning of markets. In this group of countries, mostly classified as emerging markets, capital adequacy requirements can act as an effective supervisory tool. The question here is whether the capital standards recommended under the Basel accord are the right ones for strengthening the banking systems of developing countries with an intermediate degree of financial deepening.

My assessment is that, paradoxically, the usefulness of the Basel capital standard is limited when that standard is applied in a manner similar to that in industrial countries. Indeed, I would argue that a straightforward application of that standard can actually weaken banking systems in emerging markets.

An example that serves to clarify this point is the treatment of bank credit to the government.[13] Under the current Basel accord, loans to the domestic public sector carry a zero risk weight if the country belongs to the Organization for Economic Cooperation and Development (OECD), and a 100 percent weight if it does not. The idea, of course, is that government claims from OECD countries can be considered safe assets. However, when applying the Basel recommendations to their domestic economies, most non-OECD countries attach a zero risk weight to their own government paper. That is, banks in emerging markets treat paper issued by their governments as a safe asset—a dubious assumption if one takes

---

13. See Rojas-Suarez (2001a) for additional examples of how strict application of the Basel capital standards can have unintended consequences in emerging markets.

Figure 4.2   Claims on government as percent of total assets of banks in selected emerging markets, 1980s and 1990s

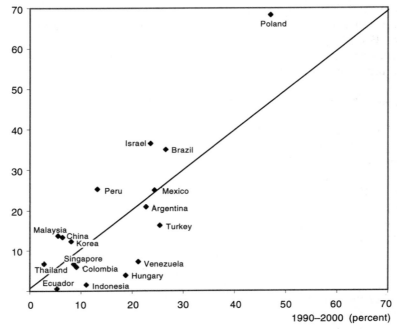

1980–89 (percent)

Note: Data are for claims on central and noncentral government by deposit money banks and are averages for the periods.

Source: International Monetary Fund, *International Financial Statistics.*

into account the default history of governments in emerging markets, highlighted by the recent defaults in Argentina, Russia, and Ecuador.[14] The problem with this practice is that, by economizing on capital requirements, banks have a strong incentive to concentrate a significant portion of their asset holdings in government paper. This incentive not only gives a false impression of bank safety but, even more important, also contributes to weakening banks' franchise value, which is rooted in their capacity to assess credit risk.

Figure 4.2 illustrates this point. It shows that, in many emerging markets (those to the right of the 45 degree line in the figure), the share of government paper on banks' balance sheets increased during the 1990s relative to the 1980s. This result is a sad irony: A significant component

14. Argentina does not attach a zero risk weight to government paper, but the weights it uses still favor this kind of instrument.

of the efforts of financial sector reform undertaken in the early 1990s aimed at decreasing the share of banks' claims on government. Of course, the results in figure 4.2 should not be entirely attributed to inappropriate implementation of regulatory reform. In a number of countries, banking crises were resolved by replacing bad loans with government paper (Mexico and the post-1997 East Asian crisis countries are notorious for this). Given the lack of access of emerging markets to international capital markets during crises, it is very difficult to conceive of alternative procedures for resolving banking crises. To take this into account, I eliminated periods of banking crisis from the sample, from the start of the crisis to five years afterward. The basic result did not change: Many banking systems in emerging markets held as much or more government paper in the 1990s than in the 1980s.[15]

As figure 4.2 shows, claims on government as a percentage of bank deposits not only increased for many countries, but by the end of 2000 were also very high in absolute terms. Several large countries such as Argentina, Brazil, India, Mexico, and Poland displayed ratios close to 30 percent. Indeed, in this sample of countries, Chile was the only country that succeeded in reducing this ratio to low levels (1.7 percent by 2000).

A thorough understanding of banks' decisions to hold public rather than private assets would require the specification of a complete model. However, it is fair to argue that the regulatory treatment of government paper has played an important role in banks' decisions. This regulatory incentive has important consequences during recessions as banks tended to magnify the downward trend in economic activity by shifting their portfolio further away from credit to the private sector and toward government paper.

The evidence presented here indicates that the regulatory treatment of banks' claims on government tends to reduce the soundness of banking systems in emerging markets.[16] This concern may seem obvious, yet it is not taken into account when assessing country progress in strengthening financial systems. Indeed, emerging markets that attach zero risk

---

15. The case of Argentina is particularly telling. During the early 1990s, following the implementation of the currency board, Argentinean banks decreased in relative terms their holdings of government paper. After the banking crisis of 1995, there was an increase in holdings of government paper, which one can associate with the restructuring efforts of the financial sector, including improving the liquidity of the banks. However, long after the crisis was completely resolved, banks continued to increase their claims on government. By the end of 2000, banks' claims on all levels of government as a share of their total assets reached 25 percent, close to the 27 percent observed in 1991 when the currency board was introduced.

16. A possible counterargument is that domestic government debt is safer than public external debt. However, given the long history of government-induced domestic defaults, in the form of either outright confiscation of deposits or sharp devaluations and inflations that drastically reduced the real value of government paper held by residents, I find this argument simply unconvincing.

weight to domestic government liabilities would not receive a warning signal from the multilateral organizations even if the government were highly indebted, because such practice is not perceived as conflicting with the international standards.

What does this all say about sequencing? The answer again lies in the level of a country's development. For industrial countries, no sequencing is necessary: They can comply with the Basel accord and even improve on it (as has actually happened in the current proposal for a modified accord, called Basel II). For the least-developed countries, where the workings of markets are highly limited, sequencing is a central issue. It is essential to first establish the appropriate legal, judicial, and accounting framework before placing high hopes on the effectiveness of capital standards. This, however, does not mean that these countries cannot design appropriate supervisory tools that work. The section below on the role of regional development banks presents some suggestions on this subject.

For the more advanced developing countries, sequencing is also important but is of a different nature. Having fulfilled the requirements for the adequate functioning of capital standards, their challenge is to adapt the Basel requirements to their own circumstances. As the example above demonstrates, it is inappropriate to attach zero risk weight to government paper if market indicators signal concerns about the default probability of such instruments. A straightforward sequencing follows: It is essential to achieve a sustainable path for public debt before treating government paper as a risk-free asset on banks' balance sheets.

Can Better Developing-Country Representation in Standards Setting Help?

Given the difficulties discussed above, it should be no surprise that developing countries feel an urgent need to participate in the design of standards for the supervision of their banking systems. The need for increased participation becomes even more pressing when one considers the issues that will arise for the stability of financial markets in developing countries if the newly proposed Basel II is implemented.

Under Basel II, banks that are large or internationally active can choose to use either ratings provided by external agencies or their own internal rating systems as a basis for classifying the credit risk of loans and for calculating regulatory capital requirements. Concerns about the adverse effects on developing countries of implementing this proposal have been widely analyzed (see, e.g., Griffith-Jones and Spratt 2001; Reisen 2001; and Latin American Shadow Financial Regulatory Committee 2001). Here I will summarize only two such worries.[17]

---

17. These concerns have been raised by the Latin American Shadow Financial Regulatory Committee, chaired by the author.

The first concern is that the adoption of either of these two approaches in industrial countries may exacerbate the volatility of capital flows to developing countries, for two reasons. First, banks in industrial countries that base their credit assessments on their own internal risk procedures will be given greater discretion in assessing the risks involved in lending to developing countries, in contrast to current practices in which all loans to non-OECD corporations and governments carry a 100 percent risk weight. If an underestimated risk from a credit to a developing country materializes, international banks will quickly reverse the inflows, to economize on capital requirements, and this will exacerbate the sharp turns in capital flows to developing countries. Second, if international banks adopt the ratings provided by external agencies, the volatility of capital flows to developing countries will increase even more. This is so because rating agencies have a track record of lowering ratings to developing countries after problems have emerged. Indeed, credit rating agencies are better at risk confirmation than risk diagnosis. This will make international bank credit to developing countries even more procyclical than it is now.

The second concern relates to the more favorable treatment of capital requirements for short-term interbank lending. Whereas the current Basel accord already requires lower capital charges for short-term interbank lending, the proposed new accord lowers even further the maturity on interbank loans subject to preferential treatment. This implies that international banks will have an incentive to reduce the maturity of loans extended to developing countries. This, in turn, will increase the vulnerability of developing countries' financial markets to adverse shocks. This strongly conflicts with the efforts of many developing countries to improve the resilience of their financial systems by extending the maturity of loans. Most important, this recommended policy strongly conflicts with the intent of the FSF to avoid the eruption of systemic crises.

This is a clear example of how particular features of developing countries warrant strong representation of these countries in international forums and standards-setting bodies. Such representation is needed to allow these countries to voice concerns about international policy recommendations that could weaken rather than strengthen their financial systems.

Role for Regional Development Banks in International Standards Setting

The conclusion to be drawn from this discussion is that policymakers in developing countries and standards-setting bodies face a difficult dilemma: how to ensure convergence toward sound international standards in the long run while recognizing that lack of preconditions for the effective functioning of some standards could render the implementation of those standards counterproductive in the short run. This chapter argues that the answer lies in the design of country- and region-specific policies aimed at dealing with the transition. This means identifying the necessary preconditions for the standards to work, designing transitional policies to deal with short-term constraints, recognizing the proper sequencing and timing for implementing the standards, and building the necessary institutional framework to make the standards sustainable.

This section advances some recommendations for dealing with these multiple tasks. The first part builds on the example of bank capital standards and suggests ways in which the issue of the lack of preconditions can be handled. The recommendations advanced here show that complementary policies, specific to each country's level of development, can go a long way toward ensuring the success of the capital standards in the long run, even if the standard should prove ineffective or even have adverse consequences in the immediate term. The second part of this section generalizes the lessons learned from the capital adequacy example and suggests that the regional development banks can play a fundamental role in supporting countries' efforts toward achieving financial stability during the transition.

Supplementing International Standards with Country- and Region-Specific Recommendations

As already discussed, a country's level of financial development is central in determining whether the Basel capital requirements are appropriate and will be effective in that country. As a consequence, policy recommendations to deal with problems associated with capital requirements also need to differ across countries and across regions.

This chapter has distinguished two groups of developing countries according to their degree of financial deepening. For the less financially developed countries, in which capital standards have no meaningful use, it is obvious that sustainable policy consists of removing the constraints on the effectiveness of the standards. This means implementing appropriate accounting, regulatory, and judicial frameworks and developing markets capable of validating banks' chosen accounting capital ratios. Such reforms, however, often take a long time to implement. During the transition, it is essential to identify and develop indicators of banking problems (other than capital ratios) that reveal the true riskiness of banks. For example, in most developing countries, deposit markets have been identified as markets that work, in the sense that they have provided effective early-warning signals about the relative strength of banks. Recommendations for policymakers in this set of countries, therefore, should focus on strengthening the role of market discipline as a substitute for the inadequacies of the regulatory capital requirements. Specific recommendations include the following:

- encourage the public offering of uninsured certificates of deposits;

- publish interbank bid and offer rates, to improve the flow of information about bank quality;

- concentrate regulatory efforts on the improvement of deposit insurance schemes, to further enhance the role of market discipline;

- avoid giving banks too much access to central bank liquidity, to contain the moral hazard problems associated with a lender of last resort;

- improve the credibility of safety nets by establishing prompt corrective actions to deal with banking problems; and

- most important, encourage the internationalization of the country's financial markets through the promotion of foreign banking, because market depth can only be achieved if a diverse group of investors and users of capital enter the market, reducing market concentration.

The policy recommendations are quite different for the second group of developing countries. In these countries, a higher level of financial development allows for meaningful capital standards, but the particular features of these countries, such as their limited access to international capital markets and, in some cases, the low quality of their government paper, imply that strict application of the Basel accord may weaken their domestic financial system. The main recommendation for this group of countries is to design a transitional capital standard that appropriately reflects the risk of banks' assets, because neither the current nor the proposed Basel accord fits the bill in the short run.

I recommend that the standard for such countries have two basic components. The first is the development of risk-based regulations for loan-loss provisions. Although this was recognized by the Basel Committee to be an essential complement to any capital standard, the proposal in this chapter is one based on prioritization: given the high frequency of adverse shocks in developing countries, the expected probability of such a shock is much higher than in industrial countries. In this environment, provisioning becomes, at times, more important than capitalization. The second component is the establishment of a reduced number of risk categories for classifying assets, with the central qualification that the categories reflect the particular features of banks' assets in developing countries. Issues that need to be considered in the design of appropriate risk categories include adequate risk assessment of government paper and the introduction of different capital charges for borrowers in the tradable and nontradable sectors.[18] This distinction responds to the well-known vulnerability of the nontradable sector to adverse shocks, such as a sudden cessation of international capital inflows.

Additional recommendations are designed to allow these countries to deepen their financial systems and so to improve the effectiveness of accepted international capital standards. They include further enhancing the mechanisms of market discipline and deepening the process of financial internationalization through the increased participation of foreign institutional investors. Needless to say, all these recommendations presuppose that those proposed for the less financially developed countries in the first group are also met.

Improving the Effectiveness of International Standards: Role of Regional Development Banks

This chapter's discussion of a key international standard, the capital adequacy ratio, has served to illustrate the validity of concerns raised by policymakers in developing countries and by a number of analysts about the effectiveness of international standards in general. The main conclusion here is that the divergence in financial deepening both between developing and industrial countries and among developing countries warrants the design of additional policies to deal with a transition period during which the standards may either lack effectiveness (in the least developed countries) or have unwanted side effects (in the more advanced developing countries).

Recognizing that there is no incompatibility between common international standards in the long run and country- and region-specific policies in the short run can go a long way toward securing financial stability for developing countries. Responsibility for setting international standards has been clearly identified, and tasks have been assigned to a number of international organizations and forums, but transitional issues and the corresponding design of policies have received considerably less attention.

Who should deal with the transition? Clearly, responsibility for policy decisions rests ultimately with the countries themselves, but a strong case can be made for a key role for RDBs. Because each RDB has extensive experience and expertise in dealing with the particular economic and financial features of its region, the RDBs are well equipped to help countries in identifying constraints on the effective implementation of standards. Furthermore, common institutional arrangements and market practices shared by countries within a region or subregion allow RDBs to exploit important synergies in designing common solutions applicable to several countries within the region.

Indeed, RDBs are ideal institutions to coordinate the tasks that I have

18. For a more comprehensive analysis of this proposal, see Rojas-Suarez (2001a).

identified here as essential for the successful implementation of international standards in developing countries in the long run. First, because countries in a region or subregion often share common goals (including in some cases regional integration), RDBs are in an optimal position to help them prioritize the implementation of standards. Second, because countries within a region often share similar experiences during the eruption and resolution of financial crises (e.g., the Latin American crises of the 1980s or the East Asian crises of the 1990s), RDBs are well aware of the constraints, both in institutional frameworks and in the development of markets, that may impede the immediate effectiveness of international standards. Third, because of their deep knowledge of the economic and political circumstances of countries in their region, RDBs can provide strong support in designing transitional policies to strengthen financial systems in the immediate future, when some international standards may not be appropriate. Fourth, because of the collaboration between RDBs and several standards-setting bodies, especially the IMF and the World Bank, RDBs can help voice the concerns of developing countries in adopting and adapting the standards. Fifth, because of their experience in advising countries on a large variety of development issues, RDBs can provide the necessary technical assistance to help countries meet the preconditions for the effective implementation of standards.

What instruments should RDBs use or develop to conduct these tasks? It is my view that the instruments needed at the regional level are similar to those employed at the global level. First, to design transition policies aimed at making international standards effective in the long run, RDBs could set up special task forces and possibly even subregional working groups. Such groups could also be of great help in dealing with the issue of appropriate representation. Consideration could also be given to the participation of global standards-setting bodies in these initiatives. Second, to disseminate information about efforts toward financial stability in a country or group of countries, RDBs could organize forums, conferences, and seminars that stress the participation of the private sector. Third, RDBs can use their financial sector reform programs to ensure progress in implementing country- or region-specific policies to strengthen financial systems. Once agreement has been reached on appropriate transition policies, there is no reason for not including them as part of the conditionality of these programs. Fourth, as countries graduate from transition policies and are ready to move to the full implementation of international standards, RDBs can coordinate their efforts with those of other multilateral organizations in the provision of necessary technical assistance.[19]

19. The need for technical assistance at the regional level to complement efforts at the global level is fully recognized in the following statement by Andrew Crockett, chairman of the FSF: "Widespread international support is needed to provide expertise and funding for the provision of technical assistance and training to assist countries in implementing international standards" (Crockett 2001, 2).

In summary, to the question posed in the title of this paper (Can RDBs help address developing-country concerns with international standards?), the answer is a definite yes, not only can RDBs help, but they should help.[20] Regional efforts are not only desirable but are, indeed, indispensable for achieving the sustainable convergence of developing countries toward international standards.

Conclusion

This chapter has argued that although international policy standards, especially those for the financial sector, should converge across countries in the long run, the pressing issue for developing countries is how to handle the transition period, when the preconditions needed for effective implementation of international standards may not yet be in place. Indeed, if the preconditions for the effective functioning of some standards are not fulfilled, it could render their implementation ineffective and even counterproductive in the short run. The ineffectiveness of international bank capital standards to control excessive risk taking by banks in a number of developing countries was presented as an example.

A second conclusion is that a country's level of development, especially with respect to financial deepening, matters significantly both in deciding whether a country is ready to implement an international standard and in designing transition policies—different from the international standards but effective in the short run—to strengthen financial systems. In addition, the degree of financial deepening is important in determining the appropriate sequencing and timing for implementing the standards. Developing countries' disastrous experiences with implementing policies in the wrong sequence (most notoriously, engaging in financial liberalization without adequate supervision of financial institutions) justify their concerns.

RDBs can play a key role in helping countries to design transition policies leading to a sustainable implementation of the standards in the long run. Indeed, here the RDBs can fill an important vacuum: Although the responsibility for setting international standards has been clearly identified and tasks have been assigned to a number of international organizations and forums, transition issues and the corresponding design of policies have not been given the attention they deserve. The existence of common institutional arrangements and market practices among countries within a region or subregion makes RDBs well equipped to help countries in several ways: in prioritizing the implementation of standards;

---

20. As reported by Crockett (2001), the FSF has recently initiated regional meetings to discuss financial sector vulnerabilities at the regional level. The need for identification and resolution of regional financial weaknesses is therefore recognized at the global level.

in identifying the constraints, both in institutional frameworks and development of markets, that may impede the immediate effectiveness of international standards; in providing strong support in designing transition policies to strengthen financial systems in the immediate term, when some international standards may not be appropriate; in helping voice the concerns of developing countries in adopting and adapting the standards; and in providing the necessary technical assistance to help countries meet the preconditions for the effective implementation of standards. Regional efforts are not only desirable but are, indeed, indispensable for achieving the sustainable convergence of developing countries toward international standards.

References

Basel Committee on Banking Supervision. 1988. *International Convergence of Capital Measurement and Capital Standards.* Basel: Basel Committee on Banking Supervision.

Basel Committee on Banking Supervision. 1997. *Core Principles for Effective Banking Supervision.* Basel: Basel Committee on Banking Supervision.

Brown, Gordon. 1998. *The New International Financial Architecture, "Codes & Standards" and the Developing Countries.* Speech to the Annual Meetings of the International Monetary Fund and the World Bank, Washington (October 6).

Calvo, Guillermo. 2000. Capital Markets, Contagion and Recession: An Explanation of the Russian Virus. In *Wanted: World Financial Stability,* ed. Eduardo Fernández-Arias and Ricardo Hausmann. Baltimore, MD: Johns Hopkins University Press.

Claessens, Stijn, Rudiger Dornbusch, and Yung-Chul Park. 2000. *International Financial Contagion: How It Spreads and How It Can Be Stopped.* Washington: World Bank.

Crockett, A. 2001. Statement delivered at the International Monetary and Financial Committee Meeting, Washington (April 29).

Diaz-Alejandro, Carlos. 1985. Good Bye Financial Repression, Hello Financial Crash. *Journal of Development Economics* 19 (September/October): 1–24.

FSF (Financial Stability Forum). 2001a. *International Standards and Codes to Strengthen Financial Systems.* Basel: Financial Stability Forum.

FSF (Financial Stability Forum). 2001b. *Compendium of Standards.* www.fsforum.org/compendium/key_standards_for_sound_financial_system.html (accessed January 20, 2002).

Fischer, Stanley. 2001. Asia and the IMF. Remarks at the Institute of Policy Studies, Singapore (June 1). www.imf.org/external/np/speeches/2001 (accessed January 20, 2002).

Griffith-Jones, Stephany, and S. Spratt. 2001. *Will the Proposed New Basel Capital Accord Have a Net Negative Effect on Developing Countries?* Brighton: Institute of Development Studies, University of Sussex. Photocopy.

Latin American Shadow Financial Regulatory Committee. 2001. *The New Basel Capital Accord and Financial Stability in Latin America.* Statement No. 2 (April 30, 2001). Caracas.

Mathieson, D., and Liliana Rojas-Suárez. 1993. *Liberalization of the Capital Account: Experiences and Issues.* IMF Occasional Paper 103. Washington: International Monetary Fund.

Pericolli, M., and M. Sbracia. 2002. *A Primer on Financial Contagion.* Rome: Bank of Italy.

Perry, G., and D. Lederman. 1999. *Financial Vulnerability, Spillover Effects and Contagion: Lessons from the Asian Crises for Latin America.* Washington: World Bank.

Reinhart, Carmen, and G. Kaminsky. 2000. On Crises, Contagion and Confusion. *Journal of International Economics* 51:145–68.

Reisen, Helmut. 2001. *Will Basel II Contribute to Convergence in International Capital Flows?* Unpublished paper. Paris: OECD Development Centre.

Rojas-Suarez, Liliana. 2001a. *Can International Capital Standards Strengthen Banks in Emerging Markets?* Working Paper WP01-10. Washington: Institute for International Economics.

Rojas-Suarez, Liliana. 2001b. *Rating Banks in Emerging Markets: What Credit Rating Agencies Should Learn from Financial Indicators.* Working Paper WP01-6. Washington: Institute for International Economics.

Rojas-Suarez, Liliana, and Steven Weisbrod. 1997. Towards an Effective Financial Regulatory and Supervisory Framework in Latin America: Dealing with the Transition. In *Safe and Sound Financial Systems—What Works for Latin America,* ed. Liliana Rojas-Suárez. Washington: Inter-American Development Bank.

Comment

CHARLES W. CALOMIRIS

I focus here on prudential standards for banks, because failure in this area has been so important for the disasters that have recently befallen developing countries. The primary purpose of prudential standards is to protect the financial sector from excessive risk, and there is clear and growing evidence that the failure to do so is at the root of the historically unprecedented instability of banking systems throughout the world over the last two decades. The problem is not one of stupidity but, rather, one of perverse economic incentives and a lack of political will within developing countries and within multilateral agencies to promote real reform.

Financial institutions that are protected, explicitly or implicitly, by taxpayer-financed deposit insurance or other similar measures tend to misallocate capital in a way that makes financial systems extraordinarily unstable. This occurs during normal times, when government protection from default risk insulates less competent management from the discipline of competition, or invites those with the greatest political influence (i.e., those with comparative advantages in arranging taxpayer-financed bailouts) into the banking industry.

The problem worsens substantially in the wake of adverse shocks to the economy: Protected banks buffeted by such shocks redouble their lobbying efforts, begging for forbearance from the enforcement of prudential regulations. (Forbearance is a polite word for a conscious political decision not to enforce prudential guidelines, such as accounting rules for

Charles Calomiris is the Paul M. Montrone Professor of Finance and Economics at Columbia Business School.

booking of losses and for measuring profits and capital.) The result has been over 100 major banking sector collapses worldwide over the last two decades, many of which have entailed costs the likes of which have never been seen before.

Politicians have been encouraged to provide such forbearance by false claims that regulatory enforcement will magnify the effects of a recession through a regulation-induced credit crunch. The evidence, however, indicates the opposite. Many researchers (e.g., Boyd et al. 2000; Cull, Senbet, and Sorge 2000; Honohan and Klingebiel 2000) have shown that failure to limit bank risk taking in the wake of a recession actually deepens the cyclical decline by allowing bankers to bet the nation's banking system on bad risks. Often these are risks that also serve their selfish economic interests at the expense of the health of the financial system or the economy. Forbearance is the opposite of a truly countercyclical policy.

In short, the record clearly shows, and the background paper by Liliana Rojas-Suarez documents this well, that prudential standards have not worked, in large part because the measures on which they are based are not credible. It warrants emphasis that this is largely a political problem—a lack of political will not just to create standards but to enforce them. It follows that the key requirement of any meaningful set of standards is a reliable enforcement mechanism. This "Prince Hamlet" is often absent from the play of global pontificating about standards, perhaps because it is an inconvenient fact for the Group of Seven to recognize, given that their own failings in this area are as obvious, if not always as spectacular, as those of developing economies. Japan is, of course, the case in which the failings of the past decade have been both obvious and spectacular.

In other words, the Basel standards are a failure—for all countries—in large part because the largest countries (the Group of Seven, or G-7) have not taken them seriously. It is worth asking, however, whether enforcing these standards could conceivably produce a stable global banking system, and whether (assuming that the standards could be made effective) doing so would be advisable for developing countries. My own view is negative on both counts. The Basel standards are not only unenforced at present, but they are unlikely to do much good if they were enforced, especially in developing countries. A new approach is needed, and luckily, one is readily available.

Before outlining that approach, let me address the second question, which I take to be the main topic of chapter 4: Do developing countries need to develop their own prudential standards distinct from those of the G-7? It depends on how one defines standards. If by standards one means a specific set of guidelines, the answer is that developing countries must adopt different banking standards that reflect the different risks and different political and institutional environments in which they operate. However, if by standards one means a standard for measuring success, and a way of establishing credible enforcement of regulatory rules, I would emphatically argue that there is no need for a double standard. It is both patronizing and counterproductive for policymakers to argue, as they typically do, that emerging market countries cannot achieve and should not target financial stability comparable to what is achievable in the G-7 countries. Ironically, the current (often unspoken) G-7 consensus is doubly wrong. It sees uniformity in specific standards as desirable (which it is not) and wrongly views uniformity in effectiveness as unachievable.

What makes emerging market countries different? First, their economic risks are different. Emerging markets have relatively underdeveloped information networks, ineffective enforcement of creditors' rights, and poor corporate governance networks, all of which increase the fundamental risks of lending. Furthermore, their economies are less diversified, often heavily dependent on a few commodities or sectors. The fact that sovereign and private sector debts are denominated in hard external currencies adds another dimension of risk in these countries, and the fiscal risk of sovereign default (particularly given the fact that banks hold enormous amounts of government debt) makes the riskiness of government debt holdings quite different in emerging markets than in industrial countries. (Argentina is the most obvious recent case of a banking sector destroyed by forced acquisition of government debt, which was encouraged by the lack of capital required as backing for those debt holdings.) In addition, exchange rate pegs increase the fragility of borrowers, particularly in the nontraded goods sector, as Rojas-Suarez has pointed out. Thus, the risk weights appropriate for sovereign debt and for different sectors of the economy differ within and across emerging markets in ways that they do not among the G-7 countries.

Second, political risk is greater in emerging markets. Greater political volatility is part of the difference. The other part is greater corruption, which translates into less reliable enforcement of laws and regulations (including prudential regulations), all of which adds to financial sector risk. Contributing to this problem is the greater concentration of wealth in many emerging market countries, which tends to encourage cronyism in the banking sector, particularly through close ties among banks, the government, and the large firms that rely on banks for financing. (These firms are often linked to bank management and to political parties in equal measure.)

Because of these greater risks, emerging market countries should require higher ratios of bank capital to assets, all else being equal, than their counterparts in the G-7. Furthermore, the need for making enforcement of these capital standards credible is even greater.

Beyond these differences, there are also special needs for augmenting capital standards with other measures that encourage stability. Such measures include liquidity standards that protect against systemic risks, not just capital standards for banks; policies that encourage free entry by foreign banks, because these provide both economic and political discipline; and limits on universal banking, motivated by political economic needs to keep banks from becoming captured by politically influential industrial conglomerates.

The Argentinean approach was a good start: limit deposit insurance to encourage market discipline; require banks to issue subordinated debt (i.e., debt that is junior to deposits), which further encourages market discipline by forcing banks to raise unprotected funds from sophisticated investors; use interest rates charged on loans as the basis for setting risk weights on loans, which are used to compute minimum capital requirements (another way that market information is brought to bear in evaluating and controlling bank risk); use stand-bys as substitutes for liquidity reserves as a means to allow the market to reward banks who can qualify for stand-bys from foreign banks at a low cost; set limits on ownership links between banks and industry to discourage cronyism; and make bank regulators independent (as much as possible) from the political process. However, one must go further (as the Argentinean experience also showed) to tie market views of bank soundness (e.g., as expressed in interest rates on uninsured bank debts) to bank actions and regulatory intervention. In other words, real regulation of risk requires discipline—a credible, predictable connection between observed increases in risk and tangible, effective actions by supervisors enforcing regulations. One must establish supervisory rules that mandate the use of useful market information and that close loopholes that are used by banks and supervisors to avoid disciplining banks when that is needed most.

Market interest rates are potentially very useful measures in emerging markets as well as in the G-7. The evidence on this is conclusive (Calomiris 1999; Demirgüç-Kunt and Detragiache 2000; Rojas-Suarez 2001; World Bank 2001; Calomiris and Powell 2001; Barth, Caprio, and Levine 2002). Contrary to what is often claimed, the difficulty is not in the absence of market infrastructure sufficient to create useful signals but, rather, in the lack of political will to use information already produced by the market.

On the role of the international financial institutions, I continue to advocate the view of the Meltzer Commission: International Monetary Fund (IMF) standards should take into account the extent of credible prudential regulation when determining the level of access a country has to IMF assistance. Countries need to know that when they fail to establish effective regulatory and supervisory systems the IMF will not step in to bail them out of the predictable financial crisis that will result. Existing IMF policy, which does not limit bailouts, encourages weakness in bank supervision and regulation.

Let the regional development banks take the lead in encouraging reform: Experimenting is good. One size indeed does not fit all. Local governments may best be able to learn from each other, and regional development banks are the organizations best positioned to encourage this kind of learning.

How does one reconcile universalism of standards with individualism of approach to implementing standards? From the standpoint of the universal standard, what matters is the level of risk and the credibility of enforcement. The establishment of market discipline is the only meaningful universal standard. The details of regulation should be left to the countries and will vary according to each country's particular history and institutional environment.

It is time to end duplicitous lip service and patronizing attitudes toward emerging market countries. Market discipline is achievable, and we should expect no less. It was a reality over 100 years ago in many of these countries, and it could be so today. The problem, of course, is that powerful special interests do not want market discipline, and myopic politicians (who want to avoid the political costs of the moment, not ensure the economic benefits of the long run) do not much like it either. Thus, it is likely that financial crises will continue to plague emerging markets for some time. Let us at least recognize this for what it is, however: a lack of political will in the emerging market countries and among the G-7 to require discipline, not an economic failure of markets or an institutional impossibility.

References

Barth, James R., Gerard Caprio Jr., and Ross Levine. 2002. *Bank Regulation and Supervision: What Works Best.* World Bank Working Paper 2725. Washington: World Bank. http://econ.worldbank.org/files/2733_wps2725.pdf.

Boyd, John, Pedro Gomis, Sungkyu Kwak, and Bruce Smith. 2000. *A User's Guide to Banking Crises.* University of Minnesota Working Paper. University of Minnesota.

Calomiris, Charles W. 1999. Building an Incentive-Compatible Safety Net. *Journal of Banking and Finance* 23, no. 10 (October):1499–519.

Calomiris, Charles W., and Andrew Powell. 2001. Can Emerging Market Bank Regulators Establish Credible Discipline? The Case of Argentina. In *Prudential Supervision: What Works and What Doesn't,* ed. F. S. Mishkin. Chicago: University of Chicago Press.

Cull, Robert, Lemma W. Senbet, and Marco Sorge. 2000. *Deposit Insurance and Financial Development.* World Bank Working Paper 2682. Washington: World Bank. http://econ.worldbank.org/files/2456_wps2682.pdf.

Demirgüç-Kunt, Asli, and Enrica Detragiache. 2000. *Does Deposit Insurance Increase Banking System Stability?* World Bank Working Paper 2247. Washington: World Bank. http://econ.worldbank.org/docs/981.pdf.

Honohan, Patrick, and Daniela Klingebiel. 2000. *Controlling Fiscal Costs of Banking Crises.* World Bank Working Paper 2441. Washington: World Bank. http://econ.worldbank.org/docs/1196.pdf.

Rojas-Suarez, Liliana. 2001. *Rating Banks in Emerging Markets: What Credit Rating Agencies Should Learn from Financial Indicators.* Working Paper WP 01-6. Washington: Institute for International Economics.

World Bank. 2001. *Finance for Growth: Policy Choices in a Volatile World.* New York: Oxford University Press.

Comment

EDUARDO ANINAT

I have witnessed a major evolution among countries as to how they view the Reports on the Observance of Standards and Codes (ROSC) process, or the Financial Sector Assessment Program process, or even the Financial System Stability Assessment—in short, the whole range of ways in which we have been using standards and codes to provide either self-assessments or more formal assessments in a process of consultation with countries since the end of 1999. My evidence comes from direct conversation with country authorities regarding, say, Article IV consultations or programs, and from listening very carefully to the intense discussion we have had on the International Monetary Fund (IMF) board about this.

Although due concern must be given to implementation difficulties, to capacity constraints, to the phasing in of the different standards, and to prioritization, I see now an overwhelming demand on the part of countries to accede in due time and to join in a cooperative and voluntary way this work of standards and codes. I observed much more skepticism about this before I came to the IMF than I do today. Why have things changed? Because countries do not want to be left out of the standards process, or left with a secondary type of standards, or left with truncated standards. They want full access with respect not only to trade markets but to financial markets as well. There is a renewed recognition of the need to clearly define the demand for access in financial markets.

Of course, this cannot be done overnight. There are ownership and transition concerns, which Rojas-Suarez has explored in her chapter. It

Eduardo Aninat was deputy managing director of the International Monetary Fund and minister of finance of Chile.

would, however, perhaps be inadvisable, irrational, and to some extent unrepresentative to deny this revealed excess demand for standards and codes, and to implement the process with a long transition phase, when instead countries can do it fully in place with their own peers. The recognition of this fact has been for me part of an interesting learning process at the IMF itself.

No one can claim that these new standards and codes, and in particular the reports on the assessments (either the ROSCs on say, the fiscal side, or the Financial Sector Assessment Programs on the financial-sector side), are going to resolve all the problems facing developing countries, or all the main problems, or even many problems. We have to remember a second, very important fact; namely, that these standards and codes are only tools in a kit that has to be used by professionals, by politicians, by legislators, and by policymakers. They are sophisticated tools that we did not have in the 1960s, the 1970s, and the early 1980s, but they are not yet as fully developed or as sophisticated as we would like them to be, and none of them on their own will solve the market's overriding concerns about structural reform or fiscal or macroeconomic adjustment.

We cannot demand from these tools, from these standards and codes, more than they can give. We must all recognize that this is a dynamic process, an input, with much that is of a transitional nature. Therefore, I find the chapter's comparisons of Argentina and Chile, and how Argentina had published more ROSCs than Chile, in a way not very appropriate. The nature of the problem is completely different in the two countries.

The IMF and the World Bank also have to pay much more attention to the ways in which countries themselves, especially the least-developed countries, with their greater institutional constraints, data problems, lack of expertise, and so forth, want to prioritize during this transition phase: which standards and codes they want to focus on first, which ones second and third, and so on. We all have to learn and listen much more carefully.

As an example, we at the IMF have lately been working with Cambodia. The Cambodian authorities have been very clear in saying they want to work first on those models that concern national economic accounts, statistics regarding the national income process, and classification of output generated by sectors, and not yet the more sophisticated models as applied to a developed, say, insurance or financial sector business. However, we have heard countries like Tunisia say they are more interested in working with the international organizations—the IMF and the World Bank and the regional development banks. There is clearly a role here for doing much more on financial sector deepening.

However, let us consider the fiscal side. When we speak of the fiscal transparency codes and the manuals and guidelines that apply to them, we are not speaking of the theoretical optimal standard. We are speaking here of reasonable best practices that can increase transparency, that can shed light on the difficult relations between the central government and the subnational governments (namely, provincial and local governments). We can think of Latin America, but many cases apply. We also have the sometimes difficult relationship between the central bank and the central government. There is nothing wrong or detrimental to the countries, the authorities, to the development process in having more transparent rules that help to improve those difficult relationships. The quicker we get there, recognizing constraints, the better for the countries, for the citizens, and for the markets in the world at large.

Finally, we need to consider the issue of improvements in the use of standards and codes. This is a very decisive issue for the success of these tools. On this issue, the IMF has looked back at many of the Latin countries of the 1980s and at several, if perhaps not all, of the countries involved in the Asian crisis of the late 1990s (the big Asian crisis, in which many of these standards were not in place, were underdeveloped, and were not adhered to). During the 1980s and 1990s, there was rudimentary application of international standards. That has changed now, since the availability and information regarding these tools has increased significantly.

In the case of the IMF, I would say there is a dynamic learning curve about the application and usefulness of the standards and codes: I think they will become increasingly useful instruments for the countries. We want to engage on the policy priorities of the countries themselves, rather than to come with a more general aggregate type of approach, as in the past.

Finally, for the private sector, I do see a gap, and I would have liked for the Rojas-Suarez chapter to address this issue more thoroughly. Multilateral organizations can help significantly: We have financial institutions—the World Bank, the IMF, and regional development banks—that can make a difference producing awareness, information, discussions, and seminars on the problems of lack of transparency, malpractice, and overlending and overborrowing. However, if the private sector, the financial markets (including commercial banks), and all the related business do not use the tools to reform their own decision-making process, then I see limits and constraints on where this approach will take us in the coming years. Here there is a tremendous task to be done cooperatively by regional development banks, by the IMF and the World Bank, and by private banking and financial institutions.

Comment

HELMUT REISEN

Since the emerging market crises of 1997–98, the international community has attached increasing importance on the design, agreement, implementation, and assessment of financial standards and codes as core elements of crisis prevention. The Financial Stability Forum, established in April 1999 as part of the effort to strengthen financial systems and improve coordination among the agencies responsible for them, posts on its Web site a *Compendium of Standards*[1] citing no fewer than 69 standards. Of these, 12 have been highlighted as being key for sound financial systems (see table 4.1).

In her excellent chapter, Liliana Rojas-Suarez avoids playing the "standards constipation blues" and instead focuses on what is arguably the most widely adopted of all recent financial standards; namely, the bank capital adequacy standard enshrined in the Basel Capital Accord. More than 100 countries claim to adhere to this standard, although it was originally designed for internationally active banks in the Group of Ten industrial countries. I will follow Rojas-Suarez's lead by first discussing general concerns about applying standards to developing countries and then turning the focus to the Basel accord (both its current 1988 version and its proposed new version) and finally by offering two policy suggestions.

The current international effort to codify best practices and disseminate them widely should help advance the seamless integration of local economies into global markets. When a country becomes globalized, its

Helmut Reisen is a counselor at the OECD Development Center.

1. The latest (June 2001) update is available at www.fsforum.org/compendium/key_ standards _for_sound_financial_system.html.

institutional, legal, and other structures need to move toward international best practices if that country wants to provide the appropriate market signals and information in the beauty contest known as attracting global capital. If designed appropriately, standards confer efficiency-enhancing value by themselves; hence, countries should have a great self-interest in incorporating these standards as they develop their institutions and markets. Bank capital standards aim at reducing bank insolvencies so as to safeguard a country's banking system, immunizing taxpayers when insolvencies occur and aligning the incentives of bank owners and managers with those of uninsured claimants (Rojas-Suarez 2001).

Whether international standards are appropriate for crisis prevention in developing countries depends much on how they are designed and owned by those countries, and when they are implemented and updated. In her chapter in this book, Rojas-Suarez lists and discusses four concerns. The first is that, for standards as for exchange rate regimes, no single model is right for all countries or at all times. The second is the proper sequencing of standards implementation, taking into account countries' institutional and market development. The third is lack of sufficient participation of developing countries in setting the standards—the ownership issue. Finally, the fourth concern is lack of effectiveness. Let me add here that other concerns have also been voiced (Griffith-Jones 2001; Park 2000; Persaud 2000; Reddy 2001; United Nations 2001; United Nations Conference on Trade and Development 2001):

- standards and codes designed to discipline debtor countries distract attention from the capital supply side (which contributed to the 1997–98 crises and contagion, notably in the form of bank credit reversals) and, thus, slow true progress toward a crisis-resistant global financial architecture;

- ignorance of investors' herding behavior in standards design, notably in standards for market-sensitive risk management and transparency, risks raising rather than reducing the crisis proneness of the world financial system; and

- too-heavy assignment of the tasks of standards design and assessment to international financial organizations introduces a conflict of interest between their assessment and their lending programs and places in doubt the emphasis on voluntary adoption, as incentives and sanctions linked to standard-setting risk become features of surveillance and conditionality.

Rojas-Suarez stresses the fact that, like the opening of countries' capital accounts, the implementation of standards faces issues of sequencing and capacity constraints. The capacity constraints on poor countries, the proliferation of financial standards in the Financial Stability Forum compendium, and the need for prioritization of standards are intimately linked. This makes it important to think about the parameters for prioritization. Rojas-Suarez shows very convincingly that the depth of local financial markets and the quality of legal and institutional frameworks are parameters of outstanding importance if unwanted side effects are to be avoided and if standards are to be effective. One can think of further parameters: Purely technical standards may be more easily implemented than those with policy implications, which would require that standards implementation form an integral part of the economic reform process, and standards that have an important sociocultural dimension may pose the most enduring challenge to credible implementation. However, the trade-off between the tendency of international organizations to proliferate standards and the capacity constraints of the poor countries will remain. It is urgent to start thinking about opportunity costs in the area of standards and codes.

It is possible that the concern about country ownership has not been overemphasized. Andrew Crockett (2000), for example, worried early on about the trade-off between the legitimacy of the Financial Stability Forum (which rises with the number of countries and the number of shades of opinion sitting in the three working groups) and its effectiveness. Emerging markets with relevant policy experience have been part of the process from early on, and regional groupings have been established. What worries me more is the potential lack of effectiveness of the entire standards and codes process. Argentina shows, in my view, Gresham's Law in action—repaying debt with Reports on the Observance of Standards and Codes (ROSCs) rather than dollars, as it were. As Rojas-Suarez points out, Argentina has been one of the most prolific developing countries in publishing ROSCs on the International Monetary Fund (IMF) Web site, yet it is in deep crisis. In a 1999 report, the International Monetary Fund praised Argentina (for exceeding the requirements of the IMF Code of Good Practices on Fiscal Transparency), just when the rating agencies were starting to downgrade the country's sovereign debt because of fiscal concerns and markets were starting to send the country's dollar bond spreads higher. The other observation that feeds my concerns about the effectiveness of the process is that private capital flows to developing countries have been declining steadily since the process began. Either investors do not, or do not yet, pay attention to ROSCs, or no progress has been made.

Banks remain the most important financial intermediaries in developing countries. Counterproductive effects of bank capital regulation will thus be particularly harmful. Significant changes to the 1988 Basel Capital Accord are currently under discussion, and a final version (Basel II) is to be published in 2002, for implementation in 2005.

Rojas-Suarez has shown in this text, again very convincingly, that unlike the situation in industrial countries, the level of bank capital in developing countries fails to send warning signals ahead of a crisis, not least because of regulatory distortions that encourage bank lending to the public sector: local-currency public liabilities were assigned a zero risk weight in the 1988 Basel accord. This problem is set to change, however: The Basel Committee on Banking Supervision is now proposing two alternative main approaches to the calculation of risk weights: a standardized approach and an internal ratings-based (IRB) approach. Under the standardized approach, debt issued by a sovereign with a triple-A credit rating would receive a zero risk weight; lower ratings would translate into a jump in risk weights to 20, 50, 100, or 150 percent, with the highest weighting being reserved for sovereigns whose credit ratings are below B-minus. The IRB approach is based on mapping risk measures derived from probability of default, or of loss given default and maturity, into risk-weight buckets. Representative values for benchmark risk weights as a function of the default probability for corporate exposures are provided in the committee's proposal. Importantly, these values indicate not a linear but, rather, a strongly exponential rise in risk weightings as one moves along the spectrum toward a higher probability of default. This again should lead to much higher risk weights being imposed on bank holdings of claims against local public authorities.

Rojas-Suarez's chapter divides the world into three country groups in terms of their response to bank capital regulation. This division, which yields many helpful insights, will be overlapped by the strong distinction between investment-grade and speculative-grade borrowers in the Basel II proposals. Simulation exercises show that speculative-grade borrowers, which include the bulk of emerging-market and other developing countries, will suffer from a dramatic rise in debt costs if the IRB approach prevails (Reisen 2001). In contrast, the standardized approach, which links risk weights to ratings by eligible external credit assessment institutions, would leave banks' regulatory capital charges, risk-adjusted returns, and, hence, required yield spreads largely unchanged for most developing-country borrowers.

The concern that Basel II will raise the volatility of private capital flows to speculative-grade developing countries, and hence their vulnerability to currency crises, is based on four aspects of the proposed new accord. The first of these is the rigidity of the 8 percent minimum capital ratio. Linking bank lending to bank equity acts as an automatic amplifier for macroeconomic fluctuations: Banks already lend more when times are good, and less when times are bad, and rigid capital requirements reinforce that habit. Second, agency credit ratings define regulatory capital needs under the standardized approach, yet the cyclical determination of these ratings and the delay in their publication mean that ratings improve, and capital charges decline, during booms, whereas ratings are lowered during busts, implying higher capital requirements. A third concern is the cyclical nature of the probability of default and of yield spreads, which determine regulatory capital needs and debt costs under the IRB approach. During the 1970–99 period, one-year default rates for speculative-grade borrowers oscillated between 1 percent in tranquil times and 10 percent in crisis years, largely as a result of global, not idiosyncratic, shocks. Such fluctuations in default probability would translate into corresponding procyclical shifts in risk weights, ranging from 100 to 500 percent for speculative-grade borrowers. Finally, the incentives for short-term rather than long-term interbank lending embedded in the Basel accord remain a concern; for speculative-grade developing countries, these regulatory incentives continue to tilt the structure of capital imports toward short-term debt and make them vulnerable to capital-flow reversals. The chapter by Rojas-Suarez demonstrates how this tilt introduces a short-term bias for domestic loans in developing countries.

Regional development banks should not only devote resources to capacity building to help their developing-country clients cope better with adherence to financial standards and codes, but they should also engage in research that investigates, under region-specific circumstances, whether standards are effective and productive or whether they risk producing unintended side effects.

Dani Rodrik (2001) reports World Bank research estimating that it costs a typical developing country $150 million to implement the requirements of just three existing World Trade Organization agreements (those on customs valuation, sanitary measures, and intellectual property rights). He points out that this corresponds to a year's development budget for many of the least-developed countries. Such quantification of (opportunity) costs would also seem necessary in view of the proliferation of financial standards as well. The estimates should be published as part of any ROSC.

References

Crockett, Andrew. 2000. Towards a Sustainable Financial System: A Role for the Financial Stability Forum. In *Achieving Financial Stability in Asia*, ed. R. Adhikari and U. Hiemenz. Paris: OECD Development Centre.

Griffith-Jones, Stephany. 2001. *New Financial Architecture as a Global Public Good*. Unpublished paper. Brighton: Institute of Development Studies, University of Sussex.

International Monetary Fund. 1999. Experimental Report on Transparency Practices: Argentina. www.imf.org/external/np/rosc/arg/index.htm (accessed January 2002).

Park, Yung Chul. 2000. On Reforming the International Financial System: An East Asian Perspective. In *Achieving Financial Stability in Asia*, ed. R. Adhikari and U. Hiemenz. Paris: OECD Development Centre.

Persaud, Avinash. 2000. Sending the Herd off the Cliff Edge: The Disturbing Interaction Between Herding and Market-Sensitive Risk Management Practices. In *2000 Essay*

Competition in Honour of Jacques de Larosière. Washington: Institute of International Finance.

Reddy, Y. V. 2001. Issues in Implementing International Financial Standards and Codes. *BIS Review* 62 (July/September). Basel: Bank for International Settlements.

Reisen, Helmut. 2001. Will Basel II Contribute to Convergence in International Capital Flows? In *Oesterreichische Nationalbank, Proceedings 29. Volkswirtschaftliche Tagung 2001,* 49–69. Vienna: Austrian National Bank.

Rodrik, Dani. 2001. Trading in Illusions. *Foreign Policy* (March/April): 54–62.

Rojas-Suarez, Liliana. 2001. *Can International Capital Standards Strengthen Banks in Emerging Markets?* Working Paper WP 01-10. Washington: Institute for International Economics.

United Nations. 2001. Information Note by Financing for Development Secretariat, 20 August. www.un.org/esa/ffd/NGO/business_site1001/meetings_at_the_federal_reserve_.htm (accessed January 2002).

United Nations Conference on Trade and Development. 2001. *Trade and Development Report.* Geneva: UNCTAD.

5

Role of Regional Development Banks in Rebuilding the International Financial Architecture

MANUEL HINDS

This chapter proposes a role for the regional development banks (RDBs) in the implementation of a modern worldwide financial architecture. The discussion of the need for this new architecture has been prompted by two problems that have become evident in the last two decades: the protracted economic instability of developing countries, which results in defaults and crises with increasing frequency, and the fact that access to international private financial markets is volatile for some developing countries and totally absent for many others. Although the more urgent of these two problems is that of instability and the resulting crises, the more fundamental one is that of inadequate access to private markets, given that the multilateral development banks are too small to supply all the financial needs of developing countries. These two problems, however, are intimately linked, because the main reason why most developing countries have no access to the private markets, and why those that have it suffer from volatility in such access, is precisely their protracted instability. Thus, the main long-term objective should be the integration of the developing countries into private financial markets. Resolving the instability problem, although it would bring about abundant benefits on its own, is a prerequisite to meeting that objective.

The need for a new financial architecture has become pressing because the official international financial institutions—the International Monetary Fund (IMF), the World Bank, and the RDBs—have worked on these problems for over two decades without finding a solution. Thus,

Manuel Hinds was finance minister of El Salvador. The author appreciates comments provided by Guillermo Calvo, Allan Meltzer, and Roberto Zahler.

the discussion largely centers on how to increase the effectiveness of the official financial institutions in solving these problems.

This chapter does not discuss the shape of the new architecture. However, it makes four assumptions regarding its workings: first, because to date there has been no credible proposal for changing the current institutional setting, this chapter assumes that it will remain in place under the new scheme. Second, given that the official international financial institutions by themselves are too small to meet the financial needs of developing countries, this chapter focuses on creating a set of economic incentives that would encourage and facilitate access of developing countries to the private international markets—the only source of funding large enough to meet these countries' needs. Third, because the future of developing countries' financing should be increasingly tied to private markets, this chapter assumes that a similarly increasing measure of market discipline should be introduced into the lending operations of the official institutions, so that the transition to the market will be carried out in a more harmonious fashion. This would also help in increasing their efficacy in resolving the problem of instability and, through this, the problem of lack of stable access. Fourth, because not all developing countries are the same, this chapter assumes that the new architecture should rely on mechanisms that allow countries to be differentiated according to their performance. The market approach implicit in the previous two assumptions should provide the mechanisms for making this differentiation in a manner consistent with the ultimate objective of integrating the developing countries into private international financial markets.

Do the RDBs Have a Role in the New International Financial Architecture?

An assessment of the problems that have inspired proposals for a redesign of the worldwide financial architecture is presented here. It argues that the RDBs have an important role to play in solving those problems, and it focuses on the two problems posed in the introduction: the protracted instability of developing countries, and their consequent lack of adequate access to private financial markets.

Instability in Developing Countries and Its Causes

The commonly held view is that problems of instability are the exclusive purview of the IMF. This is certainly true when a crisis has already exploded. However, the processes that lead to crises exceed the limitations that its own nature imposes on the IMF, which, like a central bank, operates mostly in the short-term, liquid end of the financial market. Building a resilient domestic financial system is a long-term process, well within the purview of the development banks. In addition, although short-term fiscal issues are within the province of the IMF, the longer-term issues of fiscal management—especially those concerning the allocation of fiscal resources for the country's development—are more in keeping with the role of the development banks. The two dimensions of the problem obviously interact. There is no way to say what portion of the debt of an overindebted country is the cause of its overindebtedness, and thus the development banks, like any other lender to a country, have a direct stake in preventing crises—and in solving them when they occur—beyond that dictated by their own developmental objectives.

Moreover, although financial crises by definition arise in the financial sphere, many have their roots in the real side of the economy, which is in the province of the development banks. In fact, issues associated with technological development, protection, and trade liberalization are intimately linked to the wave of instability that developing countries have suffered over the last two or three decades. Traditionally, a combination of three factors has made developing countries prone to financial instability: extreme dependence for foreign exchange earnings on commodities with volatile prices, lack of monetary and fiscal discipline, and weak financial institutional settings. This tendency toward instability has become more marked in the last two decades as a result of several developments in the world economy.

First, throughout the world economy, value added is increasingly a function of the amount of knowledge imbedded in production. As a result, real prices of nonoil commodities—goods that embody low levels of knowledge in their production—have been declining for the last 30 years, straining developing countries' ability to finance their imports (figure 5.1). Because, with some exceptions, the industrial sectors of developing countries operate behind high rates of protection, they are not competitive enough to sell their manufactured goods in international markets, and therefore these countries cannot compensate for the fall in foreign exchange revenue by increasing their manufactured exports. On the contrary, the industrial sectors of these economies typically need foreign raw materials and intermediate inputs to produce their goods, which tends to make these industries net importers. Thus, declining commodity export revenue introduces recessive tendencies in these countries' industrial sectors and in their economies in general. To counterbalance this trend, many developing countries have resorted to monetary creation, overvaluation of their domestic currencies, and foreign borrowing to keep the economy growing. Without an expansion of their export base, this has resulted in the classic cycle of overborrowing, financial crisis, and default. Through these mechanisms, the lack of competitiveness becomes manifest in the capital account of the balance of payments in both the borrowing and the defaulting phases of the cycle, even if the root of the problem is the lack of a diversified exporting base that could support

Figure 5.1 Real nonoil commodity prices, 1960–99

1995 = 100

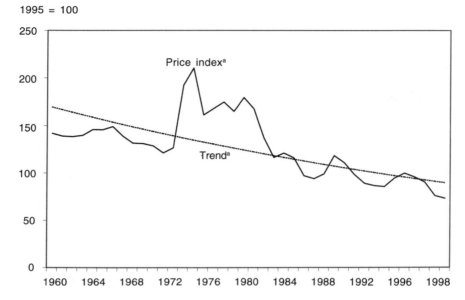

a. Nominal prices deflated by the US consumer price index.
b. Five-year moving average.

Source: International Monetary Fund, *International Financial Statistics*, various issues.

the servicing of foreign debts. For this reason, depressions in commodity markets have usually led to financial crises in developing countries.

Second, the long-term solution to these problems, namely, opening these economies to increase their competitiveness and diversification, creates transitional instability. In the 1990s, most developing countries, while remaining heavily protectionist, made some progress in liberalizing their trade regimes. Increasing competition from abroad initiated a structural transformation that necessarily implied the disappearance of inefficient activities, to be replaced by more efficient ones. This process, although necessary for solving the problem in the long run, worsened the instability in the short run, as banks experienced losses when foreign competition made the assets they had financed obsolete. Other liberalizing measures, such as the opening of the capital account and the liberalization of the financial system (including the removal of interest rate controls as well as greater ease of entry for new competitors), have also resulted in increased instability in the short term—particularly when these measures have been taken precipitously, without other measures that should accompany them, without proper analysis of sequencing issues, or without the necessary institutional support. For example, liberalizing the capital account while keeping imprudent monetary, fiscal, and foreign exchange policies in place has been a recipe for disaster. Equally disastrous has been liberalization of the financial system without adequate regulation and supervision of financial institutions.

Third, protection in the industrial countries has become a substantial obstacle to the diversification of the developing economies, even those that have made great progress in liberalizing their domestic markets. Although the trade policies of the industrial countries are relatively liberal in the complex goods and services that they trade among themselves, they are highly restrictive in those areas in which value added per worker at international prices is low, such as textiles and other goods and services in which developing countries might compete. In addition to undermining the credibility of reformers in the developing countries, the presence of high protection in the industrial countries blocks the major markets that diversified developing economies could otherwise access, trapping them in their dependence on commodities.

In combination, these problems have worsened the instability of many developing countries to the point where this volatility has become their most urgent problem. With distressing frequency, governments in these countries engage in imprudent fiscal and monetary policies to spur the growth that their dwindling foreign exchange is depressing. They then borrow abroad to finance their excessive expenditures, and eventually they default on these loans and a financial crisis begins. Such crises sweep away the gains accrued over many years in terms of increased economic activity and reduction of poverty.

The solution is not to close these economies once again—that would lead to even more instability and rapid impoverishment—but to stick to prudent fiscal and monetary policies, complete the reforms, and deal with the temporary instability to which those reforms give rise. Completing the modernization of developing economies requires heavy investment in more efficient activities. That, in turn, requires not only eliminating the distortions in relative prices that protection creates in these economies but also obtaining access to fresh financial resources, so that resources can flow to the new, more efficient activities that undistorted price systems would encourage. The main source of these resources should be the domestic market. However, the same monetary and financial policies that lead to instability also repress the growth of the domestic financial system. Fiscal and monetary prudence would open this source of financing and make it possible to solve the other fundamental problem of developing countries: their lack of access to international financial markets.

Lack of Access to Financial Markets

Sustained access of developing countries to private markets is essential, because the magnitude of the investment they need far exceeds both their current saving potential and the lending capacity of the multilateral institutions. In many of these countries, these institutions and friendly industrial-country governments are the only sources of long-term funds. This dependency must be overcome to unlock the opportunities for growth for those countries. This does not mean that multilateral institutions should disappear or be converted into grant-dispensing mechanisms. They are the equivalent of international credit unions, where countries can borrow on more favorable terms than if they borrowed individually in the markets. By enabling their members to access the market directly, the multilateral institutions would be able to concentrate on the needs of long-term financing for social purposes, which cannot be funded in the markets.

The problem of access is closely related to that of instability. The moral hazard caused by insufficient fiscal and monetary discipline, together with the volatility and long-term decline of foreign exchange revenue produced by dependence on commodities for export, poses major obstacles to the development of financial markets in the developing countries and to their integration into world markets. In combination, these trends have resulted in a strong reluctance of international markets to finance the developing countries' transition into an integrated world. As the previous section pointed out, these problems not only block developing countries' access to global financial markets but also deter the development of domestic financial systems, which remain small in most developing countries, and retard the development of regional financial markets, which are practically nonexistent in those countries.

Instability is not the only problem leading to volatile access to international markets. Although all developing countries share these problems, there are substantial differences among them. Some countries have been able to stabilize their economies fiscally and monetarily and have aligned their domestic prices with those prevailing in the international markets by reducing protection and dismantling suffocating regulations. Yet the international markets tend to see the developing countries as a whole when analyzing risks. Even if the markets have recently learned to be somewhat more discriminating, a crisis in one developing country tends to lead to a withdrawal of financing to all of them. Thus, where it exists, access to international markets has been fragile even for the most disciplined of developing countries. If this problem is not resolved, the result might be a vicious circle, in which the long-term transformation of the economy that is needed to eliminate volatility is prevented by lack of access to international markets. In this scenario, instability tends to increase, exerting unmanageable pressures on the global financial system and making it increasingly difficult for the IMF to maintain global financial stability.

Thus, resolving the long-term problems that lead to financial crises and hinder developing countries' access to financial markets is essential if the world is to have a stable and efficient financial architecture. The multilateral financial institutions, including the World Bank and the RDBs, have a comparative advantage in resolving these problems.

Competitive Advantage of Development Banks

Integrating developing countries into the global financial architecture requires dealing with four problems:

- The developing countries must carry out several tasks to stabilize their economies. These include imposing discipline on their fiscal and monetary policies, strengthening their financial systems, and diversifying their exports through trade liberalization.

- They must carry out what are often called second-generation reforms, to create an institutional setting adequate for a modern economy. These include ensuring the rule of law, facilitating the creation of and properly enforcing property rights, giving transparency to economic and political activities, improving financial regulation and supervision, strengthening banks, and undertaking other structural reforms.

- Those countries that have already accomplished these tasks, or made substantial advances toward doing so, need to overcome the resistance of international markets to financing developing countries on a sustainable basis.

- Although completing these tasks would significantly reduce the risk of financial crises, such crises are not likely to disappear. Therefore mechanisms to deal with them should be established, aimed at reducing their effect on the countries suffering them and on the rest of the developing community.

A sustainable solution to these problems goes well beyond the mandate of the IMF, which deals primarily with short-term liquidity issues and, therefore, is more naturally prepared for the third task—that of dealing with financial crises. The multilateral development banks would complement the IMF in the global financial architecture because they differ from that institution in several important ways:

- They deal with the entire range of factors influencing financial markets—including not just activities in the financial sector itself but also those in the real economy and the social sectors. Because many financial events are rooted in the nonfinancial parts of the economy, this is a clear advantage.

- They operate at the long-term end of the financing spectrum, which is essential for the long-term solution of the problems now affecting the global financial architecture.

- They work on the structural and institutional aspects of development that need to be resolved to reduce the instability of developing countries and to increase their access to private financial markets.

Competitive Advantage of the RDBs

Either the World Bank or the RDBs could play this complementary role to that of the IMF. How, then, to allocate the task between them? Answering this question requires addressing three other questions. First, can the RDBs add value to the new financial architecture beyond that which the World Bank could provide? Second, should the tasks associated with building and maintaining the global financial architecture be formally split between the World Bank and the relevant RDB in each of the regions of the world? Third, how should these institutions coordinate their activities?

Regarding the first question, this chapter argues that the RDBs are in a position to provide a distinct value added to the new financial architecture. The comparative advantage of the World Bank is that it can shift knowledge and experience across regions. However, the RDBs are best placed to help in the solution of problems that demand close regional focus and coordination.

The financial problems discussed previously tend to have strong regional differences. Although the fundamental problems are common to all developing countries, they tend to take different shapes in the different regions. For example, countries in Latin America tend to be more unstable and prone to crises than countries in Africa, whereas the problems resulting from lack of access to international markets tend to be graver in the latter. Levels of income also tend to diverge across regions, and therefore the problems that must be resolved to integrate countries in the global financial architecture also differ. Furthermore, this integration means not only bringing the developing countries to the developed international markets but also integrating the financial systems of the developing countries with each other. That task will be easier to carry out regionally, because trade among developing countries tends to develop first among neighbors. For these reasons, RDBs are ideally positioned to help in the solution of these problems.

Regarding the second question, it would not be in the interest of the developing countries to allocate tasks in a rigid manner to each of these institutions. Some overlapping of tasks between the World Bank and the RDBs is unavoidable. Regional and global issues are inextricably linked, and so the comparative advantages of both the World Bank and the RDBs are needed. Moreover, overlapping is actually desirable for three main reasons: it spurs creativity by mixing the global and the regional approaches, it introduces a healthy competition of points of view, and it allows for the strengths of some institutions to compensate for the short-comings of others. Competition need not lead to duplication if there is close coordination between institutions.

This leads to the third question. The gains of competition can be reaped only if there is close coordination not only between the World Bank and the RDBs but also between these institutions and the IMF. Such coordination may require splitting responsibilities in individual cases. The circumstances vary so much from case to case that these responsibilities should be split in a pragmatic fashion, depending on the advantages that each institution may have in dealing with specific problems in specific countries. However, all the multilateral institutions should share responsibility in building a more coherent global financial architecture—working with instruments and policies aimed at resolving the problems that this chapter has identified.

The case for giving the RDBs an important role in the new architecture can also made indirectly by asking whether there is any way they could be excluded from that architecture. It is clear that their omission would be inconceivable, because of the externalities of financial markets already mentioned. Large operators like the RDBs could easily and involuntarily disrupt any efforts of the IMF and the World Bank toward resolving the problems discussed in this chapter. In contrast, they can be of great help in solving these problems because of their competitive advantage in regional issues, their focus on the main problems of the region, and their easier adaptation to the mores of their customers. Any unnecessary duplication should be avoided through close coordination.

If these arguments are valid, the RDBs should prepare formally to help in building a more efficient and secure global financial architecture. In fact, because the problems addressed here have been around for a considerable time, all the multilateral institutions have experimented with many ideas for resolving them, most of which have proved useful, or could be useful with some modifications. These instruments, however, have been created in ad hoc ways to deal with specific crises; they have not yet coalesced into institutionally defined instruments and policies. The aim of this chapter is to put these well-tried ideas into a consistent framework that would result in a more coherent financial architecture.

Toward an Improved International Financial Architecture: Proposals for the RDBs

Objectives

The main objectives of the RDBs with respect to improving the stability of their member countries' economies and their access to financial markets would be the following:

- to help their member countries develop their domestic financial markets, so that they can mobilize their own savings for development purposes;

- to bring their member countries to the international financial markets in a sustainable fashion; and

- to mitigate, as much as they can with their scarce resources, the procyclical behavior of private sources of financing.

Meeting these objectives would have implications in several dimensions for the RDBs. They would have to

- develop new instruments,

- design special lending policies, and

- improve their capacity to generate and disseminate knowledge and best practices.

This section develops each of these aspects of the proposal and discusses the policies and instruments that RDBs could use to integrate their member countries into international markets and manage financial crises. It proposes policies and instruments that RDBs could use to integrate their private sectors into global financial markets as well as to mitigate the procyclical behavior of private financing and discusses the role that RDBs can play in generating and disseminating knowledge and experience.

Instruments and Policies to Integrate the Public Sector into International Markets

Two issues arise under this heading: improving access to financial markets and dealing with financial crises.

Improving Access to Financial Markets

To help countries acquire financial resources adequate for their needs, the RDBs' lending policies should be geared to two main objectives: developing the domestic financial markets of their member countries and bringing them to global markets, thus reducing their dependence on the development financial institutions. The design of the operations and their conditionality should be framed within this principle. As emphasized before, this would entail working to resolve the structural issues that give raise to instability, as well as assisting countries in achieving access to financial markets until they are able to do so on their own. Thus, the multilateral institutions as a whole, and the RDBs in particular, should work to reduce their own participation in the financing of developing countries (but not necessarily to reduce their lending in absolute terms), bringing their members to a more plentiful and more sustainable source of financing for their development needs. This would allow the RDBs to concentrate their operations on social projects whose benefits accrue in the long term. As already mentioned, the justification for this recommendation is simple and pragmatic: the lending power of all the multilateral institutions combined represents only a small fraction of the financial needs of developing countries. If countries fail to develop their own domestic markets and are not brought to the international markets, they will be condemned to underfinancing in perpetuity.

To accomplish this objective, the RDBs have to deal with three problems. First, they have to work closely with governments and with the World Trade Organization to liberalize trade in both industrial and developing countries, in order to reduce the dependence of the latter on a few commodities for foreign exchange earnings. Second, they have to work to improve the quality of their customers' macroeconomic management and institutions (including through the second-generation reforms mentioned before), to make the debt instruments of developing countries attractive in international financial markets and to allow for the development of a sound domestic financial system. Third, they have to help their member countries carve a niche for themselves in the global financial markets.

Regarding the first problem, the RDBs and the World Bank have already achieved substantial progress in helping developing countries liberalize their trade regimes. Exports as a percentage of GDP have increased in the last decade, particularly in Latin America, and they have tended to become more diversified. This is a long-term effort that should be continued. As discussed earlier, however, its success largely depends on the availability of domestic and international financing for the new activities that a more liberal trade regime would elicit.

Regarding the second problem, the development banks have lent substantial amounts to help countries attain stability and have introduced conditionalities in these loans to attaining the stability goals since the early 1980s. Nevertheless, after uncountable operations, true policy reform to ensure stability has not been achieved. Periodic calls to resolve this problem, by having the IMF and the development banks condition their loans on the attainment of macroeconomic stability, have proved ineffective. The reason is not that the staffs of these institutions did not know that they could use conditionality for these purposes—in fact, the IMF has used conditionality in this way since the Fund's inception, and the development banks have been doing so for more than 20 years—but because these institutions have been unable to enforce these conditions. In part, this outcome is the result of political pressure on the development institutions to lend as much as possible to all countries. This puts pressure on the staff to be overoptimistic in evaluating both the effectiveness of the measures proposed in the operations undertaken to overcome the instability problems and the willingness of the governments to put those measures in practice.

The fact that the institutions' operational staff are in charge of both assessing the likelihood of success of a given stabilization program and designing the program itself makes success very difficult to achieve, given the political pressure to lend. However, having independent agents evaluate the performance of the financial institutions would not resolve this problem, because such evaluations would be carried out years after the operations are completed. In fact, at least one of the development banks, the World Bank, carries out evaluations in this way, with the evaluating staff separated from the operational staff by a firewall. Although extremely useful, these evaluations have an effect only in the long run and are easily bypassed by arguing that conditions in whatever country one wishes to finance have changed since the evaluated operations were conducted. What is needed is a test of the real prospects of success at the time of the operation, and that is something that only the market can provide.

The solution proposed in this chapter is to give more weight in the development banks' lending decisions to the credit ratings of the professional rating companies, which, in any case, are essential if developing countries are to access private markets. Such ratings provide a quantitative assessment of the well-informed perceptions of the market. Private ratings could be used in the following ways.

- A grading from a recognized credit rating agency could be required as a precondition for any lending operation to any country.

- Such ratings, which would have to be updated from time to time, could serve as a benchmark of the success of the RDBs in enabling their member countries to access private markets. This would eliminate the conflict of interest embedded in having the same staff design the stabilization program and assess its chances of success.

- Failure to obtain progress toward good ratings should be a major obstacle in getting further financing.

One can anticipate four arguments being raised against giving such a prominent role to private credit ratings. One is the naïve argument that good ratings are the privilege of large and rich countries. This is simply not true. Ratings do not measure the wealth or size of a country but, rather, the prudence of its policies and its resulting ability to pay. Any country, whatever its size or level of income, can pursue prudent policies, and the ratings reflect this. For example, in Latin America the debts of only three countries enjoy investment-grade ratings: Mexico, Chile, and El Salvador. One of these is a large country, another is a medium-size one, and the third is a small country (or, seen from another perspective, they are two relatively rich countries and one poor one). Their favorable credit ratings translate into greater access to and lower costs of financing. For instance, whereas China, despite its gigantic size, is able to float debt of at most 10 years' maturity, tiny El Salvador can float 30-year debt at spreads over US Treasury bonds below those that China can command (in fact, on its 15-year loans El Salvador gets rates very close to those charged by the development banks).[1]

A second argument against ratings is that the accuracy of private ratings in the past has been less than flawless. This argument can be granted although there is no proof that the record of these ratings has been worse than that implicit in the repeated operations of the development banks in countries that have failed to stabilize for decades. The recommendation that private ratings be used, however, is a purely pragmatic one. Those ratings are the main piece of information that investors use in the markets. If one wants to go to the market, one has to be rated, and that rating largely determines the interest rate one pays. This is a fact of life. Thus, tracking the credit ratings of developing countries gives a good, objective measure of progress in bringing the countries to the markets, because if they do not get good ratings, they will not be able to go to the markets. The fact that they can go to the development banks without ratings weakens the effect of those ratings—the main instrument that keeps financial discipline in the industrial countries' sovereign and corporate financial markets—on developing countries' behavior.

The third argument against the use of private ratings is that the sheer number of developing countries seeking ratings would pose so great a burden on the rating agencies that they would be forced to reduce the quality of their services. This argument, however, ignores the fact that the number of developing countries is dwarfed by the number of companies that already operate in the financial markets of the industrial countries on the basis of private ratings. These companies run into the thousands, and many of them have financial operations larger than those of various developing countries. Adding the developing countries to the rating agencies' workload would represent a minor increase in the demand for their services.

The fourth argument is that the RDBs—and the World Bank—should focus their operations precisely on those countries that do not have access to the markets. Accepting this argument, however, would lead to perverse incentives: It would force RDBs to lend only to those borrowing countries with bad track records, and it would ensure financing for

---

1. In July 2002 El Salvador issued 10-year bonds at 7.2 percent interest, which is within the range charged by the development banks. A few months before, it issued 30-year bonds at 8.75 percent.

those countries, even if they do not mend their ways. Thus, it would perpetuate rather than resolve the basic problem. Furthermore, as already noted, having a good rating is a sign not of wealth but of fiscal prudence. Poor countries with a good macroeconomic track record would be denied the benefits of borrowing from the international credit unions, which they still need for long-term social projects, precisely because they have been prudent.[2]

Thus, although credit ratings are conditioned by the moods of the market, which sometimes may overreact, these ratings not only would free the operation of the development banks from political influences but also would allow for an objective assessment of the differences between developing countries (to the extent the markets' point of view is indeed objective).

Ratings are, in any case, essential for the solution of the third problem that RDBs should resolve: that of actually helping countries to float debt instruments in the markets. The RDBs should reach an agreement with each of their member countries on a long-term strategic program aimed at bringing them to the global markets, and it should evaluate the performance of their operations using their progress at completing this program as a benchmark. Domestic financial markets would be taken as part of the global system, and the proposed programs could start with issues of debt in the domestic market and then in both the domestic and the international markets.

To induce countries to access the markets, the program should also include a downward-sliding schedule of the proportion of loans that the RDB would finance in full. This is necessary because, in the short run, governments find it more comfortable to borrow from a single multilateral. The loans that the RDBs would finance in full would include all loans for social projects and a diminishing portion of all other financial needs of the state. The remainder would be cofinanced in the market with the RDB's assistance. These programs should be flexible within certain

---

2. The argument that solvent countries should be left out of the development banks' lending is based on the highly debatable assertion that the credits from these institutions are subsidized and that prudent countries should not receive subsidies. The assertion about subsidies, in turn, is based on the observation that development banks lend to countries that nobody else wants to finance and at interest rates below what even the best developing countries could get in the markets. However, the fact that a group of borrowers can lower their costs by pooling their risks is not evidence of subsidization. Those who argue that there is an implicit subsidy refer to the fact that the low cost of capital comes from the participation of developed countries in the capital of these institutions, which, through its callable portion, increases the rating that they could get. Yet, as the success of the Andean Development Corporation clearly shows, a pool of borrowers can get a rating much higher than its members can get individually—the corporation enjoys an investment-grade rating even though none of its members does. In fact, if there is subsidization, it is from the higher-rated to the lower-rated countries within the pool.

reasonable limits but should be seriously enforced. Countries approaching graduation would include their social projects in the sliding program.

Complementing this policy, the RDBs could provide enhancements for the instruments issued by the countries in the international markets, so that their exposure in these operations would exceed the amount in which they participate in the cofinancing. For example, an RDB could finance 50 percent of an operation and guarantee an additional 25 percent. The guarantees could take any form; for example, that of the familiar rolling guarantees covering the next two years, or those that guarantee the out years, or variations on these models. Cofinancing can also take several forms, including financing the out years of long-term loans and many other variations.

The RDBs can also open a new dimension of cooperation toward the integration of regional and subregional financial markets. As mentioned before, financial integration is needed not just between developing countries and the international financial markets but also between developing countries themselves. Financial flows between neighboring countries are increasing rapidly in many regions as a result of growing trade and incipient cross-border investments. This positive development is hindered, however, by a lack of coordinated financial regulation and supervision, which increases the risks of these financial flows. The RDBs are in an ideal position to help in removing those obstacles by promoting the coordination of financial regulation and supervision as well as by helping to create financial vehicles that would facilitate cross-border investments. In addition, the RDBs could help in developing regional financial institutions, such as stock exchanges.

Helping in the Prevention and Management of Financial Crises

There are four aspects to solving the problem of financial crises: preventing crises, dealing with crises when they occur, dealing with contagion, and managing the increased risks that action on the first three aspects presents for the portfolios of the RDBs. This section discusses all of these aspects, beginning with the fundamental problems caused by financial crises. The discussion of the needs posed by crises illuminates the discussion of the ways to prevent them and deal with their consequences.

Dealing with financial crises. Multilateral institutions have participated in the resolution of most recent crises, with varying degrees of success. In general, the development banks' performance has been timely and effective. However, two issues should be resolved to prevent future problems. The first is the definition of the roles of the banks—both the World Bank and the RDBs—and of the IMF in providing liquidity. The second is the potential conflict embedded in the twin objectives of providing both short-term liquidity and funds for the long-term restructuring of the banking system.

One point should be clarified before discussing these issues. In some cases the best strategy for dealing with a crisis, from the point of view of the international community, may be not to intervene but, rather, to allow the country to default and the country's financial system to fail. This discussion refers only to those cases in which the international community decides to intervene. Given that decision, the logic of events leads to the necessity of refloating the country's financial system and of creating and supporting a strategy aimed at making the country financially viable. Many critics of the official international financial institutions' handling of the recent crises see these actions as unwarranted, uneconomic, and even immoral. These arguments, however, pertain to the first issue: whether the international community should intervene. Once the decision has been made to intervene, the logic of the solution mandates that these actions should be taken. What some see as the bailout of financial institutions, others see as the enforcement of financial contracts—which, in any case, is done with resources that the country in crisis will eventually repay.[3]

Regarding the first point, it has long been recognized that the provision of emergency liquidity is an IMF responsibility, whereas the provision of financing for the restructuring of the system—plus all the required technical assistance—is within the purview of the multilateral development banks. Recent crises, however, have exceeded the IMF's financial capacity, and other institutions—the World Bank, the Inter-American Development Bank (IDB), the Asian Development Bank (ADB), and the US government, among others—have been called on to complement the IMF in the provision of emergency liquidity. This was the case in Mexico's crisis of 1994–95 and in the Asian crises of the late 1990s. As members of the international community, the development banks had no other option than to answer such calls for assistance.

Many critics of the current financial architecture point out that the provision of liquidity should be the exclusive function of the IMF. This may be a solution to the problem. However, if the development institutions are to stay away from this kind of operation, the resources of the IMF will have to be increased substantially in preparation for such contingencies. If the international community does not increase the IMF's liquidity, the development banks—including the RDBs—will have to help with their much larger liquidity in cases of emergency. Because it is difficult to anticipate the magnitude of crises, it is important that the RDBs

---

3. The impression that by saving a country's banks one necessarily bails out their shareholders is wrong. Saving one does not mean saving the other. In most, if not all, the restructuring processes supported by the development banks in the past, the shareholders of financial institutions have lost their capital—the bailout was directed to the depositors. The loans provided for the bailouts have been repaid with domestic taxes, not with the resources of the development banks' shareholders.

be prepared with appropriate policies and instruments for an emergency. If the RDBs are to continue helping to resolve liquidity problems in financial crises, they should design instruments specifically for this purpose.

To do this, they must first analyze the needs that crises present. Governments of countries experiencing financial crises need financing for two purposes: emergency liquidity, to restore the confidence of depositors and lenders in the domestic financial system and the government's ability to repay its obligations; and funds to carry out structural reforms aimed at preventing a repetition of the crisis. The latter is accomplished mainly by recapitalizing or liquidating failed financial institutions without imposing losses on depositors and by improving supervision and regulation. Each of these two problems poses different financial needs. Loans for the first purpose should be provided with short maturities, under the assumption that, as soon as confidence is restored, the country's government and financial system will recover the necessary liquidity and will repay the loans. The maturity of loans provided for the second purpose must be long, to allow the government to spread over time the losses it incurs in absorbing the losses to the financial system.[4] Also, the recapitalization of banks is a difficult task that requires substantial technical work of the highest quality.

Up to now, for lack of an instrument to convey liquidity, the multilateral development banks have used loans aimed at the subsequent recapitalization of the local institutions, so that these institutions can be used as conveyors of liquidity assistance. This has created severe tensions in the resulting operations, because the purpose of providing liquidity to restore confidence and the purpose of providing resources for the recapitalization of the banking system can easily become contradictory. By their nature, loans to recapitalize banks have to include conditions that should be met before disbursements are made: Basically, these conditions are that the banks have been recapitalized and that sufficient steps have been taken to prevent the repetition of the crisis. In contrast, the only condition for the disbursement of an emergency loan should be the

---

4. These funds, however, are not needed in all cases of restructuring: The government can cover the losses with long-term, interest-bearing bonds issued to the failed banks, using these to replace the nonperforming assets on the institutions' books. Liquid funds are needed only to liquidate institutions and, in some cases, to facilitate the sale of failed banks, because the problem facing failed banks is that their assets do not generate enough income to pay for their liabilities. Substituting interest-bearing bonds for the bad loans in the portfolio solves this problem—provided, of course, that the interest payments are calculated so as to cover the expenditures of the liabilities. Buying the bad portfolio with cash may be counterproductive, because it would give too much liquidity to the banks, which they would then have to lend quickly to generate income-earning assets. This hasty lending could lead to more bad loans as well as to inconvenient expansions of the money supply. The problem is different when the problem is a run on the banks: Stopping a run requires rapid injections of liquidity to restore confidence.

existence of a program guaranteeing its repayment. By mixing these two objectives in a single instrument, the development banks place themselves in a potentially difficult position. If a country has not complied with the conditions for disbursement but is in need of the emergency funds, any decision is bad. If the banks refuse the disbursements, they are reneging on their commitment to help in an emergency. If they do disburse, they are undermining their developmental commitment to help in the recapitalization of the domestic financial system and to improve the resilience of the system.

Thus, the following points are needed to deal with financial crises.

- RDBs need an instrument to convey liquidity help in cases of financial crisis. This instrument would have features similar to those used by the IMF in terms of maturity and conditions of disbursement.

- To complement this instrument, the RDBs should redesign the instruments used for the recapitalization of the financial system, making disbursements contingent on the occurrence of actual expenditure by the government for this purpose. Structuring these operations as classic adjustment loans, disbursed against general imports on the fulfillment of certain conditions, weakens the connection that should exist between disbursements and actual project costs, and may result in cases in which the loan is disbursed even though the banking system has not been yet recapitalized.

Preventing crises. The tasks outlined above in connection with the integration of the developing countries into international financial markets would go a long way toward preventing crises. RDBs can further this objective by supplementing an instrument already created by the IMF. This instrument, the contingent credit line (CCL) facility, aims at providing lines of credit to be disbursed in the event of a crisis that develops in a country as a result of causes other than fiscal or monetary indiscipline: The IMF interprets such a crisis as caused exclusively by contagion (IMF 2001). RDBs could enter the field of contingent operations for any of three main reasons.

- As in the case of emergency loans, RDBs might enter if the IMF facilities are too small to provide comfort to the markets. The CCLs are limited to three to five times the country's quota.

- Emergencies not rooted in fiscal or monetary indiscipline might arise for reasons other than contagion. Natural disasters and terrorist attacks are just two examples of the many events that could unravel into a liquidity crisis even in a prudently managed country. RDBs and the World Bank have facilities for this kind of need; however, such loans are not preapproved and therefore cannot provide the confidence that automatically disbursable contingent loans would provide.

- A related point is that only a third of the amounts approved for CCLs may be disbursed automatically. The rest are subject to a review of the situation at the moment of disbursal. This effectively reduces the size of the contingent loan to a third of its nominal value, or about 11.6 times the country's quota with the IMF. Here, again, RDBs could enter to fill in the gap in financing.

Thus, RDBs could make a substantial contribution by increasing the funds available for contingencies and by including emergencies other than contagion as justifications for disbursements. In these operations the RDBs should closely coordinate their actions with the IMF, although their instruments would not be exactly like the CCLs. The promise to disburse would be provided based on a program approved by the IMF and would be binding only if the government's actions coincide with what it promised when it contracted for the contingent facility. Thus, the conditionality of these operations would refer to policies and not to outcomes. A country would be able to withdraw from these facilities regardless of the depth of a crisis only if it has followed the prudent policies agreed to with the RDB when contracting the loan. Symmetrically, if the conditions established in the contract—which would be designed specifically for each country, to take into account its particular features—are met, the country would have the right to have the loan disbursed in its entirety. Given the complexity of the issues involved, the conditions would be different for each country.[5]

Dealing with contagion. Ripple effects tend to happen as a result of the sudden panic that overtakes international markets when one developing country falls into a financial crisis and defaults. As a result, even well-managed and secure developing countries find that they cannot access their private sector sources of financing. This problem is one of insufficient information, which the CCL is aimed at ameliorating. A quick-disbursing facility also should be opened for countries not contracting for CCLs. As discussed before, the IMF may lack the resources and staff to provide these facilities for countries in danger of contagion. If this is the case, the RDBs can play a decisive role by providing rapid credit to countries in this situation and, through this and other measures, by encouraging the private sector to keep on providing credit to them. As argued earlier, if the size of the IMF's resources is not increased, reality

---

5. For the need to have different indicators in the contracts with each country, see Fischer (2001).

will force these operations on the RDBs, which lack an instrument with which to carry out these operations.

Managing the risks of liquidity operations. In summary, if the IMF is not enlarged substantially, RDBs should create three liquidity facilities to deal with financial crises:

■ an emergency loan to be provided in coordination with the IMF when a crisis has already erupted,

■ a contingent line of credit to protect solvent countries against sudden and unforeseeable events that could destabilize them, and

■ a credit facility for solvent countries that fall victim to contagion as a result of a crisis in another country.

Although creation of these instruments may prove inevitable, their operation poses two serious problems for the RDBs. The first is the effect of the risks of these operations on the overall risk of the RDBs and, therefore, on the cost of their normal developmental operations. Even if carried out prudently, these operations would be much riskier than the RDBs' traditional loans. For this reason, they should be priced at interest rates higher than those applied in normal operations. The RDBs, the World Bank, and the IMF have applied this solution in the small number of operations they have carried out with instruments similar to these. Once one RDB has lent to a country that has fallen into a crisis, there is no way that institution can avoid an increase in the level of risk of its lending portfolio. In fact, liquidity loans that are well designed under a strategy coordinated by the IMF would reduce the overall risk in an RDB's portfolio at the margin, because they would eliminate the risk of default, which, in the absence of the loans, would be a certainty.

The second problem is that of the size of these operations. RDBs should avoid a situation in which liquidity loans crowd out their traditional development operations. A quantitative limit should be imposed on the former, and the costs of the staff working on them should be covered by the operations themselves, so that there is no crowding out of the staff working in traditional operations. However, this does not resolve the problem entirely, because a major crisis may explode at a time when the relevant RDB may have already exhausted its quota for these operations. This problem could be solved by allowing RDBs to invest in detached subsidiaries dedicated to these risky operations. These subsidiaries would rely on their own capital to mobilize resources and manage their risks. Of course, these subsidiaries would have a much higher cost of capital than their parent RDBs. Yet, because their operations would not be consolidated with the RDB's, the increased risk would not affect the RDBs' own credit ratings. Also, the subsidiaries would resolve the problem of crowding out, because their sources of funds would be different from those of the RDBs. This idea is worth considering.

Bringing the Private Sector to the International Markets

The main reasons for the lack of financing for the private sector in developing countries are to be found in the unstable fiscal and monetary policies prevailing in many of these countries, as well as in the inadequate regulation and supervision of the local financial system. The main efforts of both governments and the RDBs should be directed toward solving these problems. In the meantime, RDBs could help in the financing of the private sector. The objective of these operations, however, should not be to substitute for private financing (which, to the contrary, is what should be elicited) but, rather, to catalyze its development. Meeting this objective might be difficult because the presence of officially backed financing may stifle the development of domestic sources, defeating the ultimate purpose of the exercise. As in the case of the public sector, the needs of the private sector exceed by several orders of magnitude the capacity of the multilateral institutions to finance them, and creating a dependency on these institutions for the financing of the private sector would be damaging for developing countries.

There are three main issues to be resolved to ensure that financing the private sector will not damage the development of local financial systems. First is the issue of lending to the private sector with sovereign guarantees. Such lending introduces a distortion in both the local and the international markets, because other potential lenders do not enjoy such an advantage. Because governments do not have the capacity to guarantee all potential lending to the private sector, the only solution to this problem is to deny such guarantees to all of them. There is, however, another possibility; namely, lending to the private sector without a sovereign guarantee. The World Bank cannot lend without such a guarantee, but its subsidiary the International Finance Corporation not only can do so but can also invest in equity holdings. Some RDBs, such as the IDB, and some subregional institutions, such as the Central American Bank for Economic Integration and the Andean Corporation of Finance, lend directly to the private sector and can even invest in equity holdings. In addition, the IDB has a special subsidiary aimed at lending without sovereign guarantees, and this subsidiary may also invest in equity holdings.

Operations carried out without government guarantees have, in general, been financially successful, but to date the volume of resources intermediated in this manner remains small. The growth of these institutions is constrained by the very same factors that prevent developing countries from accessing private international markets. Naturally, these institutions can lend only in dollars, which poses almost intractable foreign exchange risks for most, the main exception being the relatively few companies that generate dollars in their normal operations, which tend to be large companies with good credit. In these cases, they face the competition of private international banks. The RDBs are at a disadvantage in such competition. Their credit analysis tends to be lengthy and cumbersome because, lending from afar, their knowledge of potential borrowers is scant and because their procedures tend to reflect their ultimately public sector nature. Besides, the additionality of the participation of the RDBs is questionable. In many cases, the role of these institutions is to provide comfort to large international private investors, who have access to other sources of funds but view having an RDB as a partner as reducing the risk of their investment. It can be argued that, to the extent that these investments would not take place without their participation, the RDBs' private sector subsidiaries play a useful role. However, it is clear that the market for them is very limited. Most of the domestic private sector in the customer countries is left out.

RDBs and their private sector subsidiaries have also lent to private commercial banks, which then on-lend the proceeds to private companies. These operations resolve the problem of lack of local knowledge that plagues direct lending from abroad. However, other problems conspire against these operations, particularly the already mentioned problem of foreign exchange risk, which reduces their market considerably. Overall, experience has shown that RDBs cannot become large providers of funds to the private sectors of developing countries.

Even so, the private sector subsidiaries of RDBs can continue to play a useful role, mainly through demonstration effects in innovative projects. Regional initiatives provide new opportunities for this kind of operation, particularly in cases of private international infrastructure projects, such as international electric power transmission lines, water pipelines, toll roads, and other transportation works. The presence of subsidiaries of the RDBs in these investments would provide a comfort where it is more sorely needed, rather than in cases of purely national undertakings.

One area in which these operations are badly needed is the development of credit to small enterprises and microenterprises, an area that corporate financial institutions are reluctant to enter because of the high costs and risks. As with the other operations involving the private sector, the RDBs should focus on transferring best practice while helping countries develop their own sources of financing.

Developing countries may also pool financial operations in certain sectors and gain by reducing their overall risk. One example of this is mortgage financing. Private or public financial institutions in countries with sensible monetary and financial policies can pool their mortgages and sell them in the United States or in international markets. RDBs can help in creating vehicles to carry out these operations. Their private sector subsidiaries could enhance these instruments with properly priced guarantees. Of course, these operations are more viable in countries with stable monetary and fiscal policies that make catastrophic devaluations unlikely. Otherwise, the costs of covering the foreign exchange risks would be prohibitive.

Countering the Procyclical Behavior of Private Financing

The volatility of international financing to developing countries has already been discussed in relation to the declines in lending that tend to take place after a serious crisis affects one of them. Declines may also result from global cyclical movements. The role that RDBs can play in this respect is quite modest. However, engaging in countercyclical lending activities would mean that RDBs would necessarily have to maintain excessive capital during the expansionary parts of the cycles to accumulate the financial resources needed to inject liquidity during the downturns. In fact, RDBs keep high levels of liquidity at all times, and there is no evidence that they have been unable to increase their lending during downturns for lack of financial resources. Rather, the availability of staff seems to be the binding constraint. To resolve this problem, RDBs would need to have idle personnel ready to take on the additional work when such situations arise, which would increase the overall cost of their lending. All of these problems should be studied in detail to determine whether RDBs could have lent more during contractions and, if so, to devise policies to deal with this problem. The approach to lending recommended in this chapter would provide an easy solution, as RDBs would be able to increase their share of cofinancing during times of global deceleration and also to reduce their share during times of global expansion.

Knowledge Exchange

The exchange of knowledge is one of the most important functions of development institutions, and it is one with long-lasting effects. This function has two dimensions: acquisition of knowledge and dissemination of knowledge. The staff of these institutions naturally acquires knowledge through their normal operations. However, such knowledge does not necessarily remain with, nor is it necessarily systematized by, the institution. For this to happen, institutions need two mechanisms (a small research unit and, very important, an independent system for evaluating operations) to identify both best practices and those practices that should not be repeated.

The need for research units at the RDBs may be questioned on the grounds that the World Bank already has a very good one. Other institutions could benefit from its output, which is publicized for free over the Internet. In fact, RDBs do benefit from such output. However, the research interests of the World Bank do not completely coincide with those of the RDBs: There are many subjects with which, although interesting to the RDBs, the World Bank (with its limited resources) does not deal. The World Bank provides large amounts of knowledge on issues of global importance, but not on issues that are important only, or primarily, to regions. In Latin America, for example, the IDB has been able to fill the gaps in the World Bank's research with high-quality research relevant to the region's problems.

Similar to the IDB, some of the other RDBs already have research units, but they need to develop systems to evaluate their operations. These are essential not just to control quality but also to learn what works and what does not. As mentioned before, some RDBs have proposed subcontracting these evaluations to third parties to ensure objectivity. Although this idea should be considered, an alternative might be to create, as at the World Bank, units within the RDBs to carry out these evaluations and ensure that a firewall exists between these units and the operational units. One way or the other, independent evaluation of operations is badly needed.

Conclusion

This chapter recommends that the RDBs create five new instruments or series of instruments in their core institutions:

- A series of instruments aimed at enhancing debt issued by their member countries should be created. The purpose of these instruments would be to ease the access of solvent governments of developing countries to private markets by eliminating the asymmetry of information that frequently prevents such access.

- Contingent lines of credit, to be contracted with countries in fully stable conditions and to be disbursed when those conditions deteriorate for reasons other than lack of fiscal or monetary discipline, should be formed. Countries contracting for such a line of credit would pay a commitment fee, calculated like an insurance premium. If funds are disbursed, the rate of interest would be substantially (by an amount that fully compensates for the increased risk to the institution but that is below the rates charged for emergency lending) higher than the normal rates charged by the institution.

- Emergency loans should be contracted in the midst of financial crises if and only if the country in question is putting in place a program, approved by the IMF, to resolve its problems. The approval and disbursement of each of these loans would require the approval of the IMF. Loans would have short maturities and high interest rates.

- Liquidity loans should be aimed at ameliorating the effects of contagion on financially healthy countries. These loans would have short maturities and interest rates that are below those of emergency loans but that are higher than those contracted under contingent arrangements.

- Loans specifically designed to finance the cash costs of revitalizing banks after a financial crisis should be produced. These loans would be different from those currently granted for this purpose in that they would be disbursed not against policy reforms but against actual transactions carried out to revamp the financial system. The loan amounts would be based on estimates of those costs.

Regarding lending policies, I recommend the following steps.

- A rating from a recognized credit rating agency should be required as a precondition for any lending operation to any country. Such ratings, which would have to be updated from time to time, would serve as a benchmark of the success of the RDBs in enabling their member countries to access private markets. Failure to obtain progress toward good ratings should be a major obstacle in getting further financing.

- Strict limits on the maximum exposure that any RDB can take with individual countries should be established and enforced, with an extra margin left for increasing the limit in case a major financial crisis should develop. A maximum period within which lending must return to precrisis levels should also be established.

- The RDB staff needed to manage the contingent and emergency loans should be funded with the proceeds of these operations exclusively, so that their appointment does not crowd out staff working on traditional projects.

- A schedule for graduation should be established for countries with an income level that should ensure their access to markets on their own. Graduation, however, should not be a one-step process. To entice countries to go to the market, RDBs should have a sliding schedule for the portion of financing that they would provide on projects not associated with social development, and should offer countries help in accessing the private markets for the difference. Without such a schedule, there would be no short-run incentive for countries to make the extra effort needed to integrate into the world's financial markets.

RDBs should also expand nonsovereign lending to the private sector, preferably through the subsidiaries dedicated to these operations, aiming at enhancing the access of private firms to private markets, and giving emphasis to the development of regional financial markets, the participation in the development of private infrastructure projects with a regional dimension, and the creation of markets for the financing of small enterprises and microenterprises.

RDBs should step up the evaluation of their operations and publish the results, except in those cases where sensitive information is involved. This, in addition to being an indispensable management tool, would help them to become knowledge centers.

These recommendations would help in solving the problems posed at the beginning of this chapter. Through the use of private rating agencies to evaluate countries' macroeconomic status and the mandatory cofinancing of their needs, these recommendations would help generate a harmonious integration of the developing countries into the international financial markets—which should be the long-term objective of the new global financial architecture. The use of private ratings would also allow for an objective differentiation between countries, taking into account their dissimilarities.

These recommendations would also require relatively minor changes in the way RDBs operate. The idea that RDBs should cooperate with the IMF in the solution of financial crises may elicit strong opposition. Yet there is no way in which they can be separated from the reality of their customer countries, and there are many aspects of financial crises that only the development banks can address. It is also better to address these aspects through coordination between the World Bank with the RDBs than by the World Bank in isolation, because of the externalities of financial operations. Coordination between these parties is not just desirable but also indispensable, because both the World Bank and the RDBs are large-scale lenders to developing countries.

Some of the recommendations, however, refer to the provision of liquidity loans, which RDBs have provided in the past, even though they are different from their long-term, project-oriented operations. My recommendations in this respect are contingent on what the international community decides to do with the IMF. If the community decides to fund the IMF with resources sufficient to face several financial crises simultaneously, the participation of the RDBs is not needed. Otherwise, however, the RDBs will end up participating anyway, even if doing so is inconsistent with their purpose. When the neighborhood is in flames, the firefighters must get water anywhere they can. Thus, it would be better to prepare the RDBs to play this role in a more efficient way than to pretend that they would be able to resist the pressure of the international community to help resolve an urgent crisis.

References

Fischer, Stanley. 2001. Reducing Vulnerabilities: The Role of the Contingent Credit Line. Remarks to the Latin American Central Bank and Finance Ministry Network at the Inter-American Development Bank (April 25).

IMF (International Monetary Fund). 2001. How Does the IMF Lend? A Factsheet. www.imf.org/external/np/exr/facts/howlend.htm (accessed January 2001).

Comment

ROBERTO ZAHLER

The chapter by Manuel Hinds is an important contribution to a very relevant topic in the current discussion of the new international financial architecture. The chapter is well and clearly organized in three sections. The first section assesses the problems that the new architecture is intended to solve and proposes a role for the regional development banks (RDBs) in that solution. The second proposes instruments and policies that the RDBs can use to play this role. The third summarizes the proposal and raises some issues for discussion. My comments relate to those issues about which I believe Hinds's analysis and proposals could be improved. Where I have no comments, it is because I agree with the bulk of the author's analysis and recommendations.

Hinds mentions two main problems with the functioning of world financial markets in relation to developing countries. One is the instability of developing countries, and the other is their lack, or volatility, of their access to international financial markets. He also attempts to identify the roles that RDBs can play in solving these two problems. This section, however, fails to mention some crucial problems related to the working of the international financial economy that have a direct effect on the stability of emerging market economies or on their access to international financial markets, and where RDBs could, and probably should, play an important role.

First, there is no mention of the supervision and regulation of financial markets at the international level, which is far from perfect. In particular,

Roberto Zahler is the president of Zahler and Co. and the former president of the Central Bank of Chile.

the more favorable treatment of capital requirements for short-term interbank lending, as provided in the current Basel Capital Accord,[1] adversely affects the stability of banking flows to developing countries by hampering their governments' efforts to extend the maturity structure of their foreign liabilities. Although it can be argued that the preferential treatment given to short-term interbank lending aims to strengthen banks in industrial countries, nonetheless, it has clear adverse systemic consequences, as it exacerbates the fragility of emerging markets by encouraging them to increase their short-term indebtedness.[2]

Second, although booms and busts are endemic to all financial markets, recent experience indicates that short-term financial international swings need to be brought under some kind of control. This is especially important if the main participants in the new financial architecture, which include the RDBs, are to concentrate their efforts more on crisis prevention than on crisis management. An important common feature of many of the crises we have witnessed in emerging market economies, in particular the Mexican, East Asian, Turkish, and to a certain extent, current Argentinean crises, is that the crisis originated from excessive short-term capital inflows to and from the private sector. Experience shows that, if the capital inflow booms that precede these crises can be moderated, the subsequent busts can to a certain extent be prevented. Here RDBs could play an important role by helping to place an appropriate value on the social costs and risks of short-term international lending to emerging market economies.

Hinds also fails to mention that, in many cases, instability in emerging market economies is related not to inappropriate trade policy but to inappropriate (either too sudden or wrongly sequenced) opening of the capital account of the balance of payments. In other words, in many of the recent crises the problems originated in the capital account rather than the current account (through excessive protectionism). The chapter concentrates only on the latter, as if it were the unique source of instability. In other cases, ill-conceived domestic financial reform (e.g., interest rate liberalization without proper regulation or supervision) has been the main cause of instability, rather than issues related to trade liberalization.

In addition to these general comments on the first section of Hinds's article, I have a couple of specific complaints. Hinds says that, "the in-

---

1. This favorable treatment would be augmented if the proposed revisions to the Basel accord are implemented as proposed. Furthermore, in the proposed accord, internationally active banks and large banks can choose either to use ratings provided by external agencies or their own internal rating systems as a basis for classifying the credit risk of a particular loan and for calculating the regulatory capital requirement. Adoption of either approach in industrial countries could exacerbate the already high volatility of capital flows to emerging markets (see Latin American Shadow Financial Regulatory Committee 2001).

2. The editors note that this issue is discussed in the accompanying essay of Rojas-Suarez.

dustrial sectors of developing countries operate behind high rates of protection." In many developing countries, however, this is no longer true. Nor does Hinds mention the fact that, even as many developing countries have opened their economies, liberalized, and privatized, protectionism remains quite prevalent in some industrial countries. Indeed, this is what lies behind the "declining commodity export revenue" that Hinds notes, even more than the deterioration of terms of trade.

Turning to the discussion of developing countries' lack of access to financial markets, I agree with Hinds's logic in saying that, if countries have insufficient or fragile access to foreign saving, investment opportunities cannot be realized. However, I would also mention the need for these countries to implement policies oriented toward increasing domestic saving, and especially long-term domestic saving. Here Latin America has some interesting lessons to convey from its recent experience. On the one hand, Latin America's experience shows the catalytic role that fiscal surpluses can play with regard to private saving; on the other hand, it also shows the potential contribution of social security reform to the development of bond and equity markets, which constitute the domestic basis for long-term sources of investment financing. RDBs are especially well equipped to transfer knowledge and experience in these two areas to countries in their regions.

Again I have a few comments on specific points made in this section. Hinds says that lack of access to the international markets is "the other fundamental problem of developing countries." This is a very strong statement and, as I have mentioned elsewhere, under certain and not so uncommon circumstances, it is precisely excessive access to international financial flows that has created or at least facilitated crises, even in emerging market economies that have sound macroeconomic policies.

Hinds goes on to say that "these problems not only block . . . access to global financial markets but also . . . retard the development of regional financial markets, which are practically nonexistent in those countries." This is an area in which it would be difficult to find institutions better suited than the RDBs to devoting resources and efforts to promote financial regional integration (more on this topic follows). In fact, there have been a number of interesting experiences involving regional and subregional institutions in the developing world. Examples include the agreement reached by the Association of South East Nations (ASEAN) countries, China, the Republic of Korea, and Japan to establish swap arrangements among their central banks; the ASEAN's pilot macroeconomic surveillance and monitoring schemes; the Arab Monetary Fund's provision of liquidity for intraregional trade; the Latin American Reserve Fund, which complements the International Monetary Fund (IMF) in providing liquidity financing during crises; the operations of subregional development banks such as the Andean Development Corporation; and the Arab Investment Guarantee Fund.

These experiences indicate that regional bodies can be effective in providing liquidity, sustaining trade links, and facilitating access to international financial resources through risk pooling. They can also contribute to macroeconomic policy coordination and to the adaptation of regulatory systems to regional conditions. The sense of ownership that they inspire contributes to efforts aimed at adapting stringent rules, promoting full disclosure, and undertaking joint monitoring and surveillance of regional financial markets, as well as encouraging regional arrangements for monetary, financial, and fiscal coordination to support sound macroeconomic policies. Regional and subregional institutions should actively be promoted and recognized as central players in the international financial architecture.

In particular, regional reserve funds and swap arrangements can contribute to crisis prevention and resolution, thanks to their ability to provide international liquidity. In addition, as Hinds mentions, RDBs as well as subregional development banks can complement multilateral financing by providing and facilitating access to financial resources that support activities that yield high social returns but that the private sector is not prepared to finance. They can also play a countercyclical role in providing access to financial resources at times when international private capital becomes scarce. Experiences in this area are highly specific to each region but may serve as a basis for productive interregional exchange of best practices.

In Hinds's discussion of the competitive advantage of RDBs, I suggest mentioning explicitly a very crucial event "rooted in the nonfinancial parts of the economy." This is the need for so-called second-generation reforms to improve the judiciary system, establish well-defined property rights, introduce sound bankruptcy laws, promote transparency, avoid conflicts of interest, provide appropriate corporate governance, protect minority shareholders' rights, and so on. These issues are becoming a major source of concern not only to domestic savers but also to potential suppliers of foreign savings. Again, this is an area in which RDBs could play a very significant role.

In the same discussion, Hinds mentions that "all the multilateral institutions have experimented with many ideas for resolving [these problems], . . . most of which have proved useful," but no example is given. In fact, the contingent credit lines established by the IMF for coping with liquidity problems have not yielded the expected results, probably because it takes a considerable amount of time for countries to qualify for this facility, and partly because of the possible loss of confidence or stigmatization that may be associated with its use.[3] Furthermore, only recently has the IMF declared an interest in private sector participation in

---

3. The editors note that this facility was, in fact, abandoned in late 2003.

crisis management by suggesting the implementation of an international equivalent to US Chapter 11 bankruptcy proceedings. Such an arrangement could help toward an orderly workout of debt crises in emerging market economies by mandating creditor coordination and a payments standstill.

In the section that outlines Hinds's proposals for an enhanced role for the RDBs in improving the international architecture, although he states that one of the main objectives of the RDBs would be to "bring their member countries to the international financial markets in a sustainable fashion," no suggestion is made regarding the potential role of the RDBs in improving the working of the international financial markets in this regard.[4] Hinds also states that "the RDBs . . . should work to reduce their own participation in the financing of developing countries . . . bringing their members to a more plentiful and more sustainable source of financing for their development needs." No mention is made here of the very well known procyclicality of private sources of finance, however, or of the need for the multilateral banks to play a countercyclical role when private financing is scarce. It is not clear, in my opinion, that overall financing by the RDBs should be reduced as a way to ensure that developing countries integrate more aggressively and in a stable fashion with international financial markets.

Later in the same section, Hinds says, "RDB's lending policies should be geared to two main objectives: developing the domestic financial markets of their member countries, and bringing them to global markets, thus reducing their dependence on the development financial institutions. The design of the operations and their conditionality should be framed within this principle." For reasons I gave in the previous paragraph, I consider that such a conclusion requires more grounding.

Hinds comments that the RDBs should work closely with the World Trade Organization (WTO) as part of their effort to bring developing countries to international financial markets. However, the need for such cooperation relates mainly to trade liberalization and, in my view, only in a very roundabout way to access to international financial markets. I would emphasize that, on this topic, RDBs should also work with the WTO on improving the openness of industrial-country markets to developing-country exports.

In the same paragraph, Hinds calls on the RDBs to "work to improve the quality of their customers' macroeconomic management . . . to make the debt instruments of developing countries attractive in international financial markets and to allow for the development of a sound domestic

---

4. For a recent view regarding international action required to ensure stable and sustainable access for emerging market economies to world financial markets, see *Rebuilding the International Financial Architecture*, Emerging Market Economies Eminent Persons Group, Seoul Report, October 2001.

financial system." Regarding the reasons why "true policy reform to ensure stability has not been achieved," there is no mention of mistakes made by the international financial institutions themselves in their approach to proper macroeconomic management in many countries, such as Mexico in 1994, Thailand in 1997, Turkey in 1999 and 2000, and most recently in Argentina. Some mention could be made of the need for a less narrowly ideological perspective on the part of these institutions; for example, acknowledging that corner solution exchange rate policies are not necessarily the best solution; that the current account matters, even when the fiscal sector is in equilibrium or in surplus; that capital account liberalization does not need to be implemented in an abrupt way; and so on. Often the international financial institutions have not appropriately assessed these crucial components when designing stabilization and adjustment programs, and this has been an important cause of major macroeconomic and banking crises in developing countries.

Furthermore, I have serious doubts regarding Hinds's proposed solution "to give more weight in the development banks' lending decisions to the credit ratings of the professional rating companies . . . [which] provide a quantitative assessment of the well-informed perceptions of the market." For one thing, the track record of most rating agencies has been quite mediocre. In addition, adopting such a process of qualifying countries' sovereign risk is likely to create significant demand for new and frequent ratings by governments, because they will have a strong incentive to obtain a favorable rating to lower the interest rates they pay and extend the maturity of their international loans. The existing rating agencies will probably be unable to satisfy this new demand for ratings, and although good new agencies will enter the market intending to provide fair assessments and build up countries' reputations, bad ones will enter as well, with the purpose of maximizing short-term profits through the provision of relatively favorable ratings. In these circumstances, the rating agencies, which best serve their purpose when ratings are investor-driven, not when their services are demanded by borrowers (including governments) seeking finance, will probably not contribute to market discipline in the forceful way that the chapter indicates they will.

Hinds's point regarding the need to improve coordination among supervisors of financial institutions is worth developing further because this is an area in which very little has been done. Increasing regional and subregional cooperation among supervisors and regulators would be very useful not only in relation to the stock exchange but also in relation to banks and pension funds. Improved cooperation among supervisors and regulators should become increasingly important as a way of promoting labor mobility within regions and subregions.

Turning to Hinds's discussion of the prevention and management of financial crises, it is not clear to me why it is better for RDBs to use their resources to complement the IMF in dealing with liquidity issues rather than to work more closely with the IMF in designing more effective crisis prevention instruments. RDBs could play a more active role in monitoring developments in international financial markets; for example, by designing vulnerability indicators or early warning systems, monitoring domestic macroeconomic policies, and as the chapter mentions, developing programs aimed at strengthening domestic financial sectors. RDBs could also help the IMF in designing debt workouts. These should be seen not as a substitute for emergency financing but, rather, as a complement to it, and one that would play an essential role in managing liquidity issues. Although such workouts do not eliminate the need for adequate provision of liquidity during crises, which has tended to increase given the increased severity of global financial instability, they could help substantially with this concern. Furthermore, before using the RDBs' resources, consideration could be given to the temporary issue of special drawing rights, which could become the major source of funds for IMF emergency financing.

A final, specific comment on this section is that I do not think it is convenient to say that funds being provided to recapitalize or liquidate financial institutions require that this be done without imposing losses on depositors.

Hinds offers some suggestions for complementing and improving the IMF's recently established contingent credit lines. However, this would require (for reasons I noted in my discussion of these credit lines above) using the RDBs' resources for purposes not directly related to their specific task. As already mentioned, in my opinion it would be preferable if the RDBs could devote their efforts and research primarily to helping improve the working of the international financial system. Finally, it is my impression that what Hinds proposes would require a high and difficult degree of coordination between the RDBs and the IMF. This coordination would become even more burdensome if, as seems highly probable, the World Bank would also need to become involved in these operations.

References

Latin American Shadow Financial Regulatory Committee. 2001. *The New Basel Capital Accord and Financial Stability in Latin America.* Statement No. 2 (April). Caracas: Latin American Shadow Financial Regulatory Committee.

Comment

GUILLERMO CALVO

This is certainly a very challenging topic. There are so many things that we want to do—the question is how to accomplish them as a bank. Thus, I will follow the economic tradition of being very narrow in my scope, leaving out many important issues, and concentrating on regional development banks (RDBs) as banks.

Why do we need RDBs? First, the big challenge, of which everyone is aware, is the enormous gap between developing and industrial countries that we have been trying to close for many years. We are concerned about the security implications of this gap, not to mention the miserable human conditions that it implies. I think there is a general feeling that we have not been successful, because the gap remains very large and hard to explain. If you go to the heart of those differences and approach them as an economist, however, you will certainly start to think about public goods, including regulatory reform and basic education.

Why does anyone need a bank? That is easy—because loans are needed. Why do you need a public bank? That is a harder question to answer. Before I address it, let me refer to the problem of instability of capital flows. At the Inter-American Development Bank (IDB), we believe that aside from institutional reform, developing countries need finance—they need capital. Once the conditions have been established to ensure that this capital is used in an efficient way, it will flow to those countries.

Guillermo Calvo is the chief economist at and manager of the research department of the Inter-American Development Bank.

Unfortunately, the 1990s, which started out as a very promising decade, did not turn out as we expected. As of the beginning of the 21st century we see problems ahead. Argentina is one of the latest problems, and it is a very difficult one, but I do not think it will be the last one. So we have to ask ourselves: If we want to be effective, what is missing? Why have things not worked out as we expected? What happened has to do more with moral hazard than with moral failure. What we have is a market failure problem. Economists know how to address market failure, but there are issues having to do with sounder macroeconomic policy, more adequate banking systems for developing countries, regional agreements, and so on, which are issues that may require finance—or they may not—but they certainly require knowledge.

These are other aspects closely interlinked in these banks: finance and knowledge. You can make a bigger difference with knowledge—you can identify and disseminate best practices or do policy-oriented research—than with money. However, the size of the multilateral development banks is very small, and therefore money cannot be the essential ingredient of these systems.

From the narrow perspective of an economist, one justification for international financial institutions is that they help overcome what one might call the sovereignty problem. Lending to sovereigns is not the same as lending to individuals: One country is not subject to another's legislation, a sovereign's goods cannot easily be attached, and so on. Lending to sovereigns requires an international community that will put enough pressure on sovereign borrowers to induce them to repay their loans. Otherwise, however honest a country's policymakers may be, they represent other people: They are accountable to those people, and they have to deliver.

These issues are brought up in policy discussions in every borrowing country every day, and the opposition always questions the wisdom of repaying loans. Obviously, Argentina has been forced into default, but when you look around Latin America, you see some very important politicians also questioning whether their countries' debt should be paid in full. That debate is always going to be there—the only way to deal with it, in the absence of international courts, is to exert peer pressure.

Because the international financial institutions are very small relative to the need and the markets, these institutions have to be very selective in what they do. The question thus becomes, as mentioned before, money versus knowledge. I doubt that we intended, when we created these institutions, that they would come to be thought of not so much as money banks but as knowledge banks; but that is what they have become and that is how they operate day in and day out. The academic community does not provide policy-oriented knowledge because the motivations in academia are very different. Policy-oriented research is not done in a systematic and serious way in most academic institutions. Of course, there are institutions that contribute to providing that knowledge, but in the case of the international financial institutions, I think the fact that they lend as well as preach gives some greater credibility to their preaching.

If, then, there is a role for these institutions in general, the question becomes, what is the role of the RDBs specifically? Why have them at all? Why not just have the World Bank? That is not an easy question to answer, because if one thinks of these institutions as cooperatives, there is merit in having the cooperative be as large as possible to spread the risk. Why concentrate efforts in Latin America instead of spreading them around the world? From that perspective, admittedly, the World Bank would seem to dominate.

I think the comparative advantage of the RDBs has to do more with culture than with economics, taking into account the fact that they involve countries that are closely connected culturally and geographically. I am delighted that one of the issues that has been discussed here is the issue of regional trade integration. This is an area in which the RDBs have a definite advantage, because we are at the beginning of the integration process, which, especially in Latin America, has been tried before and failed. This time we want to do it the right way and that requires much more global thinking, but at the regional level. In that sense, I can see the banks, including the IDB, playing an important role.

Of course, money is needed. Money will have to be channeled to sovereigns. However, now you are dealing not only with one sovereign but with several sovereigns at the same time. Thus, having a fluid relationship with one's region helps a lot.

To summarize, from a purely economic point of view, the need for international financial institutions has not yet disappeared. It has changed in many ways, because the world has changed, but as long as the borrowers are sovereign countries, it will be difficult to have a free market, no matter how highly one values the free, unfettered, private sector markets. It is difficult to think of a situation in which such a market by itself will be able to provide all the financial services that are necessary, because of the sovereignty problem.

In that context, I see the RDBs as playing a key role, especially in connection with issues of regional trade integration. In whatever activity the bank operates, the dissemination of knowledge and the creation of basic, policy-oriented knowledge is something that these banks can provide —and can provide effectively.

Comment

ALLAN MELTZER

I have many points of agreement with Manuel Hinds's background chapter, and a few differences. I regret Hinds's tendency to use the phrase "developing countries" as if it were a collective term, implying that one size fits all. This usage becomes particularly difficult when opportunities to borrow are discussed. Implicitly, Hinds and many others treat China, which can borrow very large sums at interest rates not much above those charged by the development banks, as on par with Zimbabwe or Kenya. The problem with this approach is that it neglects the reasons why some countries can borrow and others cannot. Despite the growing problems in Argentina in recent months, we have seen Peru come to the capital market, for the first time in living memory, and borrow for 10 years at 9 percent annual interest. Of course, within Latin America alone there are countries as different as Brazil, Chile, and Mexico, all of which have access to the capital market on quite reasonable terms.

Indeed, I see in Argentina's case the recurrence under different circumstances of a problem that has emerged several times in the last 25 years. Some countries that were able to borrow a great deal borrowed more than they could service or repay. Argentina's debt in 2000 and 2001 was unsustainable. So was that of Mexico in 1982, and that of Russia in 1998. Many other developing countries have faced the same problem: too much spending and too much borrowing. I believe we can get some idea about future capital flows if we pause to consider why lenders have

Allan Meltzer, former member of the president's Council of Economic Advisers, is a professor of political economy and public policy at Carnegie Mellon University.

been willing to lend so much to countries that eventually had to default and restructure their loans. Nobody likes lost decades, and so it is crucial to be concerned about the excessive lending and borrowing that lead to lost decades.

Why do lenders overlend? My answer is that they do it because they believe they will be bailed out, when and if a crisis comes, by the international financial institutions—especially the International Monetary Fund (IMF). As Adam Lerrick says, when creditors are asked to restructure voluntarily, they end up with more, not less. No one voluntarily takes a loss that they can avoid. Until recently, most restructurings have been voluntary. The restructuring extends the maturity of the debt, and creditors receive better terms and fees.

In the last few years, however, something has changed. Starting with Ecuador, and most recently in Argentina, countries have defaulted on their sovereign debt. In Argentina, new issues offered in July 2001 for $85 sold in November for $25 or $30, inflicting almost Enron-size losses on creditors. A reasonable guess at the time of this writing is that if the IMF continues to insist that Argentina restructure its debt before it lends any additional money, creditors will receive no more than 25 to 30 percent of the face value of their bonds.

I do not believe we can ignore this default or the defaults that preceded it when thinking about the future of international lending to developing countries. Nor should we ignore the experience itself. One remarkable fact about Argentina is that responsible observers like Charles Calomiris and Adam Lerrick predicted publicly, months before the event, that Argentina would have to default. These predictions became public in the winter of 2000–01, but despite these very public warnings, Argentina was able to sell debt at $85 as late as June 2001.

Two significant changes occurred between June and September and October 2001 that will have implications for the future. One we need not pursue today: It became clear as the summer progressed that the de la Rua government and Finance Minister Domingo Cavallo had no plan or program for restoring growth or repaying the debt. The government made promises about the budget that soon were seen to be empty. The sight of increasingly desperate ministers thrashing around was not an attractive one to Argentina's creditors.

The second big change came in August and the following months. Instead of the $30 billion to $40 billion in new loans that some at the IMF wanted to make, Argentina got only $5 billion, with an additional $3 billion earmarked for debt restructuring. This amount was too small to be useful, unfortunately. Soon thereafter, the new officials at the IMF and the US Treasury made it clear that there would be no more money until Argentina met its past commitments. These included a promise to balance the budget month by month. Default now appeared not just likely but inevitable. The days of large bailouts were not over for countries like Turkey with important systemic risks, but they were over for many countries. Creditors who had benefited from moral hazard lending now had to be more careful. The risk premiums on some emerging market debt no longer offered a windfall.

One implication is that if the IMF keeps to its new policy, creditors will be more careful about the amounts they lend and the countries to which they lend. The entire history of postwar lending to emerging market countries, particularly the last 20 years, occurred under the old rules. The new rules, if they stay in place, call for greater prudence.

What can borrowers do? They can—indeed they must—become more prudent. The report of the International Financial Institutions Advisory Commission proposed four conditions for automatic lending by the IMF to countries in difficulty. Those four conditions, perhaps supplemented by one or two others, define a prudent macroeconomic policy with diversification of risk. In Brazil, and even in Argentina, we have seen that one of these conditions—the presence of competing foreign banks—greatly increases financial stability. The largest source of capital for developing countries is private lending. Such lending dwarfs any current or prospective lending from any international financial institution—or even all of them together. If the IMF persists in its new policy, borrowers will have to show evidence that their policies are and will remain prudent.

To be lasting and effective, the adoption of prudent policy must be voluntary. The minister must go to parliament with a message that says, in effect, "We must adopt these policies because it is in our interest. We will get more capital on better terms to build our country and raise our living standards. We are not making these changes because the IMF or the Inter-American Development Bank (IDB) or the World Bank insist on it. We make them because they are in our interest."

An important role for the multilateral development banks is that of helping countries that want to attract long-term capital in the form of foreign direct investment and to attract foreign banks and participants in this market. These multilateral development banks should lend in order to permit countries to make necessary structural reforms. This means instituting the rule of law, reforming the judiciary, and establishing transparent accounting and financial practices. It means adopting financial standards, opening the economy to trade, and securing property rights. The experience of Chile and Mexico is evidence that, when these reforms are in place, countries acquire more capital at lower cost.

What is the more general role of the IMF and the multilateral development banks, and what is the particular role of the regional banks? Our commission's report saw the core competence of the IMF as the prevention and mitigation of crises and the collection and dissemination of information on developing countries. If the IMF could free itself of the bureaucratic embellishments that it puts on its contingent lines of credit and condition its commitment only on keeping prudent policies in place, it would take a large step toward a more rational financial and institutional structure. Countries would have an incentive to make structural reforms that are for their own benefit.

As for the development banks, like Jurgen Stark, I believe in specialization. The development banks should not be involved in crisis lending. Our commission proposed three major roles for the development banks. The first is to improve the quality of life in very poor countries by making grants instead of loans, monitoring the outcomes, and paying for performance. To their great credit, Treasury Secretary Paul O'Neill and the Bush administration have proposed adopting this policy, and President Bush endorsed it directly in his speech to the World Bank. Second, the development banks should lend for structural reform by making long-term commitments to continue lending for many years, provided the borrowing country continues to strengthen and extend its reforms. This proposal recognizes that reforms take time, and unlike much current structural lending, it does not confuse promise with performance. Third, the development banks should lend to support the creation of regional and global public goods. There is considerable overlap among the World Bank, the regional development banks, and the IMF. I believe that if the development banks became more effective institutions and achieved greater success in their programs, the IMF would—and should—relinquish its role in structural reform and poverty alleviation.

How should we separate the tasks of the World Bank and the regional banks? Manuel Hinds takes the position that competition between them is useful. This might be true if they actually competed, and if there were some metric by which we could compare their performances. Where Hinds sees competition, however, I see overlap and duplication. To move forward, we need to learn about the comparative advantage of the different lenders. The World Bank is generally acknowledged to have greater technical expertise than the regional development banks, over a wide range of topics. This expertise should be available as a common pool for all development banks to draw on: There is no need to duplicate it.

To learn more about what the multilateral development banks do well, I have proposed independent performance audits of the major ones. Let us learn what they do well and what they do poorly, what they should continue to do and what they should stop doing. Most of the banks do not evaluate many of their projects five or ten years after their completion, and so we have a very poor record of their accomplishments and failures. An independent performance audit is overdue.

One of the striking features of lending by the multilateral development banks is that most of it goes to countries that can borrow in the capital markets. This is as true of the IDB as it is of the World Bank. In many of these countries, the banks provide little or nothing beyond the subsidy, and there is very little, if any, addi-tionality: This money should be redirected. Our commission proposed concentrating the World Bank's lending mainly in Africa and the Middle East. It might supply technical assistance in other regions, but responsibility for lending to those regions would remain with the Asian Development Bank and the IDB. I continue to believe that this move would reduce costly duplication.

In summary, I would emphasize the need to shift to more effective policies of grants and lending. The emphasis should not be on how much is lent, but on what is being accomplished. We can wave plastic cards with the numbers of people living on less than $1 a day until eternity. We will not reduce that number until we have more effective policies. We should start with performance audits and continue with policies that reward incentives. Loans do not raise living standards unless they raise productivity, and incentives at all levels are required to raise productivity.

I dislike the word architecture, as it suggests a structure that lasts a long time. Development, however, is a process that changes as countries evolve. The key word is not architecture, but incentives.

Comment

JURGEN STARK

Neither a rebuilt nor a totally new international financial architecture is needed. By no means are all of the parts of the global financial system broken, nor has the system become obsolete. What is needed, as other collaborators in this book have already said, is a stronger and better-functioning financial system at all levels: global, regional, and national.

What has been achieved thus far in strengthening the global financial system? There has been particular progress in crisis prevention: Financial systems have been made less vulnerable through enhanced International Monetary Fund (IMF) surveillance and through improved transparency and disclosure within the setting of internationally accepted standards and codes. There have also been attempts to streamline the IMF's conditionality.

Less progress has been made in the area of crisis resolution, and we must be aware that even if the international financial system has been made safer, crises will continue to happen. Within this broader topic, one major and crucial issue still remains unresolved; namely, how to involve the private sector. This issue should be addressed in the context of the access limits to IMF resources.

What should be the roles of the different international financial institutions, including the regional development banks? And what should be the principles for their design and operation? I will begin by noting that many of the tasks of these organizations can hardly be taken over by other organizations, whether private or national. If these tasks are to be completed, it is international institutions that will do so. However, to be effective and to realize the benefits of specialization and the division of labor, each international financial institution must have a clear mandate

Jurgen Stark is the deputy director of Deutsche Bundesbank (Germany's central bank).

and clear-cut responsibilities. Overlapping mandates and activities tend to duplicate effort, waste resources, and blur responsibilities. It is obvious to me that, in the past, the IMF and the development banks either have sought on their own, or have been driven by their shareholders, to do too much. Some institutions went beyond their mandates and ended up competing with each other. Within these clear mandates, each organization should develop appropriate procedures for cooperation and make their work consistent and efficient. Finally, because official international organizations are public institutions, receiving and managing taxpayers' money (or central banks' money in the case of the IMF), their work must be transparent, accountable, and efficient if they are to be responsible to their official shareholders.

What is the role of the development banks? What should they do or not do? In my view, they should not be involved in crisis lending or crisis management, and they should refrain from publicly second-guessing the IMF's work in that area. In the crises of the 1990s, the IMF, the World Bank, and the regional development banks often pooled their funds in an attempt to resolve the crisis, but their decision to do this had little or nothing to do with the size of the crisis; it had only to do with the political approach on how to resolve the crisis.

It follows that I am not in favor of the new instruments for which Manuel Hinds called in his chapter, which would allow the regional development banks to convey financial support in time of financial crisis. These instruments would have features similar to the IMF's existing instruments. My plea is, rather, for establishing both clear-cut responsibilities for each of the international financial institutions and closer cooperation among them. Let the World Bank and the regional development banks focus on development and the IMF focus on macroeconomics and crisis management.

What should be the specific role of the regional development banks in providing development finance? Because each of the regional banks has specific knowledge about its region, in addition to financial and technical expertise, I believe they should play a more prominent role in providing technical assistance and advice in their regions; in particular, with respect to structural reform. They should work to develop regionally tailored solutions and intraregional coordination and cooperation; for instance, in the integration of regional financial markets. To reduce the vulnerabilities of their member countries, the regional banks should provide technical assistance in establishing sound financial systems and effective financial supervision. They should give advice on how to implement standards and codes in the financial sector, and on how to liberalize trade regimes and capital accounts.

Whatever the immediate source of development finance, public or private, ultimately it is funded out of the pool of world savings. On the public side of the World Bank and the regional development banks, such international or regional saving-investment channels are highly subsidized. Even here, the effectiveness and efficiency of these channels have reasonably been questioned because the real investment objectives of development lending have, in general, not been achieved—not despite their subsidization, but because of it. More often then not, the World Bank's client countries have found themselves with increased levels or subsidized external debt at an unchanged capacity of debt repayment. What we have all learned the hard way is that economic causality does not run from subsidized debt to increased economic capacity but, rather, the other way around: from increased economic capacity, including more effective, better mobilized domestic saving, to higher sustainable levels of external debt. Reasonable proposals to replace unrealistic World Bank loans with grants seek to acknowledge this experience.

The right kind of response to this experience is, therefore, to undertake a more determined and more ambitious effort to build domestic capital markets within the developing countries themselves. This is by no means an inward-looking or isolationist solution. To the contrary, broader opening of domestic capital markets would greatly improve developing countries' integration into truly global capital markets. They would also strongly stimulate intraregional capital flows, both within low-saving regions like Latin America and within high-saving regions like southeast Asia.

In my view, this approach has considerable potential for another reason; namely, that these countries' debt instruments share, broadly speaking, similar risks and rating properties. It is here is where I see the regional development banks playing an important strategic role. Each of them possesses, within its region, some natural competitive advantage over the World Bank, or at least over World Bank headquarters. Their credit officers are closer to the local investment projects being proposed. The regional banks are also constrained to deliver a solvent balance sheet at the regional level; they cannot cross-subsidize regions, as inevitably happens at the level of the World Bank. These features of regional development banks could greatly improve the overall efficiency of capital allocation.

Even more important, the regional banks could also play a catalytic role in the development of local and regional capital markets through a variety of funding instruments. They could issue instruments in local currency by assuming and pooling currency risks or by creating hedging instruments, thereby deepening markets in local currency-dominated instruments and providing necessary benchmarks. They could also help to extend the maturities of bonds denominated in local currency by assuming and pooling maturity risk. Finally, they could raise foreign exchange on global markets at market terms, which would likely be better than what individual borrowing countries could receive on their own. In all these ways, over the medium term to the long term, the regional development banks could more generally stimulate regional financial integration among emerging markets.

About the Contributors

Gun-Britt Andersson has been the ambassador and permanent representative of Sweden to the Organization for Economic Cooperation and Development (OECD) and the United Nations Educational, Scientific, and Cultural Organization (UNESCO) since June 2003. She was the head of the Swedish International Development Cooperation Agency's office in Tanzania and later, as director of the personnel division of the agency, was responsible for its reorganization. She was assistant undersecretary in the Ministry of Foreign Affairs, where she was in charge of policy planning and budgeting of the department for international development cooperation. After working as director of the United Nations Relief and Works Agency for Palestine Refugees, she became state secretary for social security and then state secretary for development cooperation, migration, and asylum policy, a post she held until her appointment at the OECD.

Eduardo Aninat, former finance minister of Chile (March 1994–December 1999), was deputy managing director of the International Monetary Fund (IMF) from December 1999 to June 2003. He taught public finance and economic development at the Pontificia Universidad Católica de Chile and was an assistant professor of economics at Boston University. He was the chairman of the Board of Governors of the IMF and World Bank (1995–96) and served for three years as a member of the Development Committee of the World Bank and the IMF, representing Chile, Argentina, Bolivia, Peru, Uruguay, and Paraguay. He was also a member of the board of directors of ACCION International and the Institute of the Americas and was the president of the Social Equity Forum organized under the sponsorship of the Inter-American Development Bank. He is a contributing editor to the Institute of the Americas official magazine.

C. Fred Bergsten has been director of the Institute for International Economics since its creation in 1981. He is co-chairman of the Shadow G-8, which advises the G-8 countries on their annual summit meetings. He was assistant secretary for international affairs of the US Treasury (1977–81); assistant for international economic affairs to the National Security Council (1969–71); and a senior fellow at the Brookings Institution (1972–76), the Carnegie Endowment for International Peace (1981), and the Council on Foreign Relations (1967–68). He is the author, coauthor, or editor of a wide range of international economic issues, including *Dollar Overvaluation and the World Economy* (2003), *No More Bashing: Building a New Japan–United States Economic Relationship* (2001), *Global Economic Leadership and the Group of Seven* (1996), *The Dilemmas of the Dollar* (2d ed, 1996), and *America in the World Economy: A Strategy for the 1990s* (1988).

Nancy Birdsall is the founding president of the Center for Global Development. Before launching the center in 2001, she served for three years as senior associate and director of the Economic Reform Project at the Carnegie Endowment for International Peace. From 1993 to 1998, she was executive vice president of the Inter-American Development Bank. She spent 14 years at the World Bank, including as director of the Policy Research Department. Among her books is *Delivering on Debt Relief: From IMF Gold to a New Aid Architecture* (Washington: Center for Global Development and Institute for International Economics, 2002, with John Williamson).

Willem Buiter has been the chief economist of the European Bank for Reconstruction and Development in London since 2000. He has held academic appointments at Princeton University, University of Bristol, London School of Economics, Yale University, and University of Cambridge. In 1997, he was appointed to a three-year term as member of the Monetary Policy Committee of the Bank of England. He has been an adviser and consultant to the IMF, the World Bank, the Inter-American Development Bank, and a number of national governments and government agencies. He has published widely on subjects of open economy macroeconomics, monetary and exchange rate theory, fiscal policy, social security, economic development, and transition economies.

Charles Calomiris is the Paul M. Montrone Professor of Finance and Economics at Columbia Business School and a professor at Columbia's School of International and Public Affairs. He also codirects the Project on Financial Deregulation at the American Enterprise Institute, where he the Arthur Burns Scholar in International Economics. He served on the International Financial Institution Advisory Commission, a congressional commission to advise the US government on the reform of the IMF, the World Bank, the regional development banks, and the World Trade Organization (WTO). Some of his recent publications include *US Bank Deregulation in Historical Perspective* (2000) and *Emerging Financial Markets* (2000).

Guillermo Calvo is the chief economist and manager of the research department of the Inter-American Development Bank. He has held tenured positions at Columbia University (1973–86) and the University of Pennsylvania (1986–89). He was senior adviser in the research department of the IMF (1988–94) and advised several governments in Latin America and Eastern Europe. His recent positions include director of the Center for International Economics and Distinguished University Professor at the University of Maryland; Carlos Diaz-Alejandro Chair of International Finance at the University of CEMA, Buenos Aires; and research associate at the National Bureau of Economic Research. He was the president of the Latin American and Caribbean Economic Association. He has published several books and more than 100 articles in leading economic journals and was awarded the Simon Guggenheim Foundation Fellowship for 1980–81 and the King Juan Carlos Prize in Economics in 2000.

Lucio Castro is a senior economist at Maxwell Stamp Plc. He has extensive experience managing trade policy, fiscal policy, and competitiveness related projects at the Ministry of Economy and other governmental agencies of Argentina, the Inter-American Development Bank, and the World Bank. He has had both government and consultancy assignments in Africa, southeastern Europe, and Latin America. His research areas include applied research, trade policy formulation, regional integration and capacity building, and design and delivery of training courses. He is the author of several publications on trade, fiscal and welfare impacts of preferential trade liberalization in Latin America and the Caribbean, southeastern Europe and Africa.

Robert Devlin has been an economist at the Inter-American Development Bank in Washington since 1994 and is the deputy manager of the Integration and Regional Programs Department there. He had worked with the United Nations Economic Commission for Latin America and the Caribbean in Santiago de Chile since 1975, where his last position was deputy director of the Division of International Trade, Finance, and Transport. He was a lecturer at the Johns Hopkins School for Advanced International Studies (1987–90). He is author or coauthor of *Towards an Evolution of Regional Integration in Latin America* in the 1990s (1999), *Some Economic and Strategic Issues in the Face of the Emerging FTAA* (1999), *What's New in the New Regionalism?* (2001), and *Macroeconomic Stability, Integration, and Trade* (2001).

Marco Ferroni is the principal officer in the Office of Evaluation and Oversight at the Inter-American Development Bank. Throughout his career in international development, he has held official posts in multilateral and bilateral agencies. He was a senior advisor at the Vice Presidency for Resource Mobilization and Cofinancing at the World Bank. He was a member of the Boards of Executive Directors of the Inter-American Development Bank and the Inter-American Investment Corporation. He occupied managerial positions in the Ministries of Public Economy and Foreign Affairs in Switzerland and held a graduate teaching appointment at the Swiss Federal Institute of Technology in Zurich in the 1990s. He has also published on foreign aid and development finance, international public goods, public expenditure reform, policy reform and social protection, and the interrelationship between trade and macroeconomic regimes and agricultural growth.

Manuel Hinds, former minister of finance (January 1995–June 1999) and minister of the economy (1979–80) of El Salvador, is a business and government consultant. He was a private consultant with the World Bank, KPMG, and the Central Bank of El Salvador before becoming the minister of finance. As a consultant, he led several financial and operational missions to Russia, Hungary, the Palestinian territories, and Venezuela, advising on the restructuring of their financial and banking sectors. He began his career at the World Bank in 1982 in the Industrial Development and Finance Division for Latin America before becoming senior financial economist and principal economist in the Financial Policy Division of the Industry Department. He also worked extensively in the private sector in El Salvador. He is the author of *The Triumph of the Flexible Society: The Connectivity Revolution and Resistance to Change* (2003).

Gary Clyde Hufbauer is the Reginald Jones Senior Fellow at the Institute for International Economics. He was the Marcus Wallenberg Professor of International Finance Diplomacy at Georgetown University (1985–92), deputy director of the International Law Institute at Georgetown University (1979–81), deputy assistant secretary for international trade and investment policy of the US Treasury (1977–79), and director of the International Tax Staff at the Treasury (1974–76). He has written extensively on international trade, investment, and tax issues. He is author, coauthor, or coeditor of *The Benefits of Price Convergence* (2002), *World Capital Markets* (2001), *The Ex-Im Bank in the 21st Century* (2001), *Unfinished Business: Telecommunications after the Uruguay Round* (1997), *Fundamental Tax Reform and Border Tax Adjustments* (1996), *US Taxation of International Income* (1992), *Western Hemisphere Economic Integration* (1994), *Measuring the Costs of Protection in the United States* (1994), *North American Free Trade* (1992), and *Economic Sanctions Reconsidered* (2d ed. 1990).

Enrique Iglesias has been the president of the Inter-American Development Bank since 1988. He began his fourth five-year term on April 1, 2003. Prior to his election as president of the Bank, he was Uruguay's minister of foreign relations (1985–88); executive secretary of the UN Economic Commission for Latin America and the Caribbean (1972–85); secretary general of the UN Conference on New and Renewable Sources of Energy, held in Kenya in 1981; and chairman of the conference that launched the Uruguay Round of international trade negotiations in Punta del Este, Uruguay, in 1986. He was the president of Uruguay's central bank from 1966 to 1968. He has taught economic development at Uruguay's Universidad de la República and served as director of its Institute of Economics. He has written numerous articles and papers on Latin American and Uruguayan economic issues, capital markets, external financing, and multilateralism.

Hilde Frafjord Johnson is the minister of international development of Norway and a member of the Norwegian Cabinet. In 1997, before taking up the position as minister of international development and human rights of Norway (1997–2000), she worked for four years as a representative in the Parliament. She was a member of the Energy and Environment Committee. In 1992–93, she worked as a consultant with the resource department in the Ministry of Foreign Affairs. She was the personal adviser to Kåre Gjønnes (parliamentary leader) and to the leader of the Christian Democratic Party, Kjell Magne Bondevik (1990–91). She was a political adviser to Bondevik, when he was minister for foreign affairs in 1989–90. She is the initiator and a present member of Utstein 4, a group of European development ministers, governors of the World Bank and members of the World Bank's Development Committee, all concerned with poverty reduction (1999–2000 and 2001).

Omar Kabbaj has been the president of the African Development Bank Group since 1995 and is the chairman of the boards of directors and the chief executive officer of the African Development Bank, the African Development Fund, and the Nigeria Trust Fund, which together constitute the Bank Group. He was a minister delegate in the Office of the Prime Minister of Morocco, where he was in charge of economic affairs from 1993 to 1995. Prior to that, he was a member of the IMF's Executive Board, representing Morocco, Algeria, Tunisia, Iran, Ghana, Afghanistan, and Pakistan. From 1979 to 1980, he represented nine countries on the Executive Board of the World Bank. He was the director of the Office of the Minister of Finance and held managerial positions in Moroccan national research, banking, finance, trade and industrial sectors, including head of the commercial department of the Bureau de Recherches et Participations Minières; head of the finance department of Banque Nationale pour le Développement Economique; managing director of Sucrerie Nationale du Tadla; chargé de mission at the Office of the Minister of Trade, Industry, Mining and Merchant Marine; and managing director of Sucrerie Nationale de Canne du Sebou.

Allan Meltzer, former member of the president's Council of Economic Advisers, is a professor of political economy and public policy at Carnegie Mellon University and a visiting fellow at the American Enterprise Institute. In 1998, he was appointed by Congress to chair a commission studying the role and effectiveness of the IMF and the World Bank. He also chaired the Shadow Open Market Committee, a self-appointed watchdog for the Federal Reserve's monetary policy. He has been an honorary adviser to the Institute of Monetary and Economic Studies for the Bank of Japan since 1986. He served on the faculty of Harvard University, University of Chicago, University of Pennsylvania, and institutions abroad. His research areas include monetary policy and history, tax and budget issues, international finance, and financial services. He is the author of several books, including *History of the Federal Reserve I: 1913–1951.*

Helmut Reisen is a counselor at the OECD Development Centre. He is working on various aspects of global, regional, and national finance, including in the OECD Task Force on the UN Financing for Development Conference. He was recently invited to join the group of international advisors for the Pacific Economic Cooperation Council Finance Forum. He served at the Institute of World Economy, Kiel, for the Confederation of German Industries, and the German Ministry of Economics and is a member of the editorial board of *International Finance.* He is author or coauthor of *New Sources of Development Finance* (2003), *Pensions, Savings, and Capital Flow* (2000), *Don't Fix, Don't Float* (2001), and *Will Basel II Contribute to Convergence in International Capital Flows?* (2001).

Liliana Rojas-Suarez is a senior fellow at the Center for Global Development. She is also the chair of the Latin American Shadow Financial Regulatory Committee. She served as managing director and chief economist for Latin America at Deutsche Bank (1998–2000) and as principal adviser in the Office of the Chief Economist at the Inter-American Development Bank. She held various posts at the International Monetary Fund (1984–94), including as deputy chief of the Capital Markets and Financial Studies Division of the Research Department. She was also a professor at Anahuac University. Among her recent works is *Can International Capital Standards Strengthen Banks in Emerging Markets?* (*The Capco Institute Journal of Finance* 2002).

Todd Sandler is the Robert R. and Katheryn A. Dockson Professor of International Relations and Economics at the University of Southern California. In 2003, the National Academy of Sciences recognized him, along with his colleague Walter Enders of the University of Alabama, for behavioral research relevant to the prevention of nuclear war. He served as a consultant with the United Nations Development Program, the Overseas Development Council, the Swedish Ministry of Foreign Affairs, and the World Bank. Some of his major publications include *Regional Public Goods: Typologies, Provision, Financing, and Development Assistance* (2002); *Economic Concepts for the Social Sciences* (2001); *The Political Economy of NATO* (1999); *The Theory of Externalities, Public Goods, and Clubs Goods, 2d ed.* (1996); *The Economics of Defense* (1995); and *Collective Action: Theory and Applications* (1992).

Jurgen Stark is the deputy director of Deutsche Bundesbank (German central bank). Before his current appointment in 1998, he served as the deputy secretary of the Federal Ministry of Finance and personal representative of the federal chancellor in preparation of the World Economic Summits. He began his career at the Ministry of Finance in 1978 after receiving a doctorate in economics from the University of Tubingen. He serves on numerous EU and German commissions and is widely published in German and English.

Roberto Zahler, former president (1991–96) and vice president (1990–91) of the Central Bank of Chile, is the president of the consultancy firm Zahler & Co. and chairman of Siemens–Chile SA. He is a member of the Latin American Shadow Financial Regulatory Committee and the Emerging Market Economies Eminent Persons Group, a board member of Banco Santander–Chile, and chairman of the Advisory Board of Deutsche Bank Americas Bond Fund in New York. He served in a range of positions at the Economic Commission for Latin America and the Caribbean (ECLAC), including chief regional adviser in monetary and financial policy (1984–89) and monetary expert (1978–83) in the UNDP/ECLAC project titled "Implications for Latin America of the Situation of the International Monetary and Financial System." He is the author of more than 90 publications and articles in books and internationals journals.

Index

ADB. *See* Asian Development Bank
AfDB. *See* African Development Bank
Africa, 48–52. *See also* African Development
    Bank; *individual countries; specific regional
    associations, agreements and initiatives*
    capital flows to developing countries in,
        4–9, 5*t*
    economic growth, 132–33
    financial and monetary cooperation in,
        48–49, 52
    international trade, 21–22
    intraregional trade, 49, 50*t*, 51
    Joint Africa Institute, 130
    New Partnership for Africa's Development
        (NEPAD), 29, 32, 107*b*, 129–30, 133
    Organization for African Unity, 130
    regional integration in, 48–49, 48*n*, 76–77
    River Blindness Control Program, 106*b*, 118
    tax revenues, 17–20
African Development Bank, 34, 107*b*, 110, 129
    annual loan disbursements and grant
        approvals, 31*t*
    current agenda, 76
    New Partnership for Africa's Development
        (NEPAD) and, 129–30
    support of regional integration, 76–77
AIDS/HIV, 114, 116
Americas, the. *See also individual countries;*
        Inter-American Development Bank;
        *specific regional associations, agreements
        and initiatives*
    dimensions of integration experience, 64–65
    Free Trade Area of the Americas, 44, 65,
        71–75, 77, 112

income growth, per capita, 97
intraregional trade, 61–64
monetary and financial cooperation in,
    65–66
multilateral initiatives, 73
North-South integration initiatives, 46–47,
    55, 71
preferential trade agreements, 60*t*
regional development banks in, 78–80
South-South integration initiatives, 69–71,
    96
Andean Community, 61, 65–66, 112, 126
Andean Development Corporation, 28, 29*n*,
    66, 66*n*, 104*n*
Andean Group, 29
Andean Pact, 2*n*
Anglo-Saxon capitalism, 97
APEC. *See* Asia Pacific Economic Cooperation
    forum
Arab Investment Guarantee Fund, 28
Arab Maghreb Union, 48
Arab Monetary Fund, 28
Argentina
    bank claims on government in, 155,
        155*n*
    capital markets and, 216–18
    financial crises in, 148, 214
    Reports on the Observance of Standards
        and Codes and, 170, 174
ASEAN. *See* Association of South East Asian
    Nations
Asia. *See also* Asian Development Bank;
    *individual countries; specific regional
    associations, agreements and initiatives*

Asian Monetary Fund (proposed), 56
  currency crisis and the bond market, 27n
  financial crisis of 1997–98, 56, 88
  forms of regional cooperation, 58t–59t
  regional integration agreements in, 52–53
  trade within regional agreements, 54t
Asian Development Bank, 89, 110, 129
  annual loan disbursements and grant
    approvals, 31t
  Greater Mekong Subregion initiative and,
    76, 113
  Long-Term Strategic Framework, 76
  projects and new initiatives, 113–14
  regional cooperation and, 112–14
  support of regional integration, 76–77
Asian model development paradigm, 131–32
Asia Pacific Economic Cooperation forum, 24,
    31, 53
  impacts of, 24
  organization and activities, 55
  origins and development, 53–55
  tariff reduction and, 54–55
Association of Eastern Caribbean States, 65
Association of South East Asian Nations, 28,
    56–57, 76
  origins and development, 53
  Surveillance Process, 56, 76
  Task Force on Currency and Exchange Rate
    Mechanisms, 57
  trade with industrialized countries, 53
  ASEAN+3, 56–57

bank capital standards, globalization and,
    172–73
bank claims on governments in emerging
    markets, 153–55, 154t, 155n
Basel Capital Accord, 148, 149, 153n, 172
  capital requirements and, 153–56
  ineffectiveness, 165
  instability in developing countries and, 207,
    207n
  interbank lending and, 157
  sequencing and, 155–56
Basel Committee of Financial Regulators, 116
Basel Committee on Banking Supervision, 145,
    151–53
Basel II proposal, 156, 174–76
Bhagwati, Jagdish, 2n
border development, regional integration and,
    69n
Brown, Gordon, 144

CACM. See Central American Common
    Market
CACs. See collective action clauses
Calomiris, Charles, 217
capital adequacy ratio, common financial
    standards and, 149, 160
capital flows
  to developing countries, 5, 109–10

by donor and recipient region, 110t
  to emerging markets and real GDP growth,
    8t
  public goods and, 110–11
capital markets
  access to, 216–20
  Argentina and, 216–18
  China and, 216
  Ecuador and, 217
capital requirements
  Basel Capital Accord, 153–56
  common financial standards, 148–57
Caribbean Community (Caricom), 44, 60t,
    61–62, 64–66, 112
Caribbean countries, regional integration in,
    57–65
Caricom. See Caribbean Community
Cavallo, Domingo, 217
Central African Economic and Monetary
    Community, 49, 52
Central American Bank for Economic
    Integration, 66
Central American Common Market, 57, 60t,
    61–62, 65–66, 112
Chiang Mai Initiative, 28, 56–57, 88
Chile, Reports on the Observance of
    Standards and Codes and, 170
China
  capital markets and, 216
  income growth, per capita, 97
CMI. See Chiang Mai Initiative
collective action clauses, 12
  sovereign debt restructuring mechanism
    proposal and, 12n
COMESA. See Common Market of Eastern
    and Southern Africa
commitments to national public goods and
    international public goods by region,
    111t
commodities exports by region, 22t
common financial standards, 138, 139t, 140,
    143
  Argentine crisis of 2002 and, 148
  capital adequacy ratio and, 149, 160
  capital requirements and, 148–57
  countries participating in setting, 146t
  country- and region-specific inputs to,
    158–60
  crisis prevention and, 173–74
  effectiveness of, 148
  emerging markets and, 166–67
  general concerns about, 145–48
  Group of Seven and, 165–68
  International Monetary Fund and, 145, 169,
    170–71
  one-size-fits-all approach, 143–44
  ownership of, 145
  policy recommendations for, 158–60
  regional development banks and, 160–62
  sequencing and implementation of, 144–45

setting, 156–57
World Bank and, 145, 170
Common Market of Eastern and Southern
    Africa (COMESA), 48–49, 52
    regional integration in, 52–57
Compendium of Standards (Financial Stability
    Forum), 148*n*, 172
Consultative Group on International
    Agricultural Research, 117, 130
contagion
    common financial standards and, 173
    definition of, 137–38, 137*n*
    global public goods and, 26
    international capital markets and,
        65, 70
    investor behavior and, 10
    minimizing negative effects of, 28, 32–33,
        88, 203
contingent credit lines, 196–97
    International Monetary Fund and, 209,
        211–12
Core Principles for Effective Banking
    Supervision (Financial Stability Forum),
    148, 148*n*
Core Principles Liaison Group, 145
corruption, institutionalization of, 98–99
credit ratings, development banks and,
    190–93, 211
Crockett, Andrew, 161*n*, 174

debt guarantees
    regional development banks and, 33
    World Bank and, 33
developing countries. *See also* financial
        instability
    access to private markets, 183–84
    instability of, 184
    integration into private financial markets,
        179
    structures and institutions of, 186–87
development banks. *See also* multilateral
        development banks; regional
        development banks; *specific development
        banks*; World Bank
    credit ratings and, 190–93
    financial crises and, 193–99
    International Monetary Fund and, 185–86,
        222
    loan conditionalities and, 189–90
    loan policies of, 192*n*
Development Committee 2001, 102
development finance
    foreign financial flows and, 7*t*
    internal economic incentives and, 4*n*
development paradigms
    Asian model, 131–32
    Washington consensus, 97, 131–32
Doha Trade Round, 28
domestic capital markets, impacts of, 223
donor system, inefficiencies of, 11*n*

East African Community, 49
Economic Community of Central African
    States, 48–49
Economic Community of West African States
    (ECOWAS), 49
Ecuador
    capital markets and, 217
    currency crisis and the bond market in, 28
El Salvador, development banks and, 191*n*
emergency liquidity
    banks and, 194*n*, 195*n*
    International Monetary Fund and, 194–96
emerging markets, common financial
    standards and, 166–67
equity growth in banking systems, pre-crisis,
    149–51, 150*t*
EU. *See* European Union
European Bank for Reconstruction and
    Development, annual loan disburse-
    ments and grant approvals, 31*t*
European Union
    Common Agricultural Policy, 94
    expansion of, 94–95
    Latin American and Caribbean initiatives,
        66
    negotiation areas with Southern Cone
        Common Market (Mercosur), 68*t*
    regional integration and, 43, 94
    tax reform and, 35
    trade with Latin America, 63*t*
exports
    commodities by region, 22*t*
    export ratios and trade diversification, 19–
        22
    as growth motor, 19*n*
    within regional agreements in Latin
        America, 62*t*

FDI. *See* foreign direct investment
financial architecture, international
    instability in developing countries and, 180
    regional development banks and, 180–87
financial crises
    development banks and, 193–99
    intervention in, 194
    origins, 196–97
financial instability
    causes, 180–83
    financial architecture, international and,
        180
    fiscal and monetary policies and, 183
    International Monetary Fund and, 179–81
    multilateral financial institutions and,
        184–85
    regional development banks and, 187–88
    trade policy and, 183
financial markets
    in developing countries, 207
    integration of regional and subregional, 193
    supervision and regulation of, 206–07

Financial Sector Assessment Program, 169–70
Financial Stability Forum of April 1999, 161*n*,
174
Compendium of Standards (Financial Stability
Forum), 148*n*, 172
creation of, 138
working groups membership, 147*t*
Financial System Stability Assessment, 169
foreign direct investment, 7, 25, 37, 46, 64.
See also specific regions and countries
financial integration and, 43*n*
foreign banks in Latin America and, 7*n*
GDP and, 5*t*, 6*t*, 7
the New Regionalism and diversion of, 47
foreign exchange
importance of, 19
trade barriers and, 19–22
volatility impacts, 19
free trade agreements, 2, 24–25, 27, 30, 37.
See also specific agreements
Free Trade Area of the Americas, 44, 65,
71–75, 77, 112
FTAs. *See* free trade agreements

G-7. *See* Group of Seven
G-10. *See* Group of Ten
Global Environment Facility, 120, 129
globalization, bank capital standards and,
172–73
global or multilateral trade systems, 2, 2*n*. *See
also specific associations, agreements, and
initiatives; specific regions and countries*
global standards setting bodies, 32, 32*n*
Greater Mekong Subregion initiative, 113
Asian Development Bank and, 76, 113
technical assistance projects, 114
Great Lakes River Basin, 49
gross private savings/gross private disposable
income, regional, 14*t*
Group of Seven (G-7), multilateral banks and,
119, 165
Group of Ten (G-10), 88, 172

Hommes, Rudolf, 5*n*

IDB. *See* Inter-American Development Bank
IMF. *See* International Monetary Fund
income growth, per capita
in the Americas, 97
in China, 97
Indian Ocean Commission, 49
Indonesia-Malaysia-Thailand growth triangle,
113
Institute for the Integration of Latin America
and the Caribbean, 74
Inter-American Development Bank. *See also*
regional development banks
Eighth Replenishment (1995), 74
Multilateral Investment Fund, 10
programs, 10

Inter-American Institute for Social
Development, 117
Intergovernmental Authority for
Development, 49
internal economic incentives, development
finance and, 4*n*
"internal ratings-based" approach, 175
International Consortium for Cooperation
on the Nile, 106*n*
international development banks, 31–32, 34,
213. *See also* regional development
banks; *specific regions and institutions*
annual loan disbursements and grant
approvals, 31*t*
characteristics of, 84
collaboration with regional initiatives, 75
development of physical infrastructure
and, 85
economic integration and, 85
economic reforms and, 85
financial crises and, 86
functions of, 84–85
innovations by, 75
Inter-American Institute for Social
Development and, 117
origins and development, 83–84
projects and new initiatives, 112
regional cooperation and, 111–12
Regional Policy Dialogue, 117
regional public goods and, 85
South American Regional Infrastructure
Plan and, 104*n*
support of regional integration, 74–75
International Financial Institutions Advisory
Commission 2000, 102. *See also* Meltzer
Commission report
lending policies and, 218
International Monetary Fund, 105, 140. *See
also* multilateral development banks;
regional development banks
common standards and, 145
contingent credit lines and, 196–97, 209,
211–12
core competencies, 218–19
development banks, multilateral and,
185–86, 222
effectiveness, 221
emergency liquidity and, 194–96
founding of, 3
instability in developing countries and,
179–81
International Tax Dialogue proposal,
23*n*
lending policies, 218
lending practices, controversy concerning,
11–12
liquidity crises and, 33
prudential standards for banks and,
167
International Tax Dialogue proposal, 23*n*

Japan, free trade agreement with Singapore, 55
Jin Liqun, 143
Johnson, Harry, 95
Joint Africa Institute, 130

knowledge exchange, regional development banks and, 201–02
Kobe Research Project, 57
Kyrgyz Republic, 93

Latin America and the Caribbean. *See also individual countries; specific regional associations, agreements and initiatives*
1990s tax reforms in, 18*n*
exports within regional agreements, 62*t*
financial integration, 27
Institute for the Integration of Latin America and the Caribbean, 74
Latin American Reserve Fund, 28, 66, 66*n*
Latin American Shadow Regulatory Committee, 156*n*
lending from foreign banks in, 7*n*
Regional Fund for Agricultural Technology in Latin America and the Caribbean, 117
regional integration, 57–65
resistance to trade liberalization, 44
South American Regional Infrastructure Plan, 104*n*
trade with the United States and the European Union, 63*t*
Latin American Reserve Fund, 28, 66, 66*n*
Latin American Shadow Regulatory Committee, 156*n*
Lerrick, Adam, 217
liquidity crises, regional development banks and, 33, 33*n*, 198, 211–12
loan conditionalities, development banks and, 189–90
loan policies, development banks and, 192*n*
Lusaka Summit, 130

Manila Framework Group, 56
Mano River Union, 49
Meltzer Commission report, 167
Mercosur. *See* Southern Cone Common Market
Mexico, 7, 97, 218
North American Free Trade Agreement and, 25, 27, 44, 64–65
Tequila Crisis, 10–11, 10*n*, 194
Miami Summit, 1994, 67*t*
Millennium Development Goals, 223
Monterrey Financing for Development Initiative, 12, 134
multilateral development banks. *See also regional development banks; specific development banks*

annual loan disbursements and grant approvals, 31*t*
financing for public goods, 116–18
overlapping functions of, 221–23
structural reforms and, 218
Multilateral Investment Fund, 10. *See also* Inter-American Development Bank

NAFTA. *See* North American Free Trade Agreement neighborhood effect, 103–04, 103*n*, 138
NEPAD. *See* New Partnership for Africa's Development (NEPAD)
New Partnership for Africa's Development, 29, 32, 107*b*, 129–30, 133
New Regionalism, 43–48
asymmetric benefits and, 47
benefits *versus* costs, 46–48
competition for foreign investment and, 46
economic transformation and, 46
examples of, 44
foreign direct investment diversion and, 47
impact on multilateral systems, 47
improved security and, 46
increasing interest in North-South agreements and, 46
increasing trade complexity and, 47
international cooperation and, 46
interregional agreements and, 43–44
loss of tariff revenue and, 47
policy environment and, 43
regional banks and, 89
restriction of trade options and, 47
trade diversion and, 47
Nile River Basin. *See* International Consortium for Cooperation on the Nile
non-oil commodities
open and radical regionalism and, 1
prices, 1960-1999, 182*t*
production, 181–82
North American Free Trade Agreement, 72, 97
benefits from, 24–25, 27, 64–65
characteristics, 61–62
financial integration and, 27
Mexico and, 25, 27, 44, 64–65, 72
open and radical regionalism and, 27
shortcomings, 30

official development assistance
characteristics, 8
GDP growth and, 8*t*
history, 9*t*
O'Neill, Paul, 219
open and radical regionalism
Asian crisis, the bond market and, 27*n*
benefits, 24
definitions, 23–24
financial integration in Latin America and, 27

open and radical regionalism (*Cont.*)
   infrastructure, economic and social
      institutions and, 25–26
   investment in public goods and, 26
   limitations of financial vulnerability and,
      26–28
   North American Free Trade Agreement
      and, 27
   regional trade agreements and, 24–25
Organization for African Unity, 130
Organization for Economic Cooperation and
   Development, 132, 134, 153–56

preferential trade agreements in the Americas,
   60*t*
private financial markets, integration of
   developing countries into, 179
private saving ratios
   GDP and, 34–35
   gross private savings/gross private
      disposable income, regional, 14*t*
   regional development banks and, 34–35
private-sector financing, regional development
   banks and, 199–201
private *versus* public saving
   in Asia, 14
   Chilean private pension scheme and, 13
   growth and, 13
   instability in developing countries and, 208
   international capital flows and, 13
   regional differences, 14
   taxation and, 12–19
   Tequila Crisis and, 13*n*
procyclical lending policies, regional
   development banks and, 201, 210
product adaptation, trade barriers and, 20
prudential standards for banks, 164–65
   common financial standards and, 165–68
   International Monetary Fund and, 167
public goods
   capital flows to developing countries and,
      110–11
   commitments to national public goods and
      international public goods by region,
      111*t*
   regional
      characteristics of, 102, 103*b*
      core and complementary functions, 108
      developing-country governments and,
         115–16
      donor countries and, 116
      examples, 101
      financing mechanisms for, 114–15, 115*t*
      financing of, 114–21, 117–18, 117*n*,
         119–20, 124–25
      functions, 123
      globalization and, 102
      grant financing of, 117–18, 117*n*
      intermediate, 102–03
      international development banks and, 85

issues concerning, 121
loan financing of, 119–20
multilateral development banks and,
   116–17, 128–29
obstacles to financing of, 124–25
regional development banks and, 125–26
spillover communities, neighborhood
   effects and, 102, 103–04
technical cooperation and, 116
public saving, 15
   industrial countries group and, 15*n*–16n
   reforms in Latin America and, 18*n*
   taxation levels and, 16–19, 16*n*

reforms, second-generation, 185
regional cooperation. *See also* New
   Regionalism; regional development
   banks
   benefits of, 104–07
   disease control and, 105
   environmental policies, resource
      management and, 105–06
   financial, 105
   international development banks and,
      111–12
   prerequisites for, 107–08
   transport infrastructure, 104
   utilities infrastructure, 105
regional development banks, 2–3, 29–35.
   See also multilateral development banks;
   World Bank
   access to financial markets and, 188–93
   in the Americas, 78–80
   building infrastructure and, 133
   capital adequacy ratio and, 160
   as catalysts for collective action, 109
   challenges facing, 130
   common financial standards and, 160–61
   debt guarantees and, 33
   developing countries, structures and
      institutions and, 186–87
   development finance and, 222
   economic stability objectives, 187–88
   financial products, 33
   general roles of, 215
   global multilateral institutions and, 125
   implementation of international standards
      and, 32
   importance in regional strategies, 30–33
   instrument recommendations for, 202–03
   knowledge exchange and, 31–32, 201–02
   lending policy recommendations for,
      203–04
   liquidity crises and, 33, 33*n*, 198, 211–12
   policies for economic and institutional
      reforms and, 32
   private saving ratios and, 34–35
   private sector financing, 199–201
   procyclical lending policies and, 201, 210
   proposed actions of, 100

public goods, regional and, 125–26
regional cooperation and integration
    programs and, 73–77, 129–30
regional financial integration and, 208
second-generation reforms and, 209
taxation systems and, 34
technical support and, 31
Regional Exchange Market of Transferable
    Securities, 52
Regional Fund for Agricultural Technology in
    Latin America and the Caribbean, 117
regional integration. *See also* New Regionalism
in Africa, 48
border development and, 69*n*
financial, equity and bond markets and,
    91–92
geopolitical benefits of, 1*n*
in Latin America and the Caribbean, 57–65
market forces and, 43*n*
monetary, 92
policy-induced, 43, 43*n*
regional development banks and, 73–77, 99
trade agreements and, 42
trends, 48
types, 41–42
in western Europe, 43, 94
regional integration agreements. *See also*
    specific regions, countries, and organizations
in Africa, 48–49, 76–77
in Asia, 52–53
impacts of, 44–46
trade liberalization and, 44
regionalism. *See also* New Regionalism,
    regional integration
as development strategy, 1
open and radical, 1, 2, 23, 29, 35
regional negotiating strategies, 28–29
regional public goods. *See* public goods
Reports on the Observance of Standards and
    Codes , 141*t*–42*t*, 148*t*, 169–70
Argentina and, 170
characteristics, 140
Chile and, 170
effectiveness of, 148, 174
standardization issues and, 140*n*
RIAs. *See* regional integration agreements
River Blindness Control Program, African,
    106*b*, 118
Rodrik, Dani, 98
ROSCs. *See* Reports on the Observance of
    Standards and Codes
Russia, 1998 crisis, foreign impacts of, 10, 10*n*

Samuelson, Paul, 102
Sandler, Todd, 128
SDRM. *See* sovereign debt restructuring
    mechanism
second-generation reforms, regional
    development banks and, 209
Siam Reap airport, 114

Singapore, free trade agreement with Japan,
    55
South American Regional Infrastructure
    Initiative, 66
South American Regional Infrastructure Plan,
    104*n*
South Asian Association for Regional
    Cooperation, 55
South Asian Preferential Trade Agreement, 55
Southern African Customs Union, 49
Southern African Development Community,
    49
Southern Cone Common Market (Mercosur),
    29, 57–65, 97, 112
European Union and, 71
negotiation areas with European Union
    Interregional Association, 68*t*
sovereign debt restructuring mechanism
    proposal, 12
Stark, Jurgen, 219

taxation
impacts on corporate and foreign
    investment, 38–39, 38*n*
in open economies, literature concerning,
    38
private saving and, 12–19
public saving and, 15, 16–19, 16*n*
regional development banks and, 34
revenue from, regional, 16*t*, 17*t*
Tequila Crisis, 10–11
private versus public saving and, 13*n*
trade and transit integration, regional, 42, 93
trade initiatives, megaregional, 10
Asia Pacific Economic Cooperation forum,
    88
ASEAN+3, 87–88
European Union–Mercosur agreement, 87
Free Trade Area of the Americas, 87
trade liberalization
in Argentina, 45*n*
in Brazil, 45*n*
regional integration agreements and, 44
resistance to, in Latin America, 44
World Bank and, 189
trade openness, regional, 21*t*

United Nations Environment Programme, 129
United States
trade with Association of South East Asian
    Nations, 53
trade with Latin America, 63*t*

Venezuela, 29

Washington Consensus development
    paradigm, 97, 131–32
West Africa Economic and Monetary Union,
    49
financial and monetary cooperation in, 52

western Europe, regional integration in, 43.
    See also European Union
World Bank, 3, 107*b*. *See also* multilateral
    development banks; regional
    development banks
  annual loan disbursements, 31*t*, 32*t*
  common financial standards and, 145, 170
  developing countries, structures and
      institutions and, 187
  grant approvals, 31*t*

international tax dialogue and, 23
investment loans and, 119
liberalization of trade policies and, 189
partial loan guarantees by, 33
World Trade Organization (WTO), 112
  integration initiatives, 71–73
  trade agreements and, 42

Zahler, Roberto, 33
Zedillo Report, 38, 101*n*